FROM
STRENGTH
TO
STRENGTH

FROM
STRENGTH
TO
STRENGTH

AN AUTOBIOGRAPHY
SARA HENDERSON

THOMAS DUNNE BOOKS
ST. MARTIN'S PRESS ✠ NEW YORK

THOMAS DUNNE BOOKS.
An imprint of St. Martin's Press.

FROM STRENGTH TO STRENGTH: AN AUTOBIOGRAPHY. Copyright © 1992
by Sara Henderson. All rights reserved. Printed in the United States of
America. No part of this book may be used or reproduced in any manner whatsoever without written permission except in the case of brief
quotations embodied in critical articles or reviews. For information,
address St. Martin's Press, 175 Fifth Avenue, New York, N.Y. 10010.

ISBN 0-312-24397-9

First published in Australia by Pan Macmillan Publishers Australia

First U.S. Edition: April 2000

10 9 8 7 6 5 4 3 2 1

This book is dedicated to
Charlie—who created the dream
Marlee—who is making the dream reality
and
Uncle Dick—whose loyalty, love and just
plain hard work are making it possible.

Create a dream
and give it everything you have,
you could be surprised just how
much you are capable of achieving.
If you don't have a dream . . .
borrow one!
Any, which way . . .
You must have a dream.

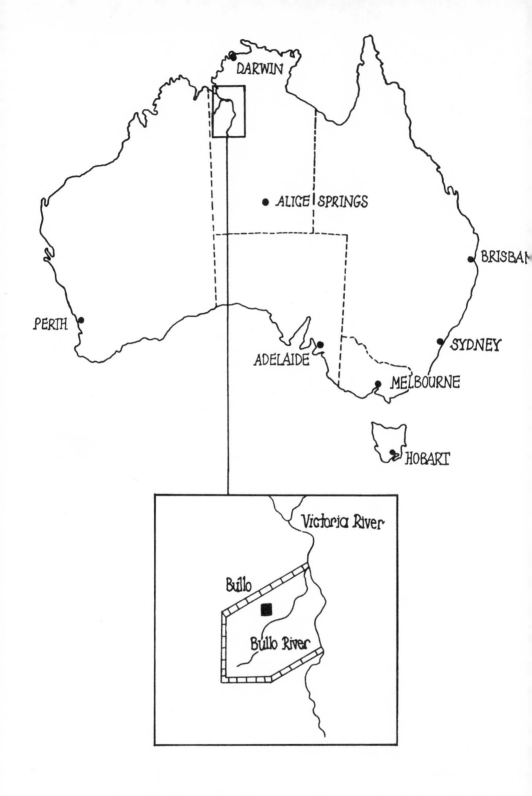

CONTENTS

ACKNOWLEDGEMENTS

I started to write this in the usual manner, but after too many pages of names and more names, I realised I was just wasting paper. Each name held a story, each person had had an effect on my life; so much so, that a name was not enough. Each person I thought of had in some way altered the path of my life or helped me along that path—family, friend, stranger, business associate, adversary and just plain straight-out enemy.

If I were writing about a part of, or even an event in, my life then a few pages of names would be acceptable, but to list names of all the people in my life to date?—forget it.

Of course, special people stand out and always will. My wonderful Mum and Dad, so sadly missed; my sister Sue and her husband Ralph, who helped me keep sane—or almost—with regular holidays during those trying, first years (about twenty) on Bullo. My wonderful daughters—Danielle, so young, yet in times of great tragedy, so wise and strong; Marlee, words are not adequate for my love and admiration for this five-foot-two dynamo. Special, special friends, always there in time of need. Complete strangers, from all over the world, whose concern, good wishes and words of encouragement came to us in letters and phone calls. I thank you all.

I even thank my enemy. Having you around makes it blatantly clear that achievement and happiness, like freedom, cannot be taken for granted and must be defended and protected, so you keep me on my toes.

I thank all the people at Pan Macmillan for their patience

in dealing with this first-time author, and for Sarah Overton for presenting my story in such a first-class manner.

And I thank Charlie who was to me all these things—family, friend, stranger, business associate, enemy, lover—plus a few thousand more, as well as teacher of some of life's greatest lessons.

Finally, I thank God for this life.

PREFACE

Well here it is, as much of my life to date as I can put down on paper and share with you.

When I wrote my draft and read it through, I thought to myself critically, well, I feel it is interesting, it is a good story, but that's what it was, a good story, not my whole life. True, I had written about my life, but I had detoured around the cruel, heartbreaking and embarrassing parts.

I worried over this for a fair time. I realised that in the book, Charles, who, let's face it, was the centre of my universe for twenty-six years, had ended up a 'goodie goodie two shoes'. In my heart of hearts I knew that this was not so. I had subconsciously recorded all my good memories and left out all the bad. I struggled with this, arguing that it was alright because most of the people who would read the book would not know me or Charles, so what did it matter? On the other hand, what of the people who did know us, together and separately? What about all the affairs he had had which I didn't know about, but other people knew about? What about the friends and employees who knew of the endless arguments, misery, money problems, family problems and so on? Why had I presented this one-sided view of my life? Only the clean and pressed linen.

I answered myself that at this time, 1991, people don't want to read about doom and gloom and misery. Indeed, the recognition I have received, due to the businesswoman of the year award, is the reason my life is being recorded. People like the story of an Aussie battler, struggling against all odds and surviving. So why not stay with this theme and leave out all the miserable, heartbreaking trimmings?

A trip to Darwin when I was around page 220 changed my mind.

I was in a taxi driving from Darwin airport to town when the lady driver said, 'You Mrs Henderson, aren't you?'

'Yes, I am.'

'I see your picture in papers, you have a hard life but you fight hard and you win. You writing a book now, congratulations.'

'Thank you.'

'I knew your husband.'

It was one of my cynical days so I said, 'Who didn't?'

She told me her life story, also a hard life. She had come to Australia from the Middle East as a young girl, to an arranged marriage, and worked very hard all her life. I couldn't help thinking her life would also make a good book, as so many other people's lives would. She was now divorced.

'I was Sammy's wife, you know Sammy?'

'Oh yes, I remember Sammy.'

When she finished I knew a lot more about Sammy. Then she moved onto Charlie. She spoke very fast, rapid fire. I was listening and not listening, if you know what I mean, when she brought me back to the past with a jolt.

'That husband of yours, don't forget to write what a bastard he was! I really hate him.'

'Oh?'

'Sure I hate him.' I think the expression 'I hate him' was supposed to be 'I do not like him', just a difficulty with the English language. But then again, maybe not.

Sometimes Charles was rude and sometimes abrupt, but he was always in such a hurry that his manner appeared rude. I tried to convey this to her, but she would not be swayed.

'I take no notice of that, I hate him because what he do to you! When I first meet him, I know nothing of you, he come to town and say "You get me girl." I say to my husband, "What wrong with this man, why not he get married always wanting girls?" I tell your husband "You go find your own

4

girls" then I meet your children, beautiful children, beautiful, beautiful. I say to my husband, "This man have beautiful children, where his wife, she dead or something?" He say you on station.'

Her eyes shot to the rear vision mirror, I was only allowed to nod.

'Right, I say to him, "The children are beautiful, so wife must be beautiful, why he always wanting girls when he have beautiful children, beautiful hardworking wife who always stay home and work? What wrong with this man?" So then I say to my husband, you'—her eyes shot to the mirror again to indicate 'you' meant me—'must be very ugly and children look like him, because even though I hate him, he all right to look at, eh?' Eyes to the mirror for confirmation. I nodded. 'Yes, so I say to my husband, "That's it, wife must be very ugly." Still this not good thing, so I still hate him, and when he say, "You get girls" I say to him "You not talk to me that way because I do not like." So after long time he stop talking to me that way, he just ask for my husband to meet him at airport, not me. Then long time after, my husband say I pick up Mrs Henderson at airport. I meet you and I am very mad.' My eyes were on the mirror waiting. 'Not at you, I mad at your husband.' I nod and her eyes go back to the road. 'I say to my husband, "What the matter with that man, he have young beautiful wife, too young for him. She beautiful lady with brains and he chase silly girls with empty heads." I hate him! Eight dollars fifty please.'

The brakes brought us to a sudden halt outside the hotel and she was out of the car with bags on the kerb before I could collect myself. She pumped my hand with four or five sharp jerks and said, 'You still beautiful lady and I was right, you have brains. Good luck.'

Then she was in the car and gone. The whole story was told non-stop, without even pause for breath.

What she said was all true and I had heard the same from many other sources, but this time it was put in such a quaint way. She was a delightful person and it was in no way meant to be hurtful. She was stating the facts and I suppose she decided if I had the brains she spoke of, I should know the truth now, even if I hadn't known it then. And she wanted to make it clear that she had in no way helped him in his nefarious dealings!

This exchange, coming at a time when I was wrestling with the problem of what to write down and what not to write, made me realise that there were many people out there who knew this side of Charles, and that to ignore it would be to leave out a lot of my life. An encounter on my subsequent flight to Kununurra was the deciding factor.

The man seated next to me was dozing when I sat down. The air hostess roused him for a snack. He smiled at me and started talking. He looked American and when he spoke, it was confirmed.

'Live in Kununurra?'

'Not really, I live on a cattle station outside Kununurra.'

He had the usual fascination with cattle stations that many people have and asked more questions.

'What station?'

'Bullo River.'

'Bullo River, eh?' I knew by the way he said it that he knew Charlie. 'I used to know the guy who owned Bullo, Charlie Henderson.'

He went on to tell me the story. Charles was his commanding officer on the U.S.S. *Enterprise* during the Second World War. 'Boy, did that guy hate me.' He didn't have the problem with 'hate' and 'not like' that my lady taxi driver may have had.

He never explained why Charles 'hated' him, he just said it caused him endless trouble. Knowing Charlie, I would say that the man would have been too goodlooking and a hit with the girls, and Charlie always had to be top dog. But that's only my guess, it could have been something completely different. He spent the first half of the flight telling me what a rotter Charles was and then he asked:

'Did you know him?'

'Oh yes,' I said with a smile.

'Have you been on Bullo a while?'

'I suppose you could say that.'

'How did you come to be connected with him?'

6

'I married him.' The poor man nearly knocked over his dinner tray.

'Oh, I am sorry. I mean . . . what I mean . . .'

'It's alright, I know what you mean.'

'Please accept . . .' He went on and on for the rest of the flight apologising.

I told him that he was not exaggerating and that Charles really was as he had said. 'I was married to him for twenty-six years and you are trying to tell me what he was like?'

He stopped when I said this and realised that he really didn't have to convince me. He introduced himself and I said I knew who he was. There weren't many Americans who had lived in Darwin for twenty years, only himself and Gus.

'And you are definitely not Gus,' I said.

'I can't believe I've been in Darwin all these years and never met you; it really is amazing. I saw Charlie plenty of times at parties . . .'

He was going to say more but lapsed into silence. The plane landed at Kununurra and he said goodbye and that he hoped we would meet again.

These two encounters in just a few days convinced me I had to put more of Charles down on paper. So I came home and put in fifty pages of inserts. I thought that was not too bad, only about twenty-five per cent gloom and doom.

Of course I couldn't possibly put down all my life with Charles as it would fill many books and would also be, to a large extent, very 'everyday'. So, I have stayed with the fast-moving parts.

Then there are parts of my life that are impossible to put down on paper. The hurt is too deep and I cannot dig it out—it has taken too much time and heartbreak to bury it. In some cases only the other party and I know the story and that is the way it must stay. Other parts are so dark and dreadful that innocent family members would have to suffer the disgrace of other family members' actions.

Other situations in my life, I would willingly write down, just to show the undesirable qualities of some humans, but the ink would not be dry before I was sued, so those secrets too will have to stay locked away. I am a great believer in my friend upstairs who said, 'Revenge is mine', so I will leave it up to Him although it is very hard to get that cheek turned, waiting for Him to get His act together. But, there is also the very true saying, 'Give them enough rope and they will hang themselves.' So I am busy plaiting rope!

CHAPTER 1

❖

1936-1954

And the winner is . . . The lights in the Regent Ballroom dimmed and a giant screen flashed scenes of my present life. As the vast expanses of the Outback invaded the room and wove their usual magic, enthralling everyone present, my mind raced back through the years.

And the winner is . . . I remember how nervous I was through the tournament. As I won each round the nerves increased. By the quarter-finals my mother was giving me a vile-tasting nerve calmer and more advice than a twelve-year-old could absorb.

I moved into the semi-finals. We played three very long very close sets. There were many times when I was within a point of defeat but I fought hard and finally it was over, the final stroke mine. Even though my backhand failed me miserably, I had won. The one day between the semi-finals and finals I spent on the tennis court coaxing my backhand to perform in a reasonable manner.

The big day arrived, my first singles final in a major tournament. More vile-tasting nerve calmer and prayers my backhand would behave.

The thrill of being a winner defies any description. The surge of adrenalin on that final stroke is very hard to put into words, even now. The cup was about twelve inches tall, all shiny with two enormous garish curved handles, but to a twelve-year-old it looked the best in the world.

I was born in the Cooinda Private Hospital in Mosman on the 15th of September, 1936. Years later, I asked Mum if she remembered the time.

'Well I was playing bridge and I remember I had to excuse myself before the hand was finished.'

So it could have been at the end of the 15th before midnight or the beginning of the 15th just after midnight.

I arrived before the doctor. Mum just made it to the hospital in time. Fortunately she was only streets away, as it was only thirty-five minutes from the first pain to my birth.

At that time, Dad had the Union Hotel on the Pacific Highway, North Sydney.

In my early childhood I remember riding my little red dinky along the upstairs hall. The hotel was on a corner and my nursery was the last room at the end of the curved hallway.

After Dad sold the hotel we lived in a house for a short time and then, when I was five, we moved to 'Halcyon' in Lakemba. This was where I grew up and where my love for tennis was born.

At a very early age Mum gave me a lightweight lady's racquet, and although it was a long time before I could hold it up with one hand, I would race around the court dragging it along and swinging at the ball. By the time I had the strength to hold it in the air, I had worn through the wooden frame.

My mother was a top district player, and no doubt if she had not chosen to marry and become a mother could have gone on to far more. My dad was also very good and my brother Warren was climbing the success ladder in tennis and soccer very fast. They all had a very definite hand in guiding me along my tennis career path.

My days revolved around tennis. I ran to school for training and ran home to have enough time for my chores and more practice before it was too dark. My dad made me a practice board and he marked out twelve-inch squares and painted a number in each one. He would call out the number and I would have to hit the ball into that square. I played tennis with anyone who had the patience to play with me. The more they ran me around the court, the harder I tried and the more I liked it. I was so dirty at the end of the day Mum said I looked like the court had been mopped with me.

We had four courts in the garden and all weekend the best teams in the district A Grade division played there. In one year, seven of the eight teams in the A Grade division for that district had their home court at Halcyon.

The courts were set in a beautiful rose garden, with over one hundred rose bushes. The rose garden bordered and crossed a long stretch of lawn which finally finished in front of the courts. There were large shade trees and two wooden tiered stands at the edge of the lawn. Next to the stands people sat on the lawns having drinks and afternoon tea. A radio and loud-speaker broadcast the Saturday horse races and the Sunday cricket. Our courts were side by side with the local lawn bowling club and all weekend bowlers and tennis players wandered back and forth listening to the races, chatting, and watching tennis. It was not unusual to have fifty or more people, other than the players, watching the tennis and sipping tea on the lawn under the shade of the plum trees.

When I look back now I realise I was privileged to have a normal childhood—my parents were loving and caring and I was part of a large robust family—something I took for granted in those days. I had four older brothers who made my life hell most of the time, and one sister, the eldest, who saved me from my brothers many times when Mum or Dad were not around.

One very precious memory from my early childhood is helping my father cut roses for the local florist. The roses had to be cut in the early morning when the dew was still on the petals. If they had cost what they do today, we would have been multimillionaires. Our house always had the smell of roses during the summer and they are still my favourite flower.

Other special times were the winter nights in front of the open fire, getting warm enough to brave the freezing dash to my bed on the sleeping porch. I would sit on the floor between Mum and Dad and he would scratch my back and head, and many a night I would fall asleep as they talked. Thinking back now, I realise he talked constantly to Mum but very little to anyone else, until he retired—then you couldn't stop him, he talked to everyone.

11

As a very young child, I listened to the horse racing on the radio on Saturdays. Apart from being fun, it was also very profitable for me. If Poppa's horse won he would pay me five shillings from his 'bank' or the 'bankroll' for barracking it home.

However, on the days when he lost not only the day's winnings, but also the reserve 'roll' things were grim. I would then have to soften Mum up for the Monday request to borrow from her 'bank', which caused endless and amazing happenings. We would keep up a happy front until Monday morning when the crunch would come and Poppa would have to ask for a loan. In those days stress levels were not monitored but I think the loss weekends would have registered ten out of ten on the stress scale. The strain was considerable.

I think Mum was a bit unfair as Dad always gave her money for her bank when he won, but she then considered it hers and was reluctant to part with it. Dad on the other hand looked at it as something like a revolving fund. I suppose, in a final audit, Dad would have had the better deal with Mum financing many of his Saturday betting flings.

The biggest trauma of those days was saving my butter rations from my brothers. As many people know, during the Second World War all food was rationed as Australia sent most of its produce to England. My earliest memories of food are rationed beef, lots of rabbit, too much shark, and one inch squares of butter, three times a day. The lengths I went to to save my butter rations from my brothers were no doubt when I first began to develop reserves of resourcefulness and determination. Most mealtimes found me sitting under the table in the kitchen eating a piece of bread spread with my precious butter ration. My brothers had to pass Mum to get to me.

As well as the butter rations, I also remember from that time the air raid warnings. When the sirens started, Mum would huddle us all under a big old desk with stacks of books piled on top. All the windows were covered with heavy drapes as no light was allowed to show. Light wardens patrolled the streets and shouted at any house that showed lights. We spent many a night under the desk fighting and pushing, with me always coming off second best. Air raid warnings were not at all conducive to developing a loving relationship between brothers and a little sister.

Eventually, after a few planes actually came over Sydney, people were advised to build air raid shelters as constant attacks seemed to be inevitable. Our shelter was built, or dug, next to the tennis shed tuck shop under a camphor laurel tree. It consisted of a hole in the ground about ten feet square with steps dug into the dirt and a domed corrugated tin roof.

So now we had to run down the garden and into the hole. Personally, I thought the desk and books were a much better and more pleasant form of protection. But the theory was that the bombs would be dropped on houses so the shelter had to be far away from the house. For good measure Mum put the shelter under the tree. Of course when it rained water simply poured in, making it unusable. So on rainy nights it was back to the desk and books, a much better alternative to slopping around in the dark and mud, running the risk of catching pneumonia.

I really do not know how Mum got us all through the war. Air raids in the middle of the night, sick children, rationing, fighting children, more air raids. Mum also had a thing about lightning, so whenever there was a storm, it was back under the desk again. Between air raids and storms, I spent most of my childhood nights during the war under the desk. I have no idea when Mum slept.

Dad left all the disciplining to Mum. I remember him quietly watching all our activities, but only stepping in when he thought it necessary—or when he could get the boys to settle their differences with boxing gloves. Dad had been a good amateur boxer and was very keen to train the boys, but Mum would have none of it. She would say, 'I did not raise healthy sons for you to put in the boxing ring and have what brains they have knocked out of their heads.' But Dad never missed an opportunity when Mum was busy or out of hearing distance. He would immediately put the boxing gloves on the two offenders, take out his stopwatch, and read them the Queensberry rules. I do believe he even went so far as to provoke arguments in order to referee a good fight.

He had a lot to do with the physical side of our upbringing. We slept on an open sleeping porch with sliding windows for bad weather. I remember at night he would check each child to make sure he or she was breathing through the nose. If someone's mouth was open, he would wake that child up and tell him or her to breathe through the nose. He would flatten our ears, straighten our arms and legs and tuck the blanket in all around. When he reached me he would take my head in his hands and kiss me on the forehead. He did not kiss the boys.

Every Saturday morning he would line us up and give out doses of senna tea. What we didn't do to get out of that little proceeding defies description.

On Sundays, having just recovered from the Saturday morning senna tea and Saturday night festivities, he would make us work our way through some exercise routine from the Sunday morning paper. We would moan and groan through page after page with Dad enthusiastically calling out, 'Stomachs in, breathe deeply, exhale . . .' When he reached the end of the article we were allowed to stagger back to bed. As we drifted back into a peaceful sleep, we could hear him reading the rest of the newspaper, page by page, to Mum in the kitchen. It was fortunate Dad's work occupied most of his time, or we would all have been total wrecks, including Mum.

I suppose the first indication of any business talent occurred when I was nine. All my brothers played football more than once a week, so their boots constantly needed cleaning. I agreed to clean them at the rate of threepence per pair. When it was time to pay, one reneged on his agreement. I asked nicely for my money and he told me to go away. I went to arbitration but she was busy with dinner and the organisation of a charity affair. I sat and thought about this situation for a long time, and came to several conclusions. First, I had done a good job and therefore I should be paid. Second, if my brother didn't pay the amount he had agreed, he would never pay again, thereby depriving me of future income. Third, if arbitration would not help me when I presented a fair and just complaint, there was only one course left open to me—I would have to deal with the problem myself. I decided I would have to make my brother realise that not honouring his agreement would be more trouble than it was worth. But how was I, a mere nine-year-old, going to achieve this? Brute strength was out—I didn't have it—so it came down to cunning.

It was Saturday night and the house was abuzz with all my brothers busy preparing for the Saturday night's festivities. Having laid my trap for revenge, I stayed very close to Mum, something like a second skin. As the howl went up, I moved in closer and closed my eyes. My brother came storming into the room.

'Look what that little brat has done!' He held out his shoes, which I had filled with honey. Mum turned to me and just looked.

'Well you wouldn't help and he owed me that money and he reneged on his agreement!'

'Did you agree to pay her for cleaning your boots?'

'Well, sort of,' he replied feebly.

'Well, did you or did you not agree?'

'She didn't clean them properly, that's why I didn't pay her.'

'The other boys paid,' I shot in. 'You ask them, Mum. I did a good job.'

'Pay her!' said arbitration. I jumped around laughing over my victory.

'What about my shoes?' wailed my brother.

'You, young lady, will pay for the honey.' That stopped me laughing. It not only wiped out my gain, but also the money from the three other pairs of shoes.

My brother started laughing and hopping around as tears streamed down my face.

My father walked into the room and said, 'You can stop laughing, because you borrowed my shoes, so you will pay for a new pair and you can keep that pair.' That certainly stopped my brother's laughter.

The case was closed but very important business procedures had been established. First, my brother learned that if he had

15

agreed to pay me it was too much trouble not to. Second, it did not pay for me to take matters into my own hands, better to just wear arbitration down. Negotiations from that point on were fairly reasonable; arbitration was called on a few times, but no more honey. If arbitration was busy cooking, I would just hide something that belonged to the offender until he paid or arbitration stopped cooking long enough to settle the dispute.

Somewhere in amongst all of this, the war ended and I didn't have to fight for my butter any more. I also became more involved in my tennis career, and I didn't have time to clean football boots. This change went a long way towards establishing more harmonious relationships between my brothers and myself.

In 1952 I was one of the junior players picked to be ballgirl for the Davis Cup—Australia versus America at White City. The junior boys were ballboys for the singles and the junior girls for the doubles. One of my great claims to fame at that early age was when Pancho Gonzales (whose serve was calculated to be over one hundred miles per hour) aced Frank Sedgman and the ball hit me in the solar plexus. I went down like a stone and Pancho jumped the net, rushed to my side, scooped me up and carried me to the first-aid room. My dizziness cleared to see his anxious face and the first-aid officer looking at me. When I was declared 'out of danger' he went back to the doubles match. I was detained under observation. When he finished the match he came back to check that I was alright. During the rest of the Cup he always spoke to me whenever he saw me, and I was the envy of all the juniors at White City.

School took a second place to tennis, but Mum made it clear that there would be no tennis unless my schoolwork was completed in an above-average manner.

At fourteen I was picked to represent New South Wales in the under-fifteen schoolgirls team. A great honour for my school and me, so I was allowed ample time for tennis practice by my school. Mum was not so cooperative and I found myself doing double time on both tennis and study.

I topped my year in physiology, my next love to tennis.

16

At the end of third year I had a choice: tennis or more study, and if I could keep up the marks, study to be a doctor? My one and only dream was to win Wimbledon, so of course I chose tennis. At fifteen it looked much easier and far more glamorous than seven years of study. But I was not to get off that easily. Mum insisted I be qualified in some field that I could, as she put it, fall back on. She would have liked to see me go on to study to be a doctor but she knew my study habits only too well and I think she realised that another seven years was not for me. Looking back now, I wish she had pushed me a little harder. Still to this day I find I would rather read the latest medical discoveries before anything, and have always loved and still would love to do research.

So it was more study. Not the intense study required to pass the grades for a doctor, but for the 'something to fall back on'. There were years of typing, shorthand, office procedure, filing, and business principles, all of which I found extremely boring. However, I still had the time I needed for tennis.

I was also enrolled in the Pat Woodley School of Modelling and Deportment to put the finishing touches to Mum's training. I cannot remember the number of girls in that particular class but we were soon all friends. We had loads of fun learning to behave as young ladies should. We walked around with books on our heads trying to look graceful—most of us looked as if we were about to be attacked from all sides. I received a diploma to say that, to the satisfaction of the school, I had acquired all the social graces necessary to pass as a well-groomed young lady. In those days it was necessary to have a diploma to prove this. During class our behaviour was extremely prim and proper, but if Miss Woodley could have seen us dashing around the streets of Sydney in our short lunchbreak, she would not have been amused.

All in all, the course has proved to be a bonus in my life. It certainly stood me in good stead when I walked across the stage at the Regent in 1990. Who would have dreamed that those madcap months of training back in 1950 would pay off so many years later?

17

I did a few swimsuit and sportswear modelling jobs but the requirements for a fashion model were tall, slim and no bust. With a thirty-six-inch bustline I was definitely not fashion material so it was fortunate that tennis was my love and not modelling.

Boys entered my life around this period but tennis still occupied most of my time, so most of the boys I found myself swooning over were tennis players or athletes.

However, the confidence and style I had on the tennis court did not extend to boys. With them I was awkward, shy and nervous, everywhere except on the tennis court. Even my confidence-building deportment course did not help in this area. I can now smile at those heart-wrenching situations which, at regular intervals, made life impossible to continue, but then it was agonising.

One heart throb was a cyclist with his heart set on the Olympics. He adored my leg muscles! He said if he had my leg muscles he would be world champion. Not exactly what a young girl dreams of hearing but he really was a gorgeous-looking boy and the fact that most of the girls were clamouring to get a date with him made me feel quite smug—at least I had his adoring attention.

However, obviously my leg muscles were not enough because the following season he fell madly in love with my doubles partner, and she didn't have any muscles at all.

CHAPTER 2

❖

1955-1959

At nineteen I got engaged. All my girlfriends were. Ben and I drove with friends to a surf carnival down the south coast from Sydney. Ben's parents had recently bought him a Triumph TR-2 sports car, and on the way back up the coast road the engine finally clocked up two thousand miles, meaning the engine was now 'run-in' and could be driven at more than thirty miles per hour without it seizing. So Ben put the car through its paces.

One of the front tyres blew on a tight bend. The car went into a slide, the back skidded into a cement mileage post and the car spun up into the air like a top. I was thrown out across the road into the oncoming traffic. The car then flipped over, trapping Ben underneath.

I do not remember much of the crash. I was turning around to see how far the lights of the other cars were behind when everything started to whirl in dizzying circles. When my vision cleared, I was on my back in the middle of the road with the bumper bar of a car almost over my head, and a nice man patiently telling the driver to back up. I think the driver was in more shock than me because there was no way he was going to get back in his car. Finally a few men pushed the car to the side of the road.

They managed to get Ben out of his car alright. He had no broken bones or serious injuries, although his face was badly cut up, leaving many scars.

I realised many years later that the nice man directing the scene of the accident saved my life. He would not let me be moved for fear of spinal injury and kept me calm during the long wait for the ambulance, talking to me about anything from dancing and tennis to flying.

Even though we were very close to Wollongong, we were just inside the St George district, so by the time this was sorted out and an ambulance dispatched, many anxious hours had passed. It was fortunate I was not bleeding from an artery or something. There was no pain—that came later. However there was a feeling of apprehension, and now and then the fear would increase but that wonderful man would see it on my face and start talking until he could see interest replace the fear. He told me about flying his plane in New Guinea, and that he was a first aid officer with St John's Ambulance. I wish I could thank him today, if only words would be adequate.

I remember the emergency ward, doctors, x-ray machines, hushed talking, blackness, my parents arriving, more blackness. Then, finally, waking up many, many days later.

When my parents arrived at the hospital, Mum could see me through the partly open door. She said I was a mass of blood from head to foot. When I was thrown from the car onto the road the gravel cut me to pieces as I rolled and skidded. I still have scars today from that tumble. She could not see my face, and said she sat there and prayed that my face was not damaged. Later she thought what a stupid thing to pray for, but by this time she was also suffering from shock.

The doctors told my parents I had five fractures in the pelvis, a crushed left hip, and an extensively damaged left knee—actually half of it was missing. There was a possibility of internal bleeding, and if this occurred things would be grim. The next two days would tell if they had to operate. The message was, prepare for the worst. All this time I was under sedation to counteract shock. After two days the doctors were pleased to announce no signs of internal injury. However, shock was now the prime worry, so more sedation. Finally I opened my eyes and they announced to my parents that I would live.

I was flat on my back on a board, with no pillow and with flannel supports around my hips like a diaper. I had no feeling in my body from the waist down. I could not lift my head as my pelvis was cracked at the base of the spine. My hair was shaved where stitching had been done and the rest had fallen out because of the massive doses of drugs given to me to counteract shock. I was gravel rash from neck to toes, and the only thing I could move without pain was my arms. *But I was alive.*

The next panic was the left leg. The doctors were concerned as the leg had no movement at all and no knee or bottom of foot reflexes. After the first month, and still no improvement, they voiced their concern to my parents. There was the possibility of losing the leg. Mum and Dad said no in very positive terms. The doctors said that if gangrene developed, they would then have to remove the leg and possibly the hip—I could even die.

My parents said they would take the chance and wait. To this day I am eternally grateful to them for taking this stand, as a doctor's opinion was almost law in those days. They said they would rather lose me than make me face life at nineteen without a leg. As a mother, I now realise how very brave they were. It is a decision I would never want to have to make.

Several months passed before the leg showed any signs of life. As it had no feeling, the trainee nurses would use it to practise on whenever I needed an injection. Then, one day, as a trainee jabbed at it with the needle, I let out a tremendous yell. The leg improved from then on. It was three years before it worked normally, but eventually after lots of training and exercise it came good and is still performing quite well today, considering its background.

I can't say anything in favour of the hospital except that I was very, very pleased to leave. However, my time there did teach me how to stand up for myself.

Because I was paralysed from the waist down, toilet procedure was via enema and catheter. The enema procedure we will leave to the imagination. The catheter, which was permanent, emptied into a small kidney dish, balanced on the side of the bed. This was so that regular checks could be made for blood in the urine. Only the checks were not regular and the kidney dish would overflow onto the bed. The matron

21

would then order the sheets to be changed and that's when the problem occurred. If the nurses did not lift together, and they didn't, the pain of the bones shifting was like being torn apart. It would completely take my breath away and I would start choking, so they would lower me back onto the bed until I regained my breath, then back up in the air, and more pain. This would take ten to fifteen minutes, depending on how many times I choked and had to be put down. Constant pain, just because a nurse did not check the kidney dish.

After going through this painful exercise a few times, I had had enough so I decided to take matters into my own hands. I could not see the dish, as I could not lift my head, so I very slowly felt down my side, picked up the dish and emptied its contents onto the floor. The matron would severely reprimand the nurse responsible and instruct her to mop the floor. The nurse would always manage to bump the bed more than necessary, but compared to being hoisted in the air by eight nurses all lifting at different times, this pain was negligible. Soon after that the checks became regular.

There was another problem I had to deal with there which was not painful, but very, very embarrassing. Apparently I was something of a medical freak. The doctors told Mum that my bones were extraordinarily strong and that most young girls with my injuries would have died—the pelvis would have shattered into the internal organs causing massive internal bleeding, whereas my bones just cracked and stayed in place. Because I was such a phenomenon, every day some doctor with a group of medical students in tow would assemble at the foot of my bed to study my bone structure. Because of the difficulty in lifting, I had just my flannel diaper and a hospital gown draped over my chest. There was a large hoop over the broken pelvic area and all was covered by a bed sheet.

The doctor delivering the address of the day would remove the sheet, gown and diaper and discuss my bone structure before them, without the least concern for the nineteen-year-old girl dying of embarrassment behind closed eyes.

When I realised this was going to be a regular event and not just a 'one off', I told my mother. She was horrified and immediately wanted to go to war with the matron for allowing it to happen.

Still flushed with my success over the kidney dish, I asked her if I could handle it, pointing out that I had to reside there for a fair while. She agreed, but told me if it was not settled by her next visit, she would take matters into her hands.

One of the few happy moments I had in that hospital occurred that afternoon.

'Now gentlemen, I want you to observe this particular bone . . .' Not a word to me, the doctor just assembled his students around the foot of the bed and started his lecture.

'No, they won't!' I said with a great deal more conviction than I thought I possessed.

He stopped, turned, glared at me, and then continued.

'No they will not observe my bone structure,' I said in a much louder voice. 'You are not my doctors and you have no right examining me!'

'Young lady, this is a medical examination, do be quiet!' He was obviously not accustomed to being challenged by someone so young.

'If you are not all out of here on the count of three I will start screaming!'

He hesitated, but the students took flight. The rush for the door saw a jumble of arms, legs, stethoscopes and displaced dignity. They managed to untangle themselves and be gone by the count of three. My hand edged down the bed, found the kidney dish and slowly emptied the contents on to the floor. I folded my hands across my chest and felt the happiest I had since the accident.

Up to this point in my life, I had always been protected by my family. This was the first time in my life I had been away from home and alone, and the first time I had had to fight for my rights. After the kidney dish and this last incident, the nurses decided I wasn't so bad after all. In fact, most of them started treating me like a human being. The matron . . . well, even the nurses couldn't get along with her.

During that painful and boring stay, I learned how very powerful the mind really is. I had been given so many drugs to pull me through the shock period that for weeks afterwards I could have little or no drugs for pain. I was only allowed painkillers twice in twenty-four hours, so the hours of pain were long and continuous. I suppose you could say I perfected self-hypnosis. I would practise at night, as the days had too many interruptions. It would take me hours, but finally I would not feel the pain and would drift off to sleep. After much practice, I could reach this desired state in about forty minutes.

Once I left that hospital my improvement was dramatic. My brother Tod made me a contraption he called a bookholder. Because I was flat on my back, my arms would ache after only a few minutes of holding a book in the air and I would have to continually rest them. Tod's invention held the book so all I had to do was turn the pages. I read many, many books that year, which helped to pass the time. My hair slowly grew back in uneven tufts, making me look like a topsy doll.

Finally, the x-rays gave the all clear, and I was told to go ahead and walk. I had dreamed every day since the accident of getting out of bed and walking. Now the time had arrived and I was terrified! I broke out in a cold teeth-chattering sweat. No one but no one could convince me I would not fall down and break my pelvis again.

Dad took over. The first step was to sit me up. I had been flat on my back for over eight months and the effect of sitting straight up was devastating. The room started spinning, I lost all sense of balance, and started vomiting and blacking out at the same time. It was back to flat on my back. The doctor said my head could only be raised a few inches at a time, so gradually I got to sitting without vomiting. Walking was another matter altogether. My muscles had not been used for so long that they would not hold my weight. With two people supporting and dragging me, I was totally exhausted after shuffling just fifteen feet.

My father was determined to prove the doctors' many grim predictions wrong. According to them I could do no strenuous exercise or sport, except maybe golf in a few years. I probably wouldn't ever be able to have children and I would almost certainly suffer from arthritis and require a constant supply of painkillers and other drugs. All in all I would lead a very sedentary life. Dad said rubbish.

I would stand between two chairs looking at him a few feet away. 'Don't give up, Sara, beat it.' Very firm, no dramatics, just quiet resolute encouragement. With muscles cramping and twitching and pain consuming me, I would struggle to force the muscles to move my legs.

Each day saw improvement until I could stand without the chairs. Then I knew the terror of a baby's first step. I had known how to walk, run and jump for nineteen years, but the terror I experienced taking that first step is indescribable. I take my hat off to babies.

More cold sweats, shakes, chickening out, Dad quietly encouraging, and then finally the first steps alone. Holding my breath, and gritting my teeth, I dragged one leg after the other until I reached the other side of the room where, shaking and laughing, I collapsed in a heap with perspiration dripping from my fingertips.

When I realised nothing was broken, I was up again and walking till I finally fell asleep in a chair. Once out of that bed I was in no hurry to go back for a while.

Within weeks I could walk without pain or exhaustion, not without a limp and other minor problems, but a reasonable imitation of the real thing. Against all doctors' predictions, I was on the road back.

My next major objective was to get back onto the tennis court. With a racquet in one hand and a walking stick in the other, I raced around the court like a three-legged rabbit. Serving was not on the agenda but I was dynamite at the net. Over the next few years tennis was of great benefit in helping my leg to mend. If I did not exercise daily my leg would stiffen up so badly that I could not walk. If I had to walk up stairs, I would turn sideways, step up one at a time with my good leg and drag my left leg after me.

I played tournaments as soon as I thought I was fit enough, but it quickly became evident that my leg would not stand up to the pressures of competitive play. It would usually give out in the second set and if the match went to a third set,

I spent most of the time on the ground. The leg would just collapse under me. There was absolutely no chance of singles. I tried, but the embarrassment of continually falling down soon convinced me to give it up. I had to accept that I would never be able to achieve my life ambition to win centre-court Wimbledon.

Suddenly there was no direction in my life, nothing to aim for, no star to reach. Ben and I had long drifted apart and depression set in. I slumped lower and lower. Mum took me to our doctor, who told her what Dad had said all along, 'She must do something to interest her until she can learn to accept the fact that championship tennis will no longer be her whole life.' Easy to say, but I was still clinging to the hope that somehow my leg would eventually be fit again.

Nevertheless, it was out into the work a day world—a job to occupy the mind. I found myself sitting in front of an electronic accounting machine taking an aptitude test. I was given a few basic instructions on how the machine operated and what it could achieve, then it was up to me. I got the job. With nine other girls I was to form a field team for Remington Rand. Training took place in the workshop, with the mechanics, from the ground up. Remington Rand offered a training and relief service to companies which bought its machines. When a firm's operator went on holidays, or was away sick, we would step in. We were very busy at the end of the financial year when companies needed the yearly profit and loss delivered by a certain date. We trained new operators, transferred written accounts to the electronic system, balanced the books, and handed the working system over.

As I became more experienced, I was sent further afield. With a senior operator, also female, I helped install, or partly install, the wage system at the Snowy Mountains Hydro Scheme. This was quite an experience as there were no women in the whole place. It was a very big sale and when the request to install the machines and system was accepted this problem was not even thought of.

When we arrived the accountant groaned, 'Oh no, women!' We looked at him, puzzled, but when he explained about the hundreds of men on the job site who had not seen women for months, we wanted to leave there and then. There were many frantic calls back to the Sydney office but the problem was time. We had to train ten operators and have a complete wage system up and running by a certain date in order to fulfil the contract. As for our safety, it was just bad luck. So life settled down to day after day of training operators. Every evening we were whisked back to our rooms before we were seen, and had to remain there until the next day. We didn't even dare venture out for a walk. At the pace the operators were progressing, it looked as if we would be there for months. Some days it was easier just to do the work ourselves but that was not getting us anywhere.

The problem was that all the operators were men. I wore out many wooden rulers slapping the knuckles of wandering hands, and learning concentration was zero. The men we were trying to teach didn't want to learn. First, they were not interested in accounting machines, but more importantly when they were trained we would leave and then they would not be able to ogle us all day.

The accountant had given us large oversized grey workcoats to wear and we were told never to remove them outside of our rooms. To say we were slightly nervous is an understatement.

Of course, like all secrets, it finally leaked out that there were two women in the office block. I looked out the window one day to see hundreds of men just staring up at the window. More frantic calls to Sydney but there was no response. So we threatened to just leave. They then sent two mechanics to guard us and the mechanics stood outside our room each night.

Finally, one night some men smuggled alcohol into the camp and there was an ugly fight outside our door. We piled all the furniture against the door and window and spent a miserable night sitting in the middle of the floor. The next morning we departed with the injured mechanics who had defended our honour. One was quite badly hurt. The system was then installed by mechanics.

After that experience I decided field work was not for me.

27

Besides, I was playing district tennis at nights and on weekends, so I did not want to be away from Sydney. Luckily, one of the teachers in the classroom was leaving and my boss asked me if I would like to take over her job. It was very interesting work as it involved teaching many different systems to different students, and I was always doing something new. I settled in quickly.

CHAPTER 3

❖

1959-1960

At twenty-three years old life was good. I was coming to terms with the new direction my life was taking, I had an interesting job and I was playing district tennis, not the tennis I had dreamed of, but nevertheless good tennis. There were some nice men in my life and one relationship was developing into something special. I had met Neville on my second job for Remington when I was installing an electronic accounting system for the Leeton Rice Co-op. He worked for a company which sold farm equipment and we were staying in the same hotel. Then suddenly life took a turn.

I was sunbaking on the deck of a sailing boat at Mosman Marina, when this very Virginian accent said, 'Permission to come aboard . . . ma'am?'

I sat up and standing before me was a tall American, judging by the accent, with the best blue eyes since Paul Newman. He was dressed in a very English suit topped off with a Homburg, carrying an umbrella, and holding his shoes in his hand.

Without waiting for permission he stepped aboard. His eyes travelled up and down my body repeatedly, so much so that I reached for my wrap. He realised my intention and went to help. Then, despite having just bragged about his prowess in sailing, he tripped on the cleat and landed on top of me, flat on the deck.

I finally managed to disentangle myself, took a few deep breaths and tried to look composed. I failed miserably.

I remember two things very clearly. The song playing softly on the radio, 'What a Difference a Day Makes', and this very attractive man standing before me, smiling.

Just then Neville walked down the wharf and onto the boat. He stood there, waiting. We all stood waiting. Neville finally said, 'Well?'

I was completely mystified. Wasn't this man one of his clients? Customers often came sailing with us on weekends. I had assumed the handsome stranger must be a hopeful buyer of farm machinery.

The American just stood there smiling. He was obviously enjoying the situation immensely. I put the ball back in Neville's court.

'Well what?'

'Aren't you going to introduce me to your friend?' he asked in a very flat tone.

'But . . .' At this point our Virginian interceded.

'Thank you for letting me look over your boat,' he said to Neville. His eyes travelled over me again. 'And your lovely crew.' This time his eyes never moved from mine. 'I see my friends have just arrived.' He indicated down the wharf. Then his eyes came back to mine.

'You, I will see again!'

He stepped onto the dock, bowed ceremoniously, put on his shoes, tipped his Homburg with the point of his umbrella and disappeared down the wharf.

'Cheeky bugger,' said Neville. It must have taken him a long time to perfect the 'Avengers' homburg and umbrella trick.

Almost all young girls have a mental picture of their Mr Right. Mine was Latin, with black hair, green eyes and very tall, around six foot three. This man did not fit the image at all. He had vivid blue eyes that were almost piercing, plain brown hair, and was just a shade under six feet. But topped off with that fabulous smile . . . The Latin image faded. What a difference a day makes.

I saw him again much sooner than expected. During the uproar on the boat he had managed to find out from one of our friends where Neville and I were having dinner.

He walked straight up to our table, and went through the 'What a coincidence . . . Come here often? My favourite restaurant actually,' routine and then, before Neville could open his mouth, whisked me onto the dance floor. He instructed the band to play 'One Enchanted Evening'. This, he told me, was now our song. He grabbed me in a clutch that would have defied Houdini and launched into a waltz that would raise the roof on any ballroom. On the tiny restaurant floor it had the effect of sending most of the other dancers spinning to the sides. I pleaded with him to slow down and he did, but intensified his grip.

The music stopped, he released the grip and I started breathing again. He helped me back to the table, bowed a goodnight and disappeared. He had impressed me, just as he had intended.

That night Neville and I had the first of many heated discussions over this man. I suppose Neville could see the writing on the wall but there was nothing he could do to fight it. He did try, he even enlisted the help of Mum, and considering Mum and Neville did not see eye to eye, that was a big step for Neville.

However, as the days after that fateful Sunday turned into weeks, the excitement of the stranger entering my life started to fade. Neville asked casually if I had heard from him again. I said no, but I had to work hard at hiding my disappointment.

It had been a very hectic day in the classroom, new students, machine bars to set for the new work, constant questions, safety lock alarms ringing endlessly, but at five o'clock this ended abruptly when, en masse, the students stampeded for the door.

I waited while the dust settled and the door slammed for the last time, and then started to catch up on the paperwork that went with the day. I was playing tennis that night so I was hurrying when interrupted on the last entry by one of the typists from the outer office.

'There's someone out here in the office wanting to enrol in your class, lucky you!'

The door whooshed open, hitting the wall with such force that the shudder reverberated around the room, and there he stood.

'Oh!' I said, and immediately cursed myself, since at least ninety per cent of my verbal exchange with this man so far had been this one syllable. He must have thought I was an imbecile.

'Hi!' was the reply. Then silence as we just stood there.

I rallied, 'What are you doing here?'

'Enrolling.'

'Don't be stupid, you can't.'

'Well, dinner then.'

I gathered the books on my desk into a neat pile and dashed for the door.

'I'm playing tennis tonight and I am already late!' Halfway out of the office I realised I was still in office uniform and had left my handbag behind. I swung around abruptly and collided with him. His arms must have been operated by snap locks—I was once again in the Houdini grip.

The rest of the evening was a delightful nightmare. His name was Charles English Henderson III. When I tried to explain him to my mother, she told me they had spent the afternoon chatting over a cup of tea.

'We had such a lovely chat, all about you.'

'What?'

'Don't upset yourself, this is not your concern,' said Charles.

I threw my hands in the air and went to dress for tennis.

The rest of the evening was along the same lines. Everyone at tennis asked, 'Who is that?' By this time my exhaustion was total so I just said, 'Don't know.'

'Don't know? He came with you!'

'Then ask him.'

Charles chatted amicably with everyone. The evening was spiced with conversations like:

'He says you're going to marry him!'

'Really?'

'When?'

'When what?'

'When are you going to marry him?'

'Ask him.'

And:

32

'He says you're going to live in Hong Kong!'

'Really?'

'Well! When?'

'Ask him.' Somehow I managed to play tennis and get home. At seven o'clock the next morning he was at the door to take me to breakfast in the Cross. He then deposited me on the office steps in time for work.

The day passed in pandemonium with phone calls, flowers, telegrams, and, somewhere in there, my work. At the end of the day I walked down the steps and he was waiting.

'You're not playing tennis, I checked with your mother, and she knows you're having dinner with me.'

I protested mildly for appearances' sake but knew that he knew he had me just where he wanted me, and where I wanted to be.

Dinner was at the Chelsea in Kings Cross, a wedge of meat big enough to feed ten people washed down by the right champagne.

The waiter watched horrified as Charles drew a map of Australia in biro on the linen tablecloth. After calming the waiter with instructions to add the cost to his bill, Charles then proceeded to mark in a spot on the top left hand corner of the Northern Territory. With a flourish of the pen he drew a circle and said, 'This is where we will live one day, when we are married.' Not a question, just a matter-of-fact statement.

After completely overwhelming me, he eventually deposited me on the doorstep, crushed me in another one of those hugs and departed. I was left with the very definite impression that he was quite mad and I should never see him again.

It continued. More breakfasts, flowers and chocolates delivered to the office at all hours, luncheons, dinners. The weeks passed in a beautiful blurred haze.

'Darling, dinner tonight at the Chelsea, okay?' A split second pause, not for an answer but for my brain to receive. 'See you tonight.' The phone went dead.

I called home and told Mum I would not be home for dinner. She said she was pleased I was with that nice American. I still had to take her to task over their afternoon chat. It seems she told him everything, including the location of birthmarks.

I arrived on time. Charles had already ordered dinner earlier by phone. I sat with two cocktails, also ordered by phone, and waited. And waited. I went home two hours later in quite a state. Emotions raced through my brain in chaotic disorder, exploding into each other.

My temper flared as I decided I had been stood up. The next emotion was terror, he had been hurt in an accident, then horror, he is dying in hospital somewhere, then despair, what will I do?

I called the police and explained the situation. They checked and I waited in agony while the checking continued.

'No, miss, no accidents in the city area involving Americans.'

My black temper returned.

My poor students felt the aftermath of the stormy temper that raged most of the night. I was finishing the day's paperwork when my boss appeared at the door.

'A few words, Sara.' It seemed that during my weeks in that blurred haze I had trained a girl from an engineering factory to be a retail operator. I assured him I was back on track, that I had been suffering from a virus and was now over it. I dragged myself back to reality and knuckled down to work. I put on a smiling face although I did not feel like smiling, and I talked to myself a lot.

I was sure my feelings were reciprocated but his behaviour did not bear this out. To just leave, not a word for weeks. It was all too much to take. I swore off men, Charles in particular, forever.

The classroom was quiet with all the students engrossed in their work. A hand appeared at the back of the room, so I walked down the aisle of noisy machines, showed the student how to correct her problem, started to walk back to my desk and stopped. He was standing in the doorway beaming that winning smile. Many, many emotions coursed through me in that split second before my temper emerged.

'You!'

34

'Now, I can explain.' The students stopped working to watch the soap opera unfolding before them.

'How dare you?' I blurted out all the pent-up feelings of anger, frustration and unhappiness of the past few weeks. There was complete silence. The students held their breath, waiting for the reply to such an onslaught.

'I'm sorry, I forgot you,' came the meek reply. Well, the meekest Charles could manage.

'Forgot her?' chorused the classroom. This brought me back to earth and I asked Charles to 'step outside'.

As in all arguments that followed, he won and had me apologising for all the dreadful things I had thought about him.

He had started a business meeting at eight o'clock and lost track of time. It was ten before he realised and he called the restaurant, but had missed me by only minutes. He then had to leave immediately for Hong Kong and could not reach me by phone before he boarded the plane. He tried to call from Hong Kong for days with no luck, and then he was travelling in areas where phones had not yet been heard of. At least that was his story.

He flashed that special smile, 'Forgiven?' What was there to say?

More months of breakfasts, flowers, telegrams, lunches, dinners, departures, letters, static phone calls from Hong Kong, arrivals, and the whole marvellous procedure all over again.

One memorable evening he called me at work to say he was playing a few sets of tennis with a friend. If I met him at the court, we could then go for dinner. I said that sounded fine. I arrived at the court after work and watched the match. Charles excelled himself. He had his friend running all over the court making Charles look terrific. The only problem was that his opponent was Martin Mulligan, my mixed doubles partner from junior days.

When they had finished they walked over to me. Charles was about to introduce Martin when Martin said, 'Hello Sara.' Charles stood there for a moment then went off to change without saying a word.

Martin and I sat and talked. Apparently Charles had wanted to impress me and Martin had been coaching him, so Charles had asked him to play up to him so he would look good in front of his girlfriend. Of course Martin hadn't known I was the girl.

Charles returned, showered and dressed for dinner. I said goodbye to Martin and we departed. Charles was very quiet. He finally said, 'How do you know Martin?' I told him we had played in the same district and were junior mixed partners. He told me I was sneaky!

'Sneaky? I'm sneaky?' He had the grace to look sheepish.

After that fiasco he moved onto his next. He told me we were having dinner in a nice quiet hotel just down the road from the tennis court. He had planned dinner in a room with violins outside the door. When Charles stopped the car, I thought I would die of laughter. Of all the hotels in Sydney, he had picked the one my father managed. Needless to say, the plot did not collapse, it exploded. Poor Charles, two complete failures in one evening. He left for Hong Kong the next day, ahead of schedule.

The letters came regularly. One would not call them love letters, I do not think I ever received a love letter from Charles. I say I do not think because most of his letters were impossible to read. I would keep them and ask him to read them to me when he arrived, but most of the time he could not decipher his own writing. They would start with 'Darling', but would then go on to list all the things he wanted me to do before his return. One time he even enclosed a draft of a business letter which he wanted me to type and send to a list of addresses.

He had been gone about a month. I was missing him, and his letters said he was missing me. However he had no return date as yet. One of his letters indicated he had business problems.

My boss opened the classroom door and said, a little too loudly, 'Sara, my office immediately!' What had I done now? Trotting down the hall behind him I ventured, 'Something wrong?' We reached his office, and there sat Charles. He had informed my boss I was leaving today and with a classroom

36

of forty students and no replacement for me, one could understand my boss's reacton.

'How? . . . What? . . . When?' I wasn't getting anywhere. He wanted me to have a week off during the time he was in Sydney. It was finally decided that I could take five days after we had called in one of the field operators, which would take two days.

During those five days we both admitted we were hopelessly in love, but although there was this declaration of love, there was no mention of the future. I found myself once again at the airport. I had the feeling he had a problem but he had never mentioned it, and I had never asked.

Sitting in the bar at the airport he dropped the bombshell— he was married! It was only a few minutes before his plane left. I just sat there. All I could think of was Mum. He said it was alright. I still just stared. They were separated, and had been for quite a while. In fact, she lived in Sydney! With the children!

'Children?' I managed feebly. He had spoken to her and they were getting a divorce which should be finalised soon. The last call on his flight was announced. He kissed me passionately and disappeared, leaving me mumbling on the bar stool, our farewell drink untouched on the bar.

I don't remember going home, and I'm not really sure of the days that followed. No one knew the agony I was going through, they mistook my dazed condition for love. What on earth was I going to do? What could I say to Mum? I decided not to tell anyone. I had read novels about such situations but never in a million years did I think it would happen to me. I kept coming back to Mum. I knew she would not be able to handle this.

Two weeks passed. His letters started arriving daily. His last letter said he was arriving next week. I could not write, I was still sorting my feelings out. I had decided that I could never see him again, or at least not until he was divorced.

A few inquiries told me this could take up to four years. This plunged me deeper into depression. I prepared myself for his arrival. Telling him my decision was going to be difficult.

A telegram arrived saying he was delayed. The letters continued and still I did not reply. The strain started to show. I was irritable, my work suffered, my tennis was atrocious, everyone gave me plenty of room. My only thought was the showdown.

He arrived and I took the day off, wanting to avoid another classroom drama. I met him at the airport, braced myself for the ordeal ahead and felt wretched. He started the 'Darling', crush, kiss, another crush routine. I was close to tears, about to turn and run, when he said, 'The divorce will be finalised in six weeks.'

He led me speechless into the bar and ordered a drink. When I recovered, I said solemnly, 'You can't get a divorce in six weeks.' More of his lies, I thought to myself sadly.

'In America you can!'

We shared another wonderful week. Everyone was pleased I was back to normal, and he departed again. Life settled down.

The feelings I had for this man I had not experienced before. When he was not with me, nothing would fill the void. I was in trouble; he was too much for me to handle, but my life was in his hands.

I had not fallen in love with any ordinary man.

Charles was born in Baltimore, Maryland, and as a young boy and in his teens he had sailed around Gibson Island and the Chesapeake Bay. He left LeHigh University in his second year of engineering to fight for his country in the Second World War, and served mostly in the Pacific.

He was a war hero, and was on the cover of *Time* magazine as 'Yank of the Week'. His war decorations included seven Battle Stars, two Silver Stars, three Distinguished Flying Crosses, three Air Medals and more. He was Lieutenant Commander of the night-bombing Torpedo 10 Squadron aboard the U.S.S. *Enterprise* aircraft carrier when peace was declared.

And now all this energy was directed towards pursuing me!

CHAPTER 4

❖

1960

I was patiently listening to a slightly hysterical mother, waiting for her to calm down. I caught words like police, international investigation, ruined, Interpol. I kept trying to interject 'Mum' into the flow, but to no avail.

My boss appeared at the door with a very sour expression on his face. What a day! 'Sara, my office now!' He was gone, without a glance over his shoulder, and Mum was still babbling. I shouted over the continuous stream that I would call her later, and ran down the hall to catch up with my boss. I entered his office and there were two more grim men.

The questioning started. My name, how long had I worked here, was I born in Australia, did I travel much, what countries . . . ? I answered all the questions until my patience started to wear thin.

'What is all this about?'

More questions. Did I know anyone in Hong Kong? I might have known it would be Charles!

'Yes.'

'Name?'

'Charles Henderson.'

'Known him long?'

'What is considered long?' And on it went.

Charles, acting true to form, had sent me a thirteen-diamond-cluster engagement ring by air freight and had not insured, registered or declared it. In the sixties, quite a lot of money could be made by buying diamonds in Hong Kong and smuggling them into Australia.

We went to the airport, my home away from home, and they showed me the ring. Charles had good taste; I liked it immediately. I quickly read the letter enclosed, which said we were to be married on the 4th of July, invitations, church and so on all arranged. My ticket was waiting at the airport. This calmed the grim men considerably but it had the opposite effect on me.

Words fail to describe the weeks that followed. What with passport arrangements, more travel injections than I care to remember, all of which made me desperately ill, dress fittings and goodbyes, it was a non-stop parade. It finally ended at the airport on the 30th of June 1960.

The whole family was there to see me off, including all my butter-stealing brothers of former years. Each one took me aside and threatened to do various things to Charles if he didn't do the right thing by their little sister. I just had to call and they would 'put him straight'. Of course I was not to mention the conversation to anyone, particularly not to my other brothers. I was very moved by these, never to be repeated, separate declarations of brotherly love.

After kissing everyone, receiving endless hugs, handshakes, and more kisses and hugs, I slowly, very slowly, started to walk that long hundred yards to the waiting plane. As much as I wanted to be with that unusual man, the times I wanted to run back to my family in that hundred yards cannot be counted. It was the longest walk of my life. It took many hours on the plane to Darwin to collect myself.

While waiting in Darwin airport for the aircraft to be refuelled, I was surprised to hear my name called over the paging system. I went to the desk and was met by a most charming American who turned out to be Charles's cousin. His name was Gus Trippe. In typical family style, he crushed me in a welcoming bear hug and promptly opened a bottle of champagne. We talked, mostly about Charles, as if we had been friends for years. When it was time to reboard, he crushed me again and poured me back on the plane.

I was just getting over the Darwin landing when the hostess appeared and said the captain had invited me up front. It seemed he knew one of my tennis friends, who had told him I would be on the flight. He asked me to have a drink with him in Manila to celebrate my coming marriage. Now in full swing, I accepted.

We were walking across the tarmac in Manila when suddenly there was Charles, looking like a thundercloud.

'Darling, what are you doing here? I'm supposed to meet you in Hong Kong.'

'It's obvious you weren't expecting me here,' he retorted.

'Oh, don't be silly. The captain is a friend of Judith's. He was just about to take me for a drink to celebrate our wedding.'

'It seems you've already started.'

'Oh no, that was your cousin Gus in Darwin.'

The captain discreetly excused himself.

'Will you please stop sulking and say you're pleased to see me.'

He didn't need much encouragement to crush me. We were definitely going to have to come to some agreement on this crushing deal—my ribs were failing fast.

'Darling, there is one problem: as a surprise I was going to join you on this flight to Hong Kong, but the airline cannot pick up passengers en route, so I will fly up on a later flight tonight.'

'What will I do?'

'I've arranged for a good friend of mine to meet you at the airport in Hong Kong. He'll take care of you until I arrive at midnight.' All this was explained to me over several cocktails, which he said would relax me. They succeeded in making me very drunk. Lots of cups of black coffee later, I was feeling deadly ill, and drunk. When it was time to leave, he kissed me several times, crushed me a little less, and poured me onto the plane with the promise to join me in eight hours time.

I was cleared through customs without much trouble and was looking for a porter to take my bags when I was told they were on strike. After dragging my luggage out into the receiving area, I certainly didn't feel like any fashion plate. I had come from winter and here it was over one hundred degrees, old style—the perspiration was pouring off me. After mopping myself down and trying to look cool, calm and collected, I looked around. In front of me was a sea of faces, all Chinese, or so it seemed. They spoke very quickly and I felt they were all looking at me. I looked for the friend in that sea and then thought, what if he's Chinese, how will I know him? I was near tears when a hand gently touched my elbow.

'You have to be Sara.'

'Oh yes!'

'Good, I'm Dick Kirby. Charles asked me to meet you.'

He spoke a few words and all those staring faces started to move in different directions. With suitcases quickly and efficiently packed in his car, he took me on a tour of Hong Kong. In those days it was a marvellous place, not yet ruined by tourism. We finished the tour in his beautiful apartment looking across Kowloon harbour to Victoria Island. After a fabulous dinner cooked by his Chinese cook, I had very hot and very cold baths, and then relaxed listening to music, to await Charles's arrival.

He turned up in his usual hurricane style and after a short business discussion with Dick, we had a romantic late supper alone.

The next day I met a most delightful person, Peggy Cater. I was to stay with Peggy and Jack at their lovely home, the White House, in Tai Po in the New Territory, for the remaining three days. Peggy, and Peggy alone, was responsible for getting me to the altar, twelve pounds lighter and doped to the gills, but nevertheless she got me there.

Each night before our wedding there was a dinner in our honour to celebrate our coming marriage. However, these Chinese wedding feasts were not dinners, they were endurance tests. Of course Charles didn't warn me they consisted of twenty-three courses, all he said was that I would be sitting next to the host who was a friend and business client, and if I refused a dish, it would offend him. Having been trained since I was a small child to eat what was set before me, I told Charles this would not be a problem. How wrong can you be? I waded through fried frogs' legs, thousand-year-old eggs, birdnest soup, steamed octopus, to mention just a few dishes. All washed down by gallons of Coke, my only sensible move in those three days. If I had used alcohol in the washing down process, I would never have made it to the altar.

My stomach had been raised on grilled steak and baked dinners, so the sudden change of diet was not appreciated. This, coupled with a bad case of nerves, meant that I spent most of each night throwing up all the food which I had spent each evening trying to eat. At least I managed to wait until the dinner was over and I was out of sight of my host.

And so it went on for three days. In between wedding feasts and throwing up, Peggy would dose me with these marvellous little brown pills which stopped the runs and the vomiting but left me in a complete daze.

The 4th of July dawned bright and sunny and Peggy whisked me off to the hairdresser. However, in July 1960, Hong Kong and Red China were not on speaking terms. People were crossing the border from Red China to Hong Kong's new territory on the mainland and Mao Tse-tung did not like it. So, to make life difficult for the colony, the water supply from China was cut off. Hong Kong did have a reserve reservoir but hairdressers were not included on the honoured list of water-users, and received minimum amounts. What they washed my hair in was, and still is, a mystery, but I think it came out of Hong Kong harbour. My hair looked great, but felt like cement.

The temperature had now reached a staggering one hundred and one degrees and the humidity was not far behind. By now I was virtually comatose. Peggy took me home and put me in alternate hot and cold baths until I could focus my eyes in unison. I rested a while and then it was time to dress for the big day of my life. I couldn't get excited, I was too doped to have any feelings at all. Poor Peggy had a dilemma. If she gave me more pills, I would probably never remember being married at all. If she didn't I wouldn't be able to stand through the ceremony without having to excuse myself, and whoever heard of a bride having to go to the powder room in the middle of her wedding? She gave me the pills.

I vaguely remember a civil ceremony in the registrar's office somewhere downtown. We sat and signed a lot of papers at a very large table and I was then whipped off to Hong Kong Cathedral to be married for the second time. After the ceremony I was led out into the bright sunlight to face a barrage of photographers.

I couldn't help wondering why Charles and Peggy had arranged so many photographers. There must have been at least twenty-five of them, all rushing around popping shots at every angle. Several hundred photos later, we finally made it to the car and off to the reception. Mr and Mrs Charles English Henderson III.

Our wedding reception was at the Repulse Bay Hotel, a few miles' drive from the Cathedral on the other side of the island. Charles told the driver to go slowly.

'Let's give the guests time to arrive and have a few drinks,' he said. I smiled, all I was capable of doing.

'Just along here a bit, there is a lovely lookout with a beautiful view of the bay and also a view of where you are going to spend your honeymoon.'

'Oh?'

'Yes, I'll have the driver stop and we can sit in the sun for a while. You look awfully pale, do you feel alright?'

'Well, I'm not one hundred per cent, but I'll improve.'

'We'll get some food into you. That'll make you feel better.'

Charles told the driver to pull over a few miles out of the city. He helped me out of the car and told the driver to wait. We went up a little path to a monument in a clearing. The bay was beautiful, and there, in the middle riding at anchor, was a long slender white sailboat.

'Do you like her?' he asked anxiously. 'I wanted to keep it a surprise for you.' Along with the other two million he had in store for me.

'Oh Charles, she's beautiful. And so big.'

'Fifty-seven feet.'

He was very proud of his sailing boat. We sat in the sun looking out over the water. It was extremely restful after what I had been through in the last few days. However, eventually it was time for us to meet our guests at the reception so we walked back down the little path. But no car. Perhaps in our driver's particular province it was customary for wedding couples to take off into the bush after being married. Anyway he seemed to think it was normal to leave us there. We were now faced with the delightful prospect of either walking or hitching a ride to our wedding reception.

However, when the driver arrived at the reception with an empty car, he was immediately dispatched again to collect us. When we finally arrived our wedding reception was in full swing. The Repulse Bay Hotel was a beautiful building in a perfect setting, a little like a time warp, a piece of England transplanted.

I met Charles' friends there for the first time, and they were all perfectly charming. After something to eat and a little champagne to relax me, all under the supervision of Charles, I did start to feel slightly human.

Before I knew it, it was time for the bride and groom to depart, so I left the party to change. It was then that I discovered the strength of the hairdressers' cement. My hair was so solid that the hairpins would not come out. Peg and I tried a few weird and wonderful things, but to no avail. I could not even sink a comb into it, let alone comb it. Finally I covered the mess with a big hat and went to say goodbye to my newfound friends.

We walked down to the beach with all our guests and stepped into the dinghy. Amid cheers, confetti, streamers and best wishes, Charles rowed us off across the calm waters of Repulse Bay towards his sailing boat. The boat was in perfect order with decks made of beautiful teak wood. With our shoes off, we relaxed. We were alone at last.

Charles then decided that a swim was in order so I went below to change. All my suitcases were in the master's cabin and I was soon dressed and ready for the swim, except for my hair. I tried vainly to make a dent but short of scalping myself, I was not going to move it. I went on deck hiding under a sun hat.

'How are you going to swim wearing that?' Charles asked.

'Oh, it's my hair, it looks terrible!'

'Never mind, we'll swim now and worry about that later.'

I was swimming around wondering what his reaction to a bald bride would be when he said, 'Look, your hair.' I looked around, fully expecting to see my concrete hairdo floating by, when he added, 'It's normal again.'

My hand went to my head and sure enough, that wild concoction made by the hairdressers had been dissolved by the salt water. After a quick towel down, we sat on deck to watch the sun set, quietly sipping a 'sunset drink'.

I didn't exactly excel in the culinary arts, so I wondered how I was going to handle the problem of feeding my new husband in the days to follow. More immediately, I was wondering about the next meal, which I was sure Charles would be looking for in the next few hours. Just as all this drifted through my mind, a sampan paddled up to the landing and waiters from the hotel scurried on board. They set out a magnificent meal on the cabin top and departed without a word. Charles sat there with a wide grin—another of his surprises.

The sun had set, it was quite dark and we were sipping our coffee quietly contemplating our life ahead. Well, at least that's what I was doing. Charles was always so completely confident about everything I'm sure he never spent a moment wondering about the future.

Charles interrupted my rambling thoughts and suggested that, after such a strenuous day, we should retire early. This threw me into complete turmoil. A loving kiss indicated the night had only just begun. I went below to dress, or should I say undress, but there were no lights. I called to Charles and he shouted back directions. Still no lights. It became evident that Charles did not know how to fix the problem and seeing as he had sent all the boys ashore for the night that was that.

'Oh well, who needs lights?' I fumbled around trying to find things. In complete darkness it was impossible.

Meanwhile Charles had arranged the bedding aft. Our first night was to be under the stars.

'What are you doing?' the question floated down to me.

'I can't find my nightgown.'

'Well, come as you are. It's dark and I'm the only one here.'

I wrapped the bed sheet around me Grecian style, and sauntered up on deck. The aft deck was a sea of foam mattresses the size of a large trampoline surrounded on all sides by buckets of champage.

We were sipping champagne, looking at the stars and snuggling into each other's arms when suddenly we were bathed in floodlights. Streaking was not yet in fashion but I can tell you, those Chinese fishermen sure had a sneak preview. Having reached the safety of below, I peeped out the porthole. Apparently we were anchored right in the middle of the regular fishing ground. For those people not exactly up on Chinese fishing methods, they use large—the largest I have ever seen— hurricane lamps. The fish come to the surface where the light illuminates the water and are caught.

Charles casually strolled below and said he had negotiated with the head fisherman to move to a better fishing ground. After he explained the situation, the fishermen were most sympathetic and apologetic, and departed. I thought this was very nice of them, seeing as we were parked in the middle of their fishing ground. Ah, love conquers all. Or it could have been the money Charles gave them.

This little event had wiped out all the effects of the champagne and left Charles with a very nervous bride. He calmly led me back on deck wrapped in another sheet, made me comfortable on the trampoline and after a few more glasses of champagne, I was laughing with him about the whole episode.

The laughter faded as we became deeply engrossed in each other. Charles's arms were wrapped lovingly around me, and he was whispering delightful things in my ear when the boat gave a terrible lurch. At this point, Charles was beginning to show slight signs of irritation.

'Damn, what a lousy landing!' a voice called out. Once again I started to streak below, this time thank goodness in darkness. I was stopped in my tracks by a man sitting on the cabin deck next to the companionway. I turned to return to

47

Charles and was horrified to see people joining him. There I was, midship and stark naked. I crouched down behind the mast and waited my chance to dash below.

It seemed we had been joined by some of our wedding guests who had thoughtfully brought the wedding cake on board for us, all five tiers of it. The most intoxicated of the mob offered this explanation, 'You can't have your wedding night without the wedding cake!'

Frankly I couldn't see his point.

'Where's the Mrs?'

Charles said I was below decks. What was I going to do? Maybe they would go. Not likely, they were too drunk. Charles would have to throw them off. But how long would they stay? Crouching there, trying to decide what to do, I felt a tap on the shoulder. It was the man who had blocked my retreat asking if I would like his coat. He was so drunk that to this day he does not remember this incident. In fact, he doesn't even remember coming out to the boat. Thanking him, I grabbed his coat, put it on in a flash and then helped him along the deck to join the others. They were by now sprawled all over my wedding bed, drinking all the champagne.

There was much ribbing as to the state in which I had been found. How they expected to find a girl on her wedding night was never explained. They settled down comfortably to our cold champagne and wedding cake.

Hours later Charles finally deposited them back on their boat, had their boat boy give us all the cold champagne on board and told him to take them away and on no condition to let them come back here. He promised, and we waved them goodbye, me still in the dinner jacket.

Quiet descended once more and Charles turned to me, 'Now young lady, I'm going to take you below and lock you in the master's cabin with the master and throw away the key. If anyone else comes, they can run around the deck all night.'

A wise move, because by this time I was very uptight about a deck performance. Arm in arm we wandered below and once more surrendered to the magic of the night. Between sips of champagne and whispers of love, I was drifting delightfully into the state of wedded bliss, when we heard knocking.

'Charles!'

'Um . . .'

'Charles, someone is knocking at the door!'

'Don't be silly,' mumbled Charles, 'we are on a boat, not in a house.'

'There it is again!' He stopped kissing, listened, and had to admit someone or something was knocking on the side of the hull. And it didn't sound as if they were going to stop. I won't print the words Charles uttered this time, but when he went up on deck, he was in a frightening mood. The next thing I heard was a thunderous, 'What!' Mumble, mumble, mumble. A thunderous, 'No!' A lot of shuffling and then silence. I went up on deck, again wrapped in a sheet, to find Charles sitting on the cabin with his head in his hands. A sampan was paddling away at the speed of a motor boat and I could see the whites of the paddler's eyes from this distance.

'Darling, what happened?'

'That idiot wanted to know if we would order our wedding photos now!'

'You must be joking?'

'No I'm not. The sample album is there on the deck. I threatened to do so many things to him he dropped it in fright and fled.'

The female is a strange creature at times. Completely ignoring my husband, I grabbed the album and started ooh-ing and ah-ing at the wedding prints by moonlight. The reason for the strange little man delivering the photos in the middle of the night was that, in Hong Kong in 1960, you didn't have to book a photographer for your wedding. You didn't have to because all the photographers in town would watch for the wedding banns to be announced in the paper and descend upon the wedding like a plague of locusts. Then the race was on to see who could get the photos to you first. I must say this little fellow was an eager beaver. Charles gently took the album from me, saying, 'How can you look at our wedding photos when we're not man and wife yet?'

True, although we had been close several times. I meekly

put down the album. Charles once more led me below and this time he locked the door. If there were lights outside, if anyone was knocking, we knew nothing about it.

I awoke the next morning with sun streaming through the porthole. I felt so warm and loving and I rolled over to kiss my husband good morning, only to find him gone. I jumped out of bed to look for him and found him in the bathroom.

'Good morning.' Kiss.

'Why are you up so early?' Another kiss.

'I have to go to the office.' No kiss.

'What!?'

'Don't shout, darling. Sound carries on water.'

'I don't care what it does on water, this is our honeymoon. You can't go to the office the day after our wedding, especially since we didn't start to be married till three o'clock this morning.

'Sorry, darling. I have an appointment in one hour.'

I know now that if I had just dropped the sheet I was wrapped in and curled a few locks of hair, that would have been the end of the office. But alas, I was young and shy and new at the game. So he left a sulky wife and departed for his office.

'What will I do?' I shouted as he departed, standing on the bow of the sampan looking for all the world like Lord Nelson.

'Oh, Ernesto will be on board soon. He has a long list of things you can help him with.' He faded out of shouting distance, which was very fortunate for him. I sat down in disgust and started to write a letter to my mother. At least someone could be happy.

Dear Mother,

You will be happy to know I am married. In fact, I am so completely married that Charles left for the office this morning, just eighteen hours after we were married. Can't say he's not the ambitious type.

I described the wedding in detail and promised to send wedding photos as soon as possible. Judging by the night before, that would not be long. I was just finishing the letter when the happiest face I had ever seen appeared out of nowhere over the side railing, followed by a body. Finally, there on the deck in front of me stood Ernesto. He was Filipino.

'Hello Mummy.' Ernesto did not have a very firm grip on the English language, in fact he frequently lost hold of it altogether. But from that day on this was the only name he ever called me. I liked him instantly.

'The master told me to look after you. I will.'

He did. He cooked breakfast, he cleaned. He wouldn't let me do a thing. I even hesitated to go to the bathroom in case he wanted to help me. So, for the next three months I spent the nights with my loving husband, after cocktails that is (before cocktails he was all businessman) and the days being watched over by the ever-devoted Ernesto. I also came to know all the strange faces at my wedding.

Most of the time things went fairly smoothly but one day when I was busy preparing for a weekend sail with a few friends on board a sampan came paddling up to the landing. On board was one of my newly acquired friends and her six-year-old son. We sat in the sun and chatted. I signalled to Ernesto to watch the little darling, as he was the type that would bore a hole in the side of the boat just for fun. Ernesto signalled back that he had gone to the bathroom and went below to the galley to make tea for us. The child surfaced again while we were having tea and jumped up and down on the deck screaming over and over again that he wanted to go. Instead of keelhauling him, his mother simply said, 'Alright, Anthony, I'm coming.'

Ernesto then discovered what he had done. While we were sipping tea, he had pressed the electric toilet flushing button until it finally gave up the ghost. Ernesto closed all the valves so we wouldn't sink, and went ashore to find someone to repair our toilet.

The next morning at some unearthly hour Ernesto appeared with five Chinese workmen all carrying dilly bags of different shapes. They were plumbers, Ernesto informed me, but he wasn't completely convinced of the fact. Unfortunately his grip on the Chinese language wasn't much better than his grip on English.

After spending an hilarious morning in the toilet with five Chinese and Ernesto, with neither myself nor Ernesto having a clue what the Chinese were saying, we were no further on. The Chinese then departed in a sampan for lunch, leaving Ernesto and me to discuss the problem. We did not resolve it and they returned and re-assembled in the toilet. I couldn't face spending the afternoon in there. The space was meant for one, it was now very hot and the men hadn't bathed recently.

I adjourned to the deck and joined the discussion by speaking to Ernesto down the air ventilator. The afternoon passed with me in serious conversation with an air vent. At sunset, I felt very weary and the only result was that the 'terrible five' wanted to take the toilet ashore. I pointed out to Ernesto that the only things wrong were the inlet and outlet valves which were attached to the side of the boat, so how could it help to take the toilet ashore?

Ernesto agreed with me, and told our waiting audience in 'Ernesto-style' Chinese. He must have said something wrong somewhere because after a few very hostile stares, they picked up their dilly bags and departed without so much as a word.

'What is wrong. Why are they leaving?'

'I don't know, Mummy.'

'What did you say to them?'

'I'm not sure.'

'Well, at least they didn't hit you. I suppose you'd better go ashore and find someone else.'

Needless to say the toilet was not fixed for the weekend and everyone had to use the crew's toilet, which was located in the sail locker. It was quite a trip there and back under full sail. Then later in the day the crew's toilet gave up the ghost and we still had dinner to go before we were back at the dock. Ernesto suggested making a Chinese junk toilet. This consists of a chair without legs and sits on the highest overhang section of the stern of junks. So if you ever see a serene gentleman sitting on the high stern of a junk contemplating the sky or reading the newspaper and you are in a small boat, steer upwind and clear.

We didn't have a high stern, but this didn't deter Ernesto. He rigged a sail across the end of the deck and hung a sign. Behind the sail on the bobtail bumpkin (V-shaped) he nailed the toilet seat from one of the other toilets. It was very ingenious, but did not really fill the bill. For the men it was easy, they just relieved themselves over the rail, but for the women it was a different story. We nearly lost a few down Ernesto's toilet. When we finally got everyone ashore that night, women scattered in all directions, leaving husbands and boyfriends standing.

The fixing of the toilet became the saga of my honeymoon. I spent more time in the head with Chinese plumbers than I spent in bed with my husband! Numerous repairmen came to examine it. They would talk a lot and gesticulate and Ernesto would try to translate and then . . . nothing. It became clear that Chinese plumbers simply did not know how to fix a western, marine-style toilet. Having tried all avenues, and tired of timing my trips to the toilet between sunset and the fishing lights, the fishing lights and sunrise, I presented the problem to Charles. He immediately had someone sent over from the shipyard who fixed the toilet in twenty minutes.

To say I was upset with Charles would be an understatement. He had let me go through endless weeks of inconvenience and trouble when he could have handled the whole stupid situation in a few minutes. I told him so in quite a few words. He said he thought I would enjoy handling small things like that— something to occupy my time. And seeing as it was a household matter, I should handle it. Did I expect him to drop everything and run home every time I had a problem?

By this time we were definitely into our first argument. I informed him that if this had been a normal situation I would have been able to get tradesmen who could speak English and who knew what they were doing. Also, that little problem he was referring to had nearly sent his beloved boat to the bottom of the bay. I then stormed below and sulked. It was a complete waste of time. He ignored my performance, finished his meal and strolled below with the inevitable champagne and that was the end of my stand.

CHAPTER 5

❖

1960

After three months our honeymoon ended. We had to head for Manila. Manila was head office for Charles's business and that was where we were to live.

The last three weeks before departure were spent readying the boat for sea. This was a long and exacting task. We had two trial runs up the coast of China. The first trip was a beautiful sail with calm water and lovely weather. The second was rather different.

We left Repulse Bay in perfect sailing weather and headed up the coast of China. With the main up and the mizzen set with loose-footed jib, the boat was sailing off the wind to perfection, her favourite position. Then, two days out of Hong Kong Charles backed into the swinging stove and spilt a pot of boiling water all over his back. I was steering when I heard Charles yell. He ran up on deck, grabbed one of the lines and jumped into the water. The first aid box was ashore being stocked for our ocean sail, so there was nothing on board. Falling back on one of Mum's old cures for sunburn, I bathed his back in cold tea while Ernesto turned the boat and headed for Hong Kong and the hospital.

The weather turned ugly. Charles did not have a radio as he felt that this made the contest with Mother Nature more interesting. So we could not receive weather reports. However, there was a barometer and it was dropping rapidly—we were heading for trouble. A typhoon was approaching Hong Kong from the southwest, and we were approaching from the northeast. Somewhere between where we were and Hong Kong, it was inevitable we would meet it head on. I was praying we would already be in the Hong Kong typhoon shelter, safely at anchor.

Charles was now in excruciating pain. His back was so bad he couldn't even move an arm. So I had to sail the boat. Charles stood behind me and told me what to do. If I hadn't been so scared it would have been a wonderful experience. She was a special boat, with a living heart. You could actually feel her challenging the sea. My sailing experience to date had only been on Sydney Harbour and certainly never on a sixty-foot, forty-ton, two-masted sailing boat. Not to mention that the China Sea can hardly be compared with Sydney Harbour.

We were flying down the China coast, and I mean flying. The closer we sailed to Hong Kong, the blacker, and thicker, and lower the clouds became. As the sun slipped below the horizon I remembered Charles's plan for the trip.

'We'll sail up the coast and anchor in a lovely bay near the border to China. There's a fishing village there and we can buy fresh fish for dinner. We'll sit on deck and watch the sunset and eat our fish with a good wine. You'll love it.'

'Look out—you're luffing the mainsail.' Charles's strong hand clamped down on mine and brought me back to the present. The waves grew by the hour and as darkness closed out the world, white foam loomed high above the spreaders, indicating their height.

'Look out!' Charles's arms locked around me and onto the wheel, holding the boat on course and me at the same time as an enormous wave dumped tons of water across the deck. By the time the water had subsided we were gasping for breath. I was about to give Charles my opinion of his idyllic night away when I saw the pain on his face caused by the action of locking his arms around me.

The hours wore on. Ernesto came and helped me at the wheel. He had trimmed and furled the sails and generally readied the deck for anything the sea might care to throw at us.

By this time Charles's back was covered with blisters the size of dinner plates. I knew he was in great pain but he never uttered a word. I had stopped using tea as the blisters had broken and I was worried about infection. All I could do was bathe his back in salt water but since meeting the typhoon there wasn't even time for that. Years later it was discovered that salt water reduces scarring. We certainly proved that as Charles's back healed with only a small scar on his waistline.

Charles was worried about the typhoon. We were racing it to Hong Kong and the problem was that if it arrived before we did, we would have to ride it out at sea. Our helmsman had to get to hospital before his back became infected. Every moment caused him pain and he would not have been able to withstand several days at sea riding out a typhoon.

We sailed into the harbour on the final alert. In fact, it would be safe to say it was a dead heat between the typhoon and us. Ernesto and Charles anchored the boat in the safe mooring harbour and we rowed to the pier. However, the ordeal was not quite over. The pier moved up and down in twenty-foot leaps. Charles told me to step ashore when the boat and the top of the pier were level. He did it so easily. After chickening out on my own judgement three times, Charles shouted, 'Jump when I tell you!' I closed my eyes and did, and found myself sprawled on the pier.

As the typhoon descended on Hong Kong, Charles and I were driving up the peak to Matilda Hospital. Normally a drive up the peak in that weather would have terrified me, but it was child's play after the last two days at sea, the trip ashore in the dinghy and the cement pier. As I helped Charles in the door of the hospital, driving rain closed out the world below, and we saw nothing but rain for the next few days.

The doctors cut the blistered skin off Charles's back and he was on his stomach for the next ten days. As the painkillers took effect, the strain gradually disappeared from his face. He had to relax as he could go nowhere and do nothing. We stayed in Hong Kong until the doctors declared Charles's back fit to sail. That took another few weeks.

Finally it was time to leave and I nervously asked if it was wise to venture forth into the China Sea considering our recent experience. Charles told me that after a typhoon the sea calms for at least five days. Plenty of time to get to Manila.

We were all set to depart. All we had to do was wait for the next typhoon to pass and then dash off from whence it came and be assured of a millpond all the way. Sound easy? Naturally it went wrong, through no fault of Charles's planning, but this time he had just omitted to check the history of nature. About every fifty years or so, some cantankerous typhoon decides to do a turn-about and retrace its path just in case it missed something. This typhoon didn't miss a thing, including us.

When the typhoon passed through Hong Kong we were in the safe cove in the lee of the typhoon and the boat rode it out without a hitch. The next day, after it had passed, was as predicted by Charles—perfect clear skies and not a ripple on the water. We were ready to lift anchor with only one small problem—from a crew of six we were now down to three, Charles, Ernesto and yours truly! This should have been enough warning but we didn't heed it.

One chap had broken his big toe in the bathtub, the second had run out of holiday time while Charles was delayed in hospital, and the third fellow's wife was sick so he had to take care of the children. However, Charles decided that because the weather would be perfect, the three of us could manage the boat.

So, we lifted anchor with Charles at the helm, Ernesto on the deck, and me in the galley. The first catastrophe befell us there and then. The moment the anchor was lifted I was sick. Sick is the understatement of the century. I couldn't stop heaving long enough to explain to my horrified sailing husband that I didn't usually get sick, well not in a bay anyway. All he could utter was, 'But I met you on a sailboat!'

After about one solid hour of throwing up I collapsed onto the deck, completely exhausted. As soon as I was in the horizontal position, the heaving stopped but the moment I took my head off the deck, off I went again. So I just had to lie flat on the deck. Fine. But this made sail-handling, cooking and steering rather difficult.

My husband was not sympathetic. He told me firmly that it was all in the mind. I told him if that was the case, my mind was in a strange position.

'You're only seasick. Take a few pills and you'll be right in no time. Take your mind off being seasick, go to the galley and cook.'

After more seasick pills than recommended, I still could do nothing in the galley except heave so violently that I had to hang onto something or I would fall over. I finally collapsed and that was how Charles found me when he came below expecting his dinner.

Eventually Charles wedged a mattress on the deck between the side of the heavy weather cockpit and the hatch opening. That way, I was under his watchful eye while I was heaving and he was steering, and, also, when I did throw up, a bucket of water would just wash it overboard, keeping belowdecks livable.

By now, after six continuous hours of throwing up in any position, even Charles was looking a bit worried. He kept assuring himself that it was the first wave of seasickness and it would pass. He was wrong, it didn't. Twice during that voyage I was not sick and one of those times was approaching. The sun was setting, the sea was very calm, too calm, and I could not understand why Ernesto was charging around the deck like a demented chicken. He changed sails at least twelve times.

'Why all the sail changing?' I groaned.

'We're getting too close to shore.'

At this stage I should point out that this enormous boat, along with no radio, had no motor of any description to drive it. She was wholly at the mercy of the wind. Just like the sailing ships of the last century, except that they were better off than us—at least they had crew. I craned my neck around, expecting to see beach or rocks looming large. 'Oh, we must be two miles away.'

'Yes I know,' he said, frowning. I knew by now that this man did not worry about trivialities, and since the danger was not being beached on the rocks, it had to be something else. I then remembered the cruiser escort that stood off shore at the entrance to Hong Kong harbour channel.

At that time Red China was not a very hospitable neighbour

and any vessel out of Hong Kong that strayed over into their three-mile limit was accompanied to Peking by patrol boats for an extended holiday! We were now one mile inside that three-mile limit and cruiser escort help was about twenty-five miles away.

For the next four hours I was not sick. I was too scared. I steered while Charles and Ernesto tried to find a sail combination that would defy the current and the inshore breeze. We were, at one stage of this hair-raising adventure, only five hundred yards from shore. We were just about to step ashore and give ourselves up when the wind changed. Charles quickly reset and trimmed the sails and we took off. We were all busy silently praying not to meet a Chinese patrol boat when we saw lights ahead. Charles studied the lights for a while and decided they were fishing boats. This did not make us safe— most of the fishing boats were lookouts for the patrols and some had radios on board.

Our predicament was this: if we changed course we would lose the wind, and if we stayed on the wind we would pass very close to the fishing boats, very close indeed. Ernesto suggested we disguise ourselves. He was fine, but we stood out like sore thumbs. I crawled below and pulled out a pair of black pyjamas, an old straw hat and a jar of make-up, then went back on deck to help Charles dress and cover his face with make-up. It was decided that there wasn't much that could be done to disguise me. I was the wrong shape to pass for a man and I had red hair. So I was to go in the bilge.

'What! I'm not going in the bilge. And that's final.'

'Would you rather go on board the Chinese boat and be at the mercy of those fishermen? You know they're fascinated by redheaded white women and . . .' I didn't want to hear anymore. I made my way to the bilge.

When we were almost in the middle of the fleet, Charles put me in there. It was dry, a little smelly and very stuffy, but I wasn't too uncomfortable. I certainly didn't want to spend a moment longer there than necessary. Ernesto was to sail the boat and Charles was to sit on deck splicing rope with his head down, way down.

I heard the first exchange of conversation between Ernesto and the fishermen. I couldn't hear exactly what was said but I wouldn't have understood anyway. Ernesto later told me that he hadn't understood a word either. The babbling went on for a few minutes. I was having a battle with my stomach. I was in its favourite horizontal position, but the stuffiness was causing problems and I was fighting to gain the upper hand.

When we had sailed out of sight of the fishing fleet, Charles released me and they told me what had happened. Ernesto had told the fishermen that he was delivering this captured sailing boat to one of the committee members in a nearby province. Considering he hadn't understood a word they had said and knowing Ernesto's knowledge of Chinese, I am quite sure the Chinese hadn't understood a word of Charles's carefully planned story. But the important thing was that they had let us go.

The moment the danger passed, my seasickness returned. I was quite sure by now that my stomach had a mind of its own. It was back to the horizontal position.

My stomach's stubbornness actually saved my life. Wedged between the framing of the sea cockpit (a four-foot-high canvas affair, rigged when at sea to prevent the helmsman from being washed overboard) and the hatch coaming, I could not be seen from the port side, the side from which the Chinese patrol boat approached.

We knew it was not a fishing boat by its large searchlight. The men quickly decided that Ernesto would stick to the same story and steer, and Charles disappeared to the bow to coil rope and stay out of the searchlight's beam. Whoever heard of a Chinese person with a Roman nose?

The patrol boat came towards us so fast that there was no time to move, let alone hide me. Charles just had time to reach the bow without running when a strong beam of light swept over the boat. Ernesto apologised and quickly threw a sail bag over me, just in case. There were several exchanges, then silence, and finally there was darkness again. Ernesto sounded the all clear and I peeped out.

In the darkness we could not see the shore, but apparently

we had been making good time and were out of the three-mile limit. Not that this by itself would have made any difference—we had been inside the limit and that was all that mattered. However they were not sufficiently game to touch us, and this was no doubt due to the approach of another light. This one turned out to be a patrol boat from the cruiser escort. As the patrol boat's crew explained when the Chinese patrol boat had departed, they had heard the fishing boat's report on the radio, and having us on their list of the day's departures from Hong Kong, thought they had better take a look.

With a good wind, we left the patrol boat behind and settled down for what I thought would be a quiet, uneventful sail. No such luck. It was well after midnight and we were tired, the men from changing sail combinations most of the night, and me, from heaving. We started the 'one awake to steer, two asleep', routine until someone was needed to handle the sails. This peaceful existence lasted almost a day, for it was then that the cantankerous typhoon decided to turn around and see if it had missed anything.

I awoke to a screeching wind and Charles and Ernesto racing around like madmen taking all the sails down. I do not know enough about sailing to be able to judge what followed from a sailor's point of view, but from the layperson's point of view, it was, and still is, the most terrifying experience of my life.

The Hong Kong Observatory recorded top winds of 128 knots, that is about 147 miles per hour. And Charles, never doing anything by halves, went right through the eye, not that he had any choice, the typhoon was calling all the shots—we were just putty in its hands. One moment we were surfing up and down ninety-foot waves, and the next moment we were sitting in a millpond of dust, rags, and debris, surrounded by an eerie howling silence.

The only time conversation was possible was when we were in the eye of the typhoon, and even then it was done on screaming level. The vacuum swirling around the edge of the calm seemed to suck out all sound. It was at this time that Charles told me that if we went back into the surrounding storm in the wrong direction to the wind, we would broach. In other words, if the boat came out of the eye facing the wrong direction, we were finished. For this reason, Charles tied me to the mizzen mast. This would also stop me being blown overboard. The wind was so strong I couldn't stand by myself, and the men were too busy to help me.

Apart from no radio and no engine, we also had no life jackets and no life raft. The dinghy was awaiting us in Manila on the mooring buoy. Of course I knew nothing of this at the time. I had put my complete faith in my husband.

The calm of the eye was the opposite of calm for us. All the damage to sails and rigging had to be repaired or lashed in order to face the rest of the storm. The trouble was, there was so much to repair and put in order, it would take weeks, not the few hours we had. The most urgent of our problems was that the steering wheel was slowly seizing. It was taking all of Charles's strength to move the wheel, and in a storm like we were encountering, you need a free steering wheel that can spin in any direction at great speed. This we did not have.

The hours passed rapidly with emergency repairs, cutting away and lashing damaged sails and rigging, and a hurried meal for the men. But before we could complete a quarter of the work, we were back in the fray.

Waiting to leave the eye and enter the storm again was completely terrifying—not knowing whether in the next few seconds you were going to live or die. Obviously more strife was planned for us in our future because we came out close to the mark. That, plus Charles's superior helmsmanship, had us before the wind surfing up and down those ninety-foot mountains of water again.

The boat would ride to the crest of each wave and then surf down the other side. She would gather so much speed surfing down the side that she would bury in the bottom of the trough up to her steering wheel every time. After about three of these breathtaking rides, I had attained the state of complete screaming hysteria. Then this passed and I moved onto silent, staring hysteria, as silent as the mizzen I was tied to (well, the mizzen did make a funny squeaking noise), while I awaited the end.

Of course this great dramatic performance was not seen or heard. If Charles or Ernesto had looked in my direction, which they didn't, they would have just seen a lot of head-shaking and eye-rolling. With winds of 128 knots, give or take a few, nothing, but nothing could be heard. In fact, seeing was near impossible. Charles had to wear diving goggles so he could keep his eyes open, not that there was anything to see. Down in the troughs it was black as death, on top of the breakers, there was about a ten-foot collar of thick yellowy-white foam. It felt rather like going through a carwash with the top down.

Some of the breakers did not behave normally and the boat, instead of surfing down the side of the wave, would catapult off the top and into the middle of the next wave. We would crash right through the wave and come out gasping for air only to fall into the trough to be buried up to the wheel again.

In the troughs the air was hot and humid; on top of the breakers, the wind was so strong it blew the foam and rain horizontally. The rain hit us so hard it felt like little needles sticking into us, and we had to turn away from the wind to breathe.

Horrified, I would watch as the bow disappeared under water at the bottom of that roaring black descent. The rest of the boat would follow in quick succession, till the water nearly reached the steering wheel. Then there would only be the stern, with the three of us holding on for dear life, sticking out of the water. She would pause in this unbelievable position for a few seconds, shudder, as if deciding whether to go on, and once more lift that graceful bowsprit to fight the next mountain of water.

Luckily, Charles had installed water-tight bulkheads, so with the two doors closed, only the main cabin had taken water. The water sloshed around until we had time to attend to it, which was many days later.

The boat had been sailing along with not only the rail underwater, but also the walkway and half the cabin house under. The main mast was touching the water many times, and after hours underwater, the portholes and hatch covers began to leak. We couldn't use the pumps because the portside pumps were completely submerged and the starboard pumps were completely out of water. Charles said the water was no danger midship, as long as it didn't get into the stern or bow and actually, because of it, the bow pointed a little higher and this was good.

As the sluggish light of dawn of the first day out of the eye battled through the murk, the wind dropped slightly. The boat kept fighting, but she became noticeably more and more unwilling to lift. Charles had Ernesto go forward and cut away the broken staysail boom, hoping this would correct her sluggishness. To do this small thing, Ernesto had to tie himself to the mainmast and go underwater every time we buried in a trough. Then, when she broke free, he had to cut the rigging and torn canvas away, and hold on for dear life when the boat went into the next trough. Every time we popped up again I would look for that small brown body wrapped around the base of the mast. Somehow he did it—how, I will never know.

Ernesto was recovering from his underwater ordeal and we were all waiting for improvement in the next trough. It never came. She groaned and shuddered and very reluctantly lifted once more, but only just. Something was very wrong. Charles signalled to Ernesto to go and check below as the trouble had to be there. It was.

The bow was so continually underwater that we were taking water through the anchor chain hole. Ernesto did not report, there was no time. He had to get the water out fast. He couldn't open the bulkhead door into the main cabin because if all that water came into the forward compartment from the main cabin we would keep going down. He couldn't open the portholes, as they were underwater on one side and above his head on the other side.

The first thing he did was stuff the anchor chain hole with clothes he found in the suitcases stored in the forward hold. In the first suitcase was my wedding dress. Only four months

64

old, it was stuffed in the anchor hole. It did the job, however, and stopped further leaking. But Ernesto was still faced with the major problem of how to get rid of the water. He sat down to think and sat right on the solution. The crew's now-working toilet. He scooped the water up in a bucket, poured it into the toilet and flushed it out. He reappeared on deck all smiles and screamed in Charles's ear what he had done. Charles was all smiles too because the effect was immediate— the boat was losing her sluggishness and was lifting better with every wave.

We continued that never-to-be-forgotten roller-coaster ride for more hours than I would like to remember, and just when we were sure it would never end and we would never survive, the wind eased. We were now down to about one hundred knots and the waves were a little smaller, only seventy feet. Several more hours and we were down to ninety knots and sixty-foot waves. It seemed like an afternoon breeze after what we had been through

By the fourth morning we were still coping with eighty knots and fifty-five-foot waves. This continued through the next day and next night. Charles and Ernesto had not had any sleep now for at least three days and they were struggling to keep the boat before the wind. The rudder, which had taken a terrible beating, was all but jammed and it took all of Charles's strength to turn it. I could not even move it. Another day passed and the wind dropped to around forty-five knots and the sea was starting to look like an ocean again. Charles set the course, balanced the boat and lashed the wheel so she sailed herself while he and Ernesto went below for a well-earned rest. By the sixth day, we were through the worst and the sun even appeared for ten minutes at a time.

The sea was still choppy—so much for the calm after the storm bit—but after what we had been through, it looked like a backyard swimming pool. Now came the cleaning up; even if the calm waters and clear skies didn't appear, we had to get the boat shipshape. What a mess.

The boat was now sailing at a reasonable angle and the pumps worked, so we started pumping. The main cabin was soon emptied of water. It was still a complete mess, but at least we didn't have to swim to the galley. We cleaned up tins of food, cushions, clothes and boxes. All these things had been neatly packed in the cupboards in the main cabin. The forward cabin was in the same state. The master's cabin was the only presentable place on the boat.

We spent the next few days drying the clothes when the sun appeared, and madly gathering them up when the rain came down. The cleaning was endless, but it was nice to eat hot meals again. Well, correction, the men ate hot meals. I had not been able to keep a mouthful down since the day we raised anchor.

The typhoon had had many effects on the land and the sea. One problem we were encountering was the tides. We had been blown off track a few hundred miles and were southwest of our landfall, Manila Bay. We were sailing into the tides and flood waters coming from the rivers along the coast of Luzon. Our second problem was our main halyard. One and a half inches thick, it had chafed through during the typhoon and we could not hoist the mainsail. The boat, being forty tons, could not buck the tide with only the mizzen and foresail hoisted, so we were standing still and some days going backwards as the tides pushed us away from land.

The most pressing problem was that I could not keep a mouthful of food down, not in any position, and I was losing weight rapidly. We had now been ten days at sea, with no radio to contact help and only a rough idea of where we were. Even Charles started to look worried. I was so weak I was confined to the bunk.

Charles had to get a new halyard to the top of the mast to hoist the mainsail, but the mast was seventy-five feet high and the only way to the top was in a bosun's chair. With Ernesto in the chair, it was impossible for Charles to hoist it more than fifteen feet before the weight defeated him, and Ernesto was small.

The boat had no engine and no modern winches. It was all hard work and muscles and there were not enough muscles to do the job.

Charles knew he had to find a solution. No one on land knew where we were. Eventually we would land somewhere, but if it took too long, Charles could be landing without his bride of four months. I was looking decidedly grey.

He and Ernesto went into deep discussion and the next morning I heard hoorays. They had conquered the problem. Charles had made a drag attached to a rope which went through a few pulleys and under a cleat and around a winch. The drag was thrown into the water and its movement through the water helped Charles hoist Ernesto to the top of the mast so he could thread the new halyard through the pulley on top of the mast.

Charles carried me on deck to see the big mainsail unfurl. We felt the difference immediately. The boat seemed to leap out of the water. Charles quickly trimmed and balanced the boat and she was like a thoroughbred with the bit between her teeth. The bowsprit crashed through the waves with a vengeance and we headed for land.

Charles assured me we would be on land soon. I was past caring. Twelve days without food had made me lightheaded and dizzy and even the prospect of dying didn't faze me. All I could think of was at least I would no longer have to endure the relentless up and down motion of the boat.

CHAPTER 6

❖

1960-1962

On the thirteenth day, we limped into Manila Bay and, just to top everything off, were becalmed in the middle of the bay, with not a breath of wind. We finally had to be towed to anchor by a passing barge.

By the time we stepped ashore, I was a very peculiar shade of green and I had lost so much weight that I was too weak to stand on my own feet. I put one foot on blessed ground and collapsed in a heap. Charles decided he had better get me straight to hospital. After a few days, the heaving stopped and after lots of medication, my stomach finally accepted some food. After a few more days of tests, we found out we were going to be three. It seemed that all my throwing up was morning sickness; the only hitch was it lasted for twenty-four hours instead of just the mornings. That damn stomach of mine couldn't even tell time, and it never improved. Helped along by dysentery and a few other tropical bugs, I threw up for the next eight months.

Living on board the boat didn't help. As the months went by, I became an expert on the marine life that lived around the bottom of the boat. One evening, when the bay was unbelievably calm and I was not hanging over the rail, Charles came on board all smiles. Apparently a friend of his, Nick, had sent his girlfriend on a trip and her apartment was just sitting there with maids, airconditioning, the lot. When he heard how sick I was he had offered it to Charles. I didn't waste any time moving in. Early next morning I was packed and ready. By the end of the day I was comfortably settled

in a lovely airconditioned apartment being waited on, hand
and foot, by three maids. To say the next three months were
bliss would be an understatement. Being cool had a marvellous
effect on my stomach—it actually stopped throwing up for
a few hours a day—and being waited on hand and foot had
a similar effect on me as a whole. If I could have stopped
my stomach from demanding centre stage for most of the day,
things would have been perfect.

Well, almost. Charles was rebuilding his business again.
He finally told me that he and Gus had lost their shipping
company after defending a long court case. They won the court
case but had gone out of business in the meantime. They had
decided to start again, but this time not as partners. Charles
would start again in the Philippines and Gus in Australia. So
Charles was picking up what was left of the Manila office
of their old company. We were living on the sailing boat because
we did not have enough money to rent an apartment and the
unplanned pregnancy didn't help the budget at all.

At that rather down time in our life Nick, the owner of
the apartment, was a wonderful friend to have. In fact Nick
was a wonderful friend to have at any time in one's life. He
owned a restaurant, legal, and a gambling den, illegal, the real
McCoy. You went into a type of airlock room where I suppose
they looked at you, then certain types were frisked for weapons.
Another door opened and you could go into the den. It was
right out of the prohibition days of America. The girlfriend's
apartment was just across the road. His wife and various children
lived a few miles away.

One evening Charles arrived at the apartment via the Casino
and threw a large paper bag on the bed. I was hoping it contained
food. It turned out to be full of money.

'How much? Where did you get it?'

'A loan from Nick, count it,' he said casually. I did—
there was 100,000 pesos in cash. We had no food in the house.

'Can we buy hamburgers?'

'You can buy caviar if you want.'

'No, hamburgers will be just fine thank you.'

I quickly dispatched one of the maids, who returned with

hamburgers, thick chocolate milkshakes and delicious nut and cream-covered jelly rolls from the American Country Bake Shop.

We had a picnic on a towel on the bed, and washed it down with San Miguel beer. And all during the meal, I counted out little piles of money, surrounding us with a ring of notes. It was a dinner that is imprinted in my memory bank forever.

We were happily enjoying our last mouthful of jelly roll when the maid brought in a note from Nick. She said the messenger was waiting for a package. Charles read the note and told me to pack the money back into the bag. It seemed someone had had a run on the bank and Nick needed the 100,000 back for the night. We had to borrow 25 pesos from one of the maids to make up the 100,000 again.

We never did see the loan again. Nick had a bad run at the gambling tables, and the lady friend whose apartment we were occupying had a few health problems. By the time this was all sorted out Charles had progressed far enough to earn food for the table. So I never did get to spend 100,000 pesos. Thank heavens I didn't order caviar.

The entire time I had been in Manila, I had seen nothing but the marine life around the waterline of our boat and the inside of a friend's mistress's apartment. So after the traumatic event of the birth of our first, and the recovery period, I was ready to explore Manila.

We had now moved into our very own apartment, a surprise Charles had in store for me when I came out of hospital. After a few weeks of rest and not having to consider my stomach any more, I was very anxious to attack the shops, wherever they were. All my clothes had floated in sea water for the best part of two weeks so I really didn't have much left. And our little girl was equipped to pose on a bearskin rug. So I asked Charles to take me shopping.

He took me downtown and told me to sit in the foyer of a pleasant and very cool hotel. It was just around the corner from the bank, so I was to wait in comfort till he returned with some money. He wouldn't be long and then I could shop till I was tired and he would take me home. After outlining this acceptable plan, he kissed me and departed. I didn't see him again until five p.m. When he was ready to leave the office, he suddenly remembered that five hours previously he had left a wife sitting in a hotel foyer.

There were many problems that prevented me from venturing forth, not the least of which were that I had no money, not one cent, and no idea where I was. Also, Charles had just moved into new offices and I could not remember the new number. After thinking it through many times, I decided that he would remember he had left me sitting there when it came time to eat, so I settled down to a long wait.

However, I soon realised that the men who kept sitting next to me whispering sweet nothings and amounts of money in my ear were not telling me the latest stock market reports. It turned out that this particular hotel was a lucrative pickup centre for the white slave rings that were operating in the Far East at that time. Being a well-shaped redhead I was a very saleable product. So I spent the day moving round and round the horseshoe lounge. Eventually the girl on the magazine counter took pity on me and gave me a few magazines to read. Apparently she could tell I was not in the business. I buried my head in these but it made no difference. They still sat next to me.

I was so pleased to see Charles when he charged through the door, I forgot how angry I was. He came out with the same classic line of many months before.

'Darling, I forgot you!'

I burst into tears and he tenderly led me out.

While we were waiting for our car, one of the unsuccessful bidders sidled up to Charles.

'How much?' he asked.

Charles just stared at the chap, puzzled. Feeling much better, I replied, 'Seven hundred and fifty.'

'Wow, I hope you get your money's worth!'

'Oh he will,' said I.

Our car pulled up and we stepped in.

'What on earth was that all about?'

'Well, it seems you left me in the best pickup centre in town, and I have had a roaring day.'

'What do you mean "seven hundred and fifty"? Over-rating yourself a bit, aren't you?'

'Oh, I don't know, one guy got up to five hundred.'

'I don't know why I'm wasting my time at the office, better to put you in business!'

He told the driver to take us home and, over champagne and strawberries, succeeded in making up for forgetting me. During that night he promised me he would never forget me again, and if he did, at least he would not say so. The next morning I awoke to find he had already departed for the office, but pinned to his pillow was a cheque.

From that day on, I studied the city map and took money with me before I ventured forth. Having a husband like Charles, I knew it would happen again but this time I would be prepared.

I was now into my second typhoon season on land, and it was well and truly with us. The weather had been low and overcast for many days, but then the skies took on a different appearance. A dark sludgy grey barrier hung menacingly over the city.

I knew before Charles could tell me that I was about to experience my first really serious typhoon ashore. Manila has between ten and fifteen typhoons each year and usually three or four of them are equal to the ferocity of Cyclone Tracy, putting Manila out of action for about five days. After the water and flooding subside, people straighten their nepa huts and get on with living. The more substantial houses have air vents in the walls under the eaves, so that the air can flow through, leaving the roof behind.

Charles came home from the office at about four-thirty. He had sent all the staff home to prepare their houses and families. Once the flooding started they would not be able to travel. Manila is built on a swamp, with very casual landfill, so after a few inches of rain, the whole city is awash. Charles was worried about the boat. He was not sure if the mooring would hold. If it did give way, the boat would smash to pieces on the sea wall. He decided he would go on board for the night and anchor her in the middle of the bay. If she did drag, there was plenty of room to manoeuvre and time for him to get under sail. The plan was, we would drive down to the boat and I would bring the car home. Our house was about fifteen miles from the boat.

On the drive out there visibility was almost zero. But there weren't too many other idiots out driving, just Charles and me. The last three miles of road was along the waterfront. Water was already running across it—it was like driving down a riverbed. It took about an hour for Ernesto to get the dinghy ashore, and for both of them to get back out to the boat. I anxiously watched every move, and by the time Charles turned to wave goodbye, I was exhausted.

It was only then that I realised I still had to get home, and by myself. I drove off the wharf and turned onto Dewey Boulevard. My heart gave a lurch. In the last hour, while my eyes had been glued to Charles and Ernesto, the storm had intensified. Huge waves were breaking over the sea wall and crashing onto the road. I went to turn inland and saw that the water level for the first hundred yards was as high as the top steps of the houses. That meant the water was over three feet in depth. If the car stalled, I would have to spend the night there, as in those days, in Manila, there were no rescue teams like the NRMA.

Not wishing to spend all night in the car, I decided to brave the waterfront. It was only about three miles!

I had downtown Manila to myself. The typhoon had well and truly arrived. Driving on the right side of the road had me close to the wall. There was an area of grass between the wall and the road, but on this day it was far too narrow for my liking. I looked at that stretch of horror in front of me and hesitated. If the decision faced me today, I would turn left and drive one hundred yards to the Manila Hotel. But I was young and my one dramatic thought was, I must get home to my child.

I edged gingerly onto the road, deciding to creep along slowly. The first wave hit the car, making it veer right across the lanes. It hit the gutter with such force that it lifted up on one side and balanced for a few split seconds. If a wave had come then

73

it would have gone right over.

The car came down with a crashing thud. It was clear I had to get to the other side of the road, as far away from the sea wall as possible. Another wave hit, the car jerked violently but it was up against the gutter, so no skidding. A few more of those waves and the engine would be swamped. I decided to surge ahead in between waves and stop as they hit. I could see an opening in the median strip—if I could get to the wrong side of the road I would be further away from the crashing waves.

I gunned the engine. As the car came level with the opening, I hit the brakes, but no response—they were too wet. I could see the opening going by. I wrenched the wheel into a sharp turn just as the next wave hit. The car swung sideways and sailed through the break in the median strip. It was on a bed of water and the steering wheel had no effect. The amount of water was so great, the car was actually surfing. This time I knew it would turn over, it was travelling so fast.

It whooshed into a tree with a deafening thud. The wave subsided and I looked around. The tree had struck the car just behind my door. I had turned one hundred and eighty degrees and was facing back the way I had come.

Waves were still hitting and rocking the car, but nothing like on the other side of the median strip. She wasn't even lifting off the ground. I was twenty feet down a side street, up against the tree, on the edge of a lawn.

I put my hand on the ignition key and prayed. She started— great cars, Cadillacs—and I drove onto the wrong side of the road, very sure I wouldn't meet any traffic.

The 'dash–stop theory' was now out as I had no brakes, so I wedged the car in the gutter and drove steadily all the way. There was a side-rocking motion every time a wave hit the car, but with the wheels up against the gutter, she would give a few jerky movements and then settle. I made it home without further mishap. I was very glad when I switched off the engine in the garage.

Of course Charles later told me all the things I should have done, and that everything I had done was wrong.

Apart from the occasional typhoon, life was now going along very well. Business was on an upward trend and our number one had started to walk and talk and was an absolute delight. Then suddenly my stomach demanded centre stage again. This time we were in an airconditioned apartment and on solid ground, but it made no difference. It performed just as it had out in the middle of the China Sea. It was back to the apartment again. This time I threw up for six months—the first five, and just when I thought things were settling down, the ninth month as well, in fact right up until the time the doctor slapped our second little daughter on the bottom.

As a surprise, Charles had arranged tickets on the *Oriana* for Mum and Dad to come and stay with us for the birth of our second child. Mum would not fly in an aeroplane— this was a genuine fear, she could not even bring herself to get on a plane to fly to Hong Kong for my wedding. And if Mum didn't go Dad didn't go. But the cruise ship was quite acceptable, so they came to visit.

Our second daughter owes her life to my mother. If Mum had not been with me, I would never have gone to the hospital when I did and she would have died before she was born. I had no contractions at all, just this constant dull pain. I vomited most of the day.

Mum finally said, 'This is not right, we have to go to the hospital.' My doctor had doctors on duty around the clock, and he would arrive in time for the delivery or if things were not proceeding according to schedule.

The doctor on duty examined me and said there was nothing wrong and that I had not even started stage one yet. Mum wouldn't take no for an answer.

'Doctor, the baby is ten days overdue and my daughter has been vomiting all day. There is something wrong. She is not leaving this hospital until her doctor sees her.'

'He won't be in until morning.'

'Then we'll stay.' He was sensible enough not to take on Mum. I was put in a private suite with a bedroom for Mum, and later another bed next to mine for Charles. He refused to stay at home and moved into the hospital, generally throwing the whole place into chaos.

With Mum and Charles in charge, everyone was bumping into each other in the rush to do their bidding. Meanwhile I felt so miserable, I wished I could just pass away. The pain had been too much. I had not slept for days, and despite constant concern from all quarters all night I still had no rest. When my doctor arrived I was on the verge of total exhaustion.

He was met with a feeble smile. I barely had the energy to move my facial muscles. Not the case with Charles, Mum and the assistant doctor. They were all shouting at each other across the bed. I was so ill by this stage, I started to cry. Dr Monahan moved everyone out of the room except the assistant and quietly started to examine me. A few seconds into the examination the silence was exploded by rapid-fire Spanish verbal abuse. The assistant doctor started running, other people came running, doors slammed. Faces and voices flashed at me at a thousand frames per second. Dr Monahan's face appeared.

'The baby is too big to enter the birth canal, I will have to perform a Caesarean section,' he told me calmly. I was beyond caring what he did. In any case I wasn't asked what I wanted, I was just informed of what was about to happen. I moved my hand in a gesture of hopelessness as he instructed the nurse to give me an injection to knock me out.

As the room started to become fuzzy around the edges I was lifted onto a trolley and taken to the operating room. Then just as I was being lowered onto the operating table a contraction hit me with such force that my knee knocked a nurse off her feet.

More panic, people shouting, doors slamming, but it was all becoming fuzzier and fuzzier and I slipped into welcome oblivion. Not for long. I could hear my name being shouted down a long tunnel. The noise was deafening. I tried to cover my ears. I then realised I was being slapped very hard on the face—I was being rudely jerked back to consciousness by injections, shouting and more slapping. I forced my eyelids to open, they weighed a ton. I was sitting, well not really, I was slumped over with many hands holding me. My doctor was holding up my head. He was looking into my drugged eyes and shouting.

'The baby has moved into the birth canal. You must push. Push!'

'Push' was screamed at me for what seemed like forever. I finally blacked out to the words, 'There's the head.'

During all that panic, chaos, pain and fear, one clear thought came through my poor drugged and fuzzy brain—never again.

I awoke in blessed silence, a lovely pastel room, the sun shining through the window and Mum holding my hand. I remember being mesmerised by the dancing light of the sunbeam across the room. I tore my eyes from the sunbeam and looked at Mum.

'Mum?' I waited for the worst. She just shook her head.

'The baby is dead?' I was drained of all emotion.

'Oh no, she is well, ten and three quarter pounds, no wonder you had trouble. But they nearly killed you to save her. I have never seen so much blood come out of one person and you should see the mess you are down below, they virtually ripped her out. I have never seen anything like it in all my experience.'

Mum was right. It took months and a few operations to repair the physical damage done during that rushed birth. I don't think I ever got over the mental experience. So, as far as I was concerned, there would be no more offspring.

It was alright for Charles. He would hand me over at the white double doors, wave goodbye and go and relax while I went through the agonies of childbirth. I informed Charles I thought the whole thing was very one-sided and he had better be satisfied with what he had. I just didn't have another six months of throwing-up energy in me, let alone the strength required to deliver.

However, Charles requested four or five more and said he would put me on a build-up programme. So, taking matters into my own hands, I joined the pill brigade and Charles couldn't do anything about it. Oh, he did try, and how he tried. He even told my doctor not to renew my prescription. I simply went on strike and that soon changed his tactics.

He did everything he could to make me miss the pill. He

would say 'We're going somewhere for a few hours' and we would end up staying the night, a very loving night. Then there were unexpected weekends when we departed with no time to pack—'You can buy all the clothes you need there'. He never did find out that I kept ten pills in a locket around my neck.

CHAPTER 7

❖

1962-1965

By this time we had moved into the 'correct suburb' and had a lovely old house close to the Polo Club. Charles bought me a horse for my birthday and we started riding every afternoon just before sunset.

One evening we were on one of these peaceful rides when he said, 'Oh hell, I forgot!' Not me this time.

'What have you forgotten?'

'I invited the Baltimore Harbour delegation for cocktails. They're in town for a few days and dropped by the office yesterday.'

Now rather concerned, I ventured, 'When?'

'When? Oh, tonight. I can't understand how I forgot.'

'Yes, it's so unusual for you to forget something.'

He sat there shaking his head, actually amazed that he had forgotten.

'What time did you say?'

'Six o'clock.'

'Charles, it's a quarter to six now. How many?'

'Oh I don't know, fifteen or so.'

'Oh Charles, you are impossible! Fifteen minutes to get ready and I'm out in the middle of the Polo Club riding.'

We galloped home and I jumped off and sprinted to the house while Charles casually strolled the horses back to the stable. I raced in the door yelling to the cook to take the reserves out of the deep freeze.

By now I had learned that my husband would often turn up with anything from six to twenty people without a moment's notice. So to keep the cook, and my sanity, I always had a whole line of frozen meal and snack standbys on hand. Wilma, the cook, also used to his 'nibs', went straight into action the moment I charged through the door. I rushed into the bedroom and had started to change when I realised that Charles was not there to take off my long riding boots and there was no way in the world I could get them off by myself. I called one of the girls from the kitchen to come and help, but it was hopeless. Every time I put my other foot on her behind to push, she would vault across the room and land in the corner in hysterics. No amount of persuasion could get her to stand still while I pushed. I would never get my boots off with her help, so I sent her back downstairs to help Wilma.

I now had about three minutes to go and I was stripped to the waist with boots and riding pants still firmly in place. I did a very tricky manoeuvre and showered to the waist, donned an evening sweater and a long flowing skirt over my riding pants and boots, and after drowning the horse smell in expensive perfume, went downstairs to greet my guests. They all arrived en masse and were a very nice group of men.

Charles arrived not long after and I went to help the girls in the kitchen while he and several of the men went through the, 'Do you know Whimpy?', 'Do I know Whimpy! Why, we were at high school together!' routine. They all had a go, and by the time they had exhausted this avenue and settled down to how to save the world, I had the girls circulating with the snacks.

I ended up having dinner with jodhpurs and boots still under my evening skirt and I nearly had to sleep in them as Charles was so tired he fell asleep while I was in the nursery checking the children. After a short nap, my boots were finally removed, along with everything else.

I had a few problems catching on to the local habits and customs. About six weeks after the riding boots incident we were invited to dinner by a Spanish business client. I hadn't eaten since breakfast and I was very peckish but I assumed we would have dinner around eight or at the latest nine. No such luck. The house was built on the side of a very high hill and had a magnificent terrace built out over the valley. We were led to this terrace and there we stayed while drinks and more drinks were poured into us. After two hours, I was dizzy as a top and still starving. I did the circuit of that terrace many times but I never once encountered food.

Charles, having discussed all his business long ago, had gone to sleep next to a man who wouldn't stop talking. He had an intelligent expression on his face, and in the dim light, he looked for all the world like he was deeply engrossed in the conversation.

I started drinking Coke so I would be able to walk to our car. The hostess finally appeared at about ten-thirty dressed in a bath robe, with a wet poodle under each arm. She wandered vaguely around the terrace, said something to the waiters in rapid Spanish and then disappeared without a word to any of the guests.

We finally sat down to dinner at midnight. Charles, having had several hours sleep, enjoyed a hearty meal but I was so full of Coke I felt sick and couldn't manage a bite.

After that I never went to any dinner without a snack first, and a few snacks in my evening bag and Charles's pockets.

I was keeping up nicely with the hectic social and business rat race, when one day Charles told me that because I had done such a good job with all the dinner parties, he had a surprise for me. We were going away for a weekend sail. Some surprise. The thought terrified me. He assured me I would be safe, we would sail to Bataan and all we would do was swim, rest and enjoy ourselves. No clients, no phones and, most of all, no Timothy telex.

Who was Timothy telex? Well, he was an innocent telex machine except that he lived right next to our bed. This unusual state of affairs was due to the fact that the European shipping market was in full swing at two a.m. Manila time, so if Charles was closing a ship or cargo deal, he would have to either sit up in the office all night or drive back and forth every time a message came in. Charles, liking his comfort, had a telex installed right next to his favourite place, the bed. It was very unnerving to say the least. It would whir and click at the most inappropriate times. Sometimes I felt it was almost human.

Just to be away from Timothy telex for three nights was enough to induce me to venture onto the water again. Not to mention having my husband alone for a whole weekend. I agreed to go.

We sailed across the bay Friday night. The heavens behaved, the water was flat as a board and a beautiful full moon bathed the whole bay in light. It was magic. We dropped anchor in a small cove just inside the Bataan point at about three a.m., went to bed, and slept the whole morning till lunch.

I was sunning myself on deck thinking what a perfect day it was when Charles had one of his brilliant ideas. He was going to teach me to sail. From the bottom up. He had Ernesto rig the small sailing dinghy. All my protests were like water off a duck's back. It was knowledge one must have, he said. So, I was deposited in the twelve-foot sailing dinghy, told to sail in that direction and then turn and come back to the boat. Simple. Even if I capsized I would be quite safe. The dinghy could not sink as it had an airtight compartment, so all I had to do was hang on and I would just float back.

I sailed off as directed, keeping the wind in the sails. I didn't mind as I was heading towards the shore and I liked that. Charles was screaming instructions and everything was working as planned until I turned to make my home run. 'It was just one of those unpredictable things,' he said later.

I ended up in a rip and instead of drifting back to the boat in the cove, I was going sideways out to sea at an alarming rate. The China Sea! Charles was frantically shouting directions to me but by this time I was so terrified I was not receiving. I stopped pulling ropes and sails and just stared. What to do? I certainly couldn't swim for it. Even with sails and a strong wind, the boat was making no impression on that riptide at all.

Once out of the protection of the point, I hit stronger tides and winds from a different direction. Trying to sail the dinghy in high wind on open water was beyond my experience and it was not long before I capsized. I went around the point watching a crazy Charles and an equally crazy Ernesto trying to pull up the anchor, which had decided at this moment to jam. The last words my darling husband shouted to me as I drifted around the point out of sight were, 'The bloody god damn anchor is jammed, swim for it!'

I was now passing Bataan point, which was sheer rockface with rocks jutting out of the water at its base in a mad foam of surf. The distance of about one thousand yards, against the current that was taking me swiftly out to sea, was completely beyond me as a swimmer. On my left was the fortress island of Corregidor in the middle of the channel with cliffs straight into the water on all sides.

If only I could make it there, but I couldn't. No way in the world a sparrow could find a footing on those rocks, not to mention the six-foot swells racing by. With these alternatives facing me, I decided to take a chance and stick with the dinghy. So I curled myself tighter around the centreboard and cried.

I kept my eyes glued to the point, hoping every moment that a big white boat would sail around it and come to my rescue. It didn't. The point became smaller and smaller. Frantic thoughts raced through my mind. What direction was I going in? As if it mattered. The obvious question was how long could I hold onto the centreboard.

An hour passed and land was fading out of sight. Watching the sun drop lower in the sky, I realised my situation was grim. What about the night? Would I make it through till morning?

I was so engrossed in my morbid thoughts that I didn't hear the outboard motor until the fishing bunker was nearly on top of me. I couldn't believe it; there was a native fishing bunker right next to me. The men helped me aboard, tied the upturned dinghy to the stern and headed slowly back to Bataan. They started questioning me and I knew I was in more trouble. Out of the frying pan into the fire. I had been picked up by Cavite pirates! Oh well, it was better than floating around in the China Sea, at least I would be on dry land. But when I told them I was from the large white boat inside the point, things changed dramatically.

'Ernesto?'

'You know Ernesto?'

'Oh, Ernesto always feeds us. He's our best friend. He hides us when we are being chased. You are very safe. We take you back to Ernesto.'

Thank heavens for Ernesto! It was sunset when we reached the boat, still with its jammed anchor. I thanked them and they departed, very happy that they had helped Ernesto. Both Ernesto and Charles were out looking for me, so I had one of the boat boys go ashore to contact the search boat.

Having done all I could, I sat on deck and waited. Charles saw me on the deck when the boat was a fair distance away.

'Thank heavens. I was so worried. When it came over the radio on the patrol boat that you were back here, I couldn't believe it. You couldn't have sailed the dinghy?'

'Yes, I did!' I said smugly.

'Sara!'

I couldn't keep a straight face. 'The Cavite pirates brought me back.'

'Cavite pirates? Why, they're the worst cutthroats in the world. You must be mistaken.'

'No. I don't think their first intentions were very honourable, but when they found out I was from the big white boat and Ernesto was our boat boy, I was safe as a bank.'

'How come?'

'It seems he feeds them now and then and hides them when they're being chased by the police around the wharves. They think the world of him.'

That night Ernesto had his own bottle of champagne and he disappeared ashore for a big night. Charles said I could give up the sailing lessons, for a while at least, and we had a very peaceful Sunday on the beach with the children. Late that night, we reluctantly returned to the mad social/business merry-go-round.

The riding, tennis, dinner party, entertaining clients circuit continued and the months went by. We enjoyed the riding parts of this busy schedule, but even these were not without unexpected excitement.

Apparently, before my horse belonged to me, she was owned

by a polo player and as soon as the chukka whistle or the referee's whistle blew, she would take off like the wind straight for the polo field. I would find myself in the middle of the battle with mallets whizzing in all directions. She must have been a good polo pony in her day because she was always right on the ball, and would become quite agitated when I did not hit it.

This embarrassing situation improved my riding at a very fast clip. The players were good sports about the whole thing and I was never actually flattened by a mallet. They had only one request, that I refrain from going riding when a match was on.

For my approaching birthday, Charles arranged a cruise to Japan on the *President Roosevelt*. Unfortunately, to fit in with business, it had to be in the middle of the typhoon season again. No, not another typhoon, in fact the complete opposite. The sea was like a sheet of glass the entire trip. I couldn't believe it.

We didn't board till two a.m., so we skipped breakfast the first morning just for the pleasure of sleeping in and being alone. At lunch we went to the swimming pool when all the people were in the dining room. It really is amazing how people become regimented on board a cruise ship, they jump at every bell. Charles, of course, did the opposite. So, when everyone was eating, we went swimming, then retired to our cabin before they all returned to take up their positions till the next bell. We returned to the pool in the early afternoon for another swim and some sun while afternoon tea was served on top deck.

By this time we also were feeling a little peckish so Charles hailed a passing waiter, told him we wanted to be alone and could he arrange somewhere private where we could eat an early evening meal. He said yes and set up a card table on the side deck under one of the lifeboats. We had a marvellous meal with not a soul in sight. Charles tipped the waiter generously and said we would have our meal there at the same time each day. The waiter said he would arrange it.

We retired to our rooms and had a very pleasant evening

alone. It was like a real honeymoon, at last. We were together day and night with no interruptions, and enjoying it tremendously. The following days passed as pleasantly as the first, with a few late night and early dawn walks around the deck.

By the third day, the only person who had spoken to us was the waiter who fed us each afternoon. We had not made the dining room once and no food orders had gone to our room. This was puzzling the steward in charge of our rooms. The other thing that was puzzling him was that only one bed was being used. No matter how small the bed, Charles always insisted that we share it. When we ordered the first breakfast in our cabin, this was the final straw for the steward. Charles ate a heavy breakfast and I just had fruit juice, tea and toast, so the order only seemed to be for one. When the steward delivered the breakfast, I was asleep, wedged down between the wall and mattress with Charles's back on me and a pillow over my head. I was completely hidden, and Charles was reading. When Charles woke me for my tea and toast he commented on the strange behaviour of the steward. Apparently he had looked through each room in the suite, in the cupboards, and asked a lot of odd questions. He finally left when Charles was very short with him. We had breakfast and chatted about many things and forgot our steward.

After breakfast Charles was called to the purser's office to answer an urgent telex from the office. I showered, dressed and went shopping, leaving a note for Charles to meet me at our private eating spot under the lifeboat at four-thirty. In typical form, Charles did not see the note and assumed I had gone swimming. Or at least that's what he told the purser and security guard who came to the suite. They were very persistent and insisted that they meet me. When Charles asked why, they told him that the steward suspected he had 'done me in'! No one had seen me since I boarded the ship.

'Well, if you would like to meet her, she's up by the swimming pool.'

They accompanied Charles to the swimming pool and no me. More questions.

'Is there anyone who has seen your wife in the last four days?'

'Yes. I have.'

'Besides yourself, sir?' They asked quietly.

'Well, we have kept to ourselves mostly, that's why we came on a cruise, to be alone. Anything unusual about that?'

'You haven't had a meal in the dining room since you boarded, and the only meal that has been delivered to your rooms was breakfast, and that was only for one. Is that all you've both eaten in four days, sir?'

'No, of course not. We have a mid-afternoon meal up on the deck. The waiter can tell you my wife is alive and well. He's seen her every day.'

Unfortunately our waiter was one of the drink waiters from the lounge, and when the men lined up all the food waiters, our special one was sadly lacking. Charles was very close to losing his temper but the two men were now convinced he had murdered me.

'Look, as soon as my wife comes back I'll present her to you and this whole silly affair will be settled once and for all!'

'I'm afraid we'll have to stay with you until then.'

Meanwhile I had decided to have my hair set, thus keeping me away for another hour. At four o'clock the two men accompanied Charles to our special eating spot, and there was our waiter setting up the table. Charles was very pleased to see him and asked him to tell the two men that he had served me a meal there every day.

The two men started to question the waiter. All the time we were with the waiter Charles had jokingly told him that I was his girlfriend. And, as the waiter put it, 'they certainly didn't act like a married couple'. Also, to the best of his knowledge, he had never heard Charles call me by my name, only 'Darling'. The men asked Charles to come with them to the office.

I arrived at our dinner spot and the waiter told me my husband was being held on suspicion of murder. I hurried down to the office and walked in all smiles. Charles leapt to his feet.

'Darling, at last, tell these men who you are for heaven's sake, and get this silly thing over with.'

'Why of course, darling.' I turned to the men. 'I'm his girlfriend.'

'Sara!' threatened Charles.

On our arrival in Tokyo, Charles had many business appointments, but he promised that when that was over, we would spend the rest of the week together. I was to busy myself shopping.

The first morning while I was dressing, Charles casually asked if I would like some shopping money. I readily accepted. I was not exactly up on the current exchange rate, so when Charles asked me, 'Will two and a half thousand be enough?' I nearly collapsed. He threw me a stack of Japanese money that would choke a horse, gave me a long kiss and departed. I gathered myself and the money and tried to work things out. That's it, it's counterfeit. No, he wouldn't. I might end up in jail. Why on earth would he give me all this money?

I finally decided he was in a sane state when he gave it to me so it was mine to spend!

Feeling on top of the world, I started out for a marvellous day. It didn't last long. I had decided one of the first things I would buy was Japanese pearls for Mum. Breezing into a jeweller's in the hotel's arcade, I came back to earth with a thud. There in the showcase before me was displayed a beautiful single strand of pearls, and the price tag: 85,000 yen.

He had done it again. As the shop assistant kindly informed me, the total extent of my shopping wealth was $25. I stormed out, leaving a very bewildered shop assistant.

Mad wasn't the word for it. Some way, some day, I would get even. I spent my fortune on a few souvenirs in about two seconds flat, so I had all day to think up some devious revenge.

Charles arrived back at about five. He'd forgotten all about the morning's episode. I sulked, he apologised, we went out and had a delicious Japanese dinner and he promised me more shopping money in the morning. I never did think up any devious revenge, not then, or at any other time in the following years, but I sure was practised and successful in the sulking department.

The next day I was to meet Charles and a client for lunch at a small restaurant in the Ginza. When I say small, I mean small. You couldn't swing a cat without being cruel. Our host ruled supreme as he owned the restaurant. We were waited on hand and foot and served fabulous food. By this time my stomach was completely broken in and I enjoyed whatever was set before me, from raw fish to smoked octopus. Our host was a monster of a man, in size, I mean. It is unusual for a Japanese man to be six foot two inches tall. I later learned he was half American.

Four of us sat at the table, but only three of us spoke. I hesitated to speak in case I upset the applecart. He was Japanese in every way and I didn't want to spoil Charles's business negotiation by being a talkative wife. But the host kept bringing me back into the conversation. It became clear that, as a European woman, I was allowed to speak, but the cute little Japanese girl with us was not.

She wasn't a day over sixteen and was in full traditional dress with rice flour on her face. He was fifty-eight. I had a few words to say to Charles on the subject on the way back to the hotel. He told me not to interfere with the customs of the country.

Dinner brought more surprises. This time we dined with his delightful wife, who was the same age as himself and the mother of his seven children. The unnerving thing about it all was that the lunchtime companion sat off in one of the corners of whatever room we happened to adjourn to. This confused me terribly. I didn't know whether to ignore the young one and only speak to the older one, or the other way around, or speak to both. I decided that the best policy was to sit and smile, as they did, and wait to be spoken to. This procedure was praised by our host, who said that my husband was most fortunate to have other than the usual babbling western wife. Charles's response was to burst into loud laughter. It was then arranged that we would spend the weekend at his mountain retreat.

Saturday was a beautiful day with a clear blue sky, and our drive through the country and up the mountain was breathtaking. We visited all the sightseeing spots along the way, much to Charles's disgust, and arrived at the mountain establishment at about mid-morning. We were greeted by four great danes of magnificent proportions and a lovely Japanese girl of about twenty-eight, in traditional dress minus the rice powder. She ushered us into a large house which, in traditional Japanese style, consisted of numerous sliding screens.

We spent a pleasant afternoon looking at the beautiful gardens and finished the day with a perfect meal cooked by number three, who appeared to be mountain or high altitude wife. As usual, she went through the entire meal without uttering a word and sat in the corner or shuffled in and out of the room.

Dinner was long and all business talk, so I shuffled over and tried to ask 'Silent' to teach me some of the arts of the Japanese wife. She smiled and immediately started to instruct me in various Japanese cooking secrets. I was enjoying myself so much that I didn't hear the men leave. After a while she beckoned to me to follow her and led me into another room, opened one of the hundreds of screens and there in front of me was a beautifully furnished living room, western style.

Charles and our host were sitting there enjoying drinks. The screen closed behind me and she disappeared. My host gave me a scotch and dry and I sat patting the four great danes in rotation while the business droned on. The screen opened again and there stood number three, this time in full western rig. The biggest surprise was yet to come. She was a university graduate, spoke four languages, including English, fluently, and was one of Japan's top woman golfers. The host imparted all this information with a satisfied grin. He said he always invited business clients and their wives here for the weekend before he signed a contract, just to see what they were like as people. And number three was his little bait and trap combined, although he didn't say this.

I had the distinction of being the only western wife to ask to be taught the arts of the Japanese wife, and to not tell the Japanese wife to rebel. This, according to him, indicated Charles was in command of his household, and would therefore be a good man to deal with in business. This time I wanted to laugh, but contained myself. Charles was speechless. I had won the contract for him on, I might say, completely false pretences. I was all for a woman standing up for her rights. The only reason I hadn't voiced my opinion was because I was still in a state of shock. It was the first time I had ever met a man who had a wife or mistress for every thousand feet of altitude.

The weekend passed pleasantly. I continued to play the role of meek and dutiful wife and Charles acted as if I had never been any other way. We left number three at three thousand feet on Monday morning, picked up number two around two thousand feet, and lunched, hit sea level late in the afternoon, and dined with number one that night. A most confusing day.

Two days later Charles's business was complete. We left the hotel early in the morning and had a pleasant drive out to a little inn. Having received the impression that Charles could do everything, I was quite sure he could speak Japanese. He couldn't.

'Why on earth did you book into an inn where no one can speak English?'

'Actually, I didn't think of that. I just thought it would be nice to stay at an authentic Japanese inn, off the beaten track.'

'Well, this is a nice cup of tea. Between us we can say, "rice", "thank you", "good morning", and "good night"! That's not going to get us far.'

'Now don't get upset, everything will be just fine.'

A pint-size of Japanese femininity shuffled up to us and after a tremendous game of charades, we discovered we were to follow her. We ended up in a charming suite of little rooms with hundreds of sliding screens. Our problems started right there. Charles requested champagne and strawberries and the bedding to start the holiday. This entailed many, many more charades, but I didn't dare laugh as he was on the brink of exploding. I quickly ushered the girl from the room and started to investigate the inn with her in tow.

I soon found the liquor and the champagne was under

control; we then came across the kitchen and the strawberries became a reality. The bedding was more difficult. After going around the inn several times, I was just about to give up when I picked up a magazine and there was an ad for sheets, with a girl asleep. I showed her the picture and presto, we found the bedding, behind one of the screens in the hall near our suite.

I triumphantly returned to our room with our little waitress and displayed my achievements to Charles.

The bedding was arranged and the champagne and strawberries deposited on a low table nearby. The afternoon passed very pleasantly with fresh orders of champagne and strawberries appearing regularly with a little food here and there. Our waitress had the message and, right or wrong, she was going to keep the champagne and strawberries coming. Around sunset, Charles tried to convince her we didn't want any more, but once she had an idea, it seemed she would not let go. The snacks continued till the kitchen closed, and the champagne and strawberries, till the bar closed.

The constant interruptions then ceased and after a pleasant few hours, we drifted into a restful sleep, very grateful that the hotel did not provide twenty-four-hour room service.

Unfortunately, it was not to last. Charles developed indigestion. I struggled out of my sleepiness to try and remember which suitcase contained the indigestion tablets.

'I think it's the small blue suitcase in the closet, darling.' And turned over and snuggled down again. I couldn't sleep. Charles was tugging and pushing and swearing in the dark.

'Please be quiet, darling, you'll wake everyone in the inn. These walls are very thin.'

'For a thin door this one sure is stubborn.'

I turned over and switched on the light. He was not at the closet door. I looked around the room and there he was on the other side of the room, trying his best to slide part of the wall dividing us from the next room. I shouted a warning, but it was too late. Just as I uttered, 'No, Charles, that's not the closet!' that section of the wall came away in his hands to reveal the couple in the next room holding the covers up to their eyeballs. I also grabbed for a cover.

So the situation was thus: they were Japanese and, judging from the barrage of Japanese that was flying through the hole in the wall, couldn't speak English; Charles was naked behind the screen; and the rest of us were naked in bed.

As it was our blunder, I decided the ball was in our court. I wrapped the cover around me, grabbed a bottle of champagne from our staggering stock, shuffled across the room past my bewildered husband, deposited the bottle on their bed and backed out bowing and uttering 'Sayōnara'. Once back in our suite, I moved the screen and Charles back into position, turned out the light and listened. The chatting died down to whispering which was soon replaced by the popping of a cork, followed by giggles.

Charles put a large pot plant in front of the screen and it held. He congratulated me for being such a clever girl and after promising me not to open any more closets, returned to bed.

The next day dawned with our waitress popping through one of the screens with, you guessed it, champagne and strawberries!

'Oh no, not again!' said Charles. Then he paused, turned to me and said, 'How in the hell do you act out "no"?'

'How about shaking your head?'

He gave me a very disgusted look but proceeded to shake his head furiously and push her out of the room with tray intact.

We dressed, ate a suitable breakfast, and left for our day in the country. It was a perfect day. The inn had packed us a picnic lunch, obviously under the supervision of our girl because the champagne and strawberries were there in full force. We walked and talked and felt very relaxed. On a lovely hillside covered with wildflowers, under a magnificent old tree, we decided to have lunch. The lunch was fit for a king, and we spiced it liberally with champage and strawberries. After indulging ourselves lavishly, we stretched out in the sun and fell asleep.

The next thing I was aware of was waking up feeling very

cold and wet. I opened my eyes and the friendly sky that had lulled us to sleep had changed drastically. It was now pitch black and raining very hard. We jumped up and huddled under the tree.

'We can't stay here, and it doesn't look as if it's going to let up.' We looked around and all we could see through the downpour was that we were completely alone on a hillside.

'Hang on, I'll look over the other side of this hill.'

I sat there shivering while Charles dashed up the hill. 'Come on, we're in luck, I can see lights over there in the distance.'

I wrapped the blanket around me and started up the hill. Distance was the word for it, and the terrain wasn't exactly flat. We fell into creeks, and after many stumbles, cuts and bruises, arrived at a farmhouse door. We were so cold that our teeth were dancing their own tango.

A darling little woman opened the door, took one look at us and ushered us in. At the same time she issued orders in the quietest tones to several children of various sizes. In no time at all we were plunged into steaming hot baths, fed soup, wrapped in kimonos and seated around the sunken fire in the middle of a large room. Again, they spoke only Japanese.

In the next few hours the rest of the family arrived and we settled down to a wonderful family dinner. I offered to help during the preparation and the women were happy to teach me.

After dinner, the whole family entertained us with many hours of songs and dances. At the end of a very pleasant evening, we bedded down to sleep. All together! Boards were put over the sunken fire and bed rolls laid out. Charles and I were given honoured position over the fire with the parents, so feet to feet we settled down for the night.

The next morning we were given a royal sendoff and started down the road back to the inn in the beautiful sunshine.

By now we had our waitress well trained, and after a pleasant day shopping in the village, she served us a lovely dinner in bed. Hoping for an uninterrupted sleep, I snuggled up to Charles for another blissful night. But as usual, at around one o'clock in the morning he developed indigestion and had to go to the bathroom. I carefully directed him towards it and watched to make sure he made it. He did.

I was completely unprepared for what happened next. Charles staggered out of the bathroom still half asleep, tripped on the floor matting and crashed through the wall which had just been repaired. Being two hundred pounds, he just kept going straight and landed on the bed of our friends in the next room. Both lights went on and there we were again, only with one difference; this time they had my naked husband sprawled across their bed.

I quickly wrapped myself in the bedcover, grabbed a bottle and a sheet, shuffled in, threw Charles the sheet, handed them the champagne and backed out holding up the sheet so Charles wouldn't trip again. Once through the hole, I hung some of the bedding over it, and turned out the light.

The next day the screen was repaired again.

It was our last night at the inn and we were very sad to be leaving. There was a full moon, so we sat in the garden till quite late and went to our room very sleepy. We undressed each other slowly and had just snuggled down into the fluffy bedding to enjoy the rest of the evening when there was a tremendous crash.

We jumped up, switched on the light, and there was our friend from the next room holding a large bottle of sake! He bowed, handed us the sake, and grabbed a bottle of our champagne. He then covered the hole with a screen and switched out the light. We heard the popping of the champagne cork.

'I suppose they think it's some kind of custom!' commented Charles.

'Well, you must admit, you did it with regularity!'

The entire staff of the inn turned out to see us leave, as well as our friends from the next room. I suppose they had never seen anything like us before.

We went back to Tokyo for a few days while Charles finished his business, but it was a letdown after our swinging inn.

Back in Manila, life continued with the usual proportions of fun, laughter and tears, and we busied ourselves with riding, tennis, children and social commitments, and Charles with his business.

The children were growing up fast and we were really enjoying them. The eldest was now riding and Charles had bought her the funniest little pony. It was one of the native horses, a little bigger than a Shetland but with the sweetest nature. It was so fat that Murray Lee did the splits just sitting on him.

So now our afternoon rides included the two little girls, Murray Lee on her own pony, and Bonnie sitting in front of her father. Our eldest seemed to be a natural rider and it wasn't long before she was riding very well. Her sister was only one and a half, so you couldn't tell, although she seemed very at home perched up in front of her father.

Charles spoilt his children rotten but would hotly deny it. Of course I had to do all the disciplining, so naturally by the time Charles came home he was given a right royal welcome as they knew there would be no more spankings. He was thrilled to be the most popular member of the team.

One afternoon the children and I were out playing in the garden when Charles arrived home and said, 'Hurry and pack, you and I are leaving at first light in the morning.'

'Where are we going?'

'One of our ships is loading timber in Mindanao and there is some delay.'

We left the next morning in a small four-seater plane. Charles was the pilot. The weather was perfect and we landed in Cebu for lunch with friends, and then continued on to the timber camp. In his usual teasing manner, Charles had me navigate and to spice the whole deal, he would say, 'Quickly, engine trouble, nearest landing field!'

I finally convinced him I didn't need this type of entertainment and we settled down to a peaceful flight. Of course it didn't last. We were about eighty miles from the timber camp, when the sky started to turn an ugly black. The flying became very bumpy and Charles stopped talking and concentrated.

The weather did not improve and the rest of the trip was

most unpleasant. We finally made a low, low water approach to the grass strip and not a moment too soon. Just as we touched down, we were engulfed in the thickest, blackest cloud imaginable.

'Something tells me this is going to be some weekend!'

'Now don't let your imagination run away with you. What could possibly happen here in this out of the way place?'

Famous last words. We were met by the engineer and he drove us to the mill, which was right on the water's edge. As the hold-up was loading, we went staight down to the ship. I followed Charles down the rickety wharf and up the boarding ramp. We were staying on board for the evening so I went to the cabin, washed my face and then went out on deck to join Charles. He was in deep conversation with a variety of men, European, Filipino and Chinese, and some local natives in very little clothing. I was reluctant to join them so I walked around the upper deck to enjoy the view. After a while I realised that they had all stopped talking and were looking in my direction. Charles left the group and joined me.

'Darling, come and meet everyone.'

'Oh no, I'll wait till you're finished. They all look a bit too formidable for me.'

'Don't be silly, they're harmless, come along.'

And promptly dragged me over to the group. The next minute I was standing in the middle of the mob. One of the natives stepped forward, and mumbling something started to walk around me in circles. When he touched my hair I nearly launched into space! I threw frantic looks at Charles, who merely nodded and smiled. I excused myself and went to the cabin.

Charles joined me an hour or so later looking very cheerful. 'Well, everything is settled. They start loading immediately.'

'Oh that's marvellous, darling. When do we start back to Manila?'

'I'll have to stay until they finish loading, which should be tomorrow.'

'Can we look around and have a picnic?'

'As a matter of fact, I've arranged an outing for you.'

'An outing? What do you mean? What about you? Charles, what have you done?'

97

'Now, it's perfectly alright, you'll be absolutely safe.'

'Safe? What do you mean "safe"?'

Charles then told me what he thought was safe. Apparently the chief of the local natives wanted to go fishing with me and if I did the ship would be loaded.

'Charles, you didn't say "yes"?' Complete silence. 'You did!' Now in complete hysterics.

'Now, Darling, it will be alright, Ernesto will go. Besides, the chief just wants to catch some fish for you. He's very attracted to the colour of your hair. He's never seen red hair before.'

'He's probably a head-hunter,' I said gloomily.

'Don't be silly, they gave that up long ago.'

'What do you mean, "gave that up"? Oh Charles, how could you?'

'Well, if I didn't agree, the ship would sit there for heaven knows how long. And we can't afford that.'

'But we can afford to lose me.'

I cried and performed, but to no avail. Charles had promised I would go fishing and he wouldn't go back on his word.

It was now late in the afternoon and our fishing date was no rod and reel on some quiet river, but a full-scale deep sea fishing operation. At least we had the company of twenty other native fishing boats, but they were all on his side. Charles waved goodbye to me and I completely ignored him. We headed out to sea and the sun slowly set in the west, for the last time as far as I was concerned.

Well, I was wrong. It was a beautiful evening, the terrible storm that had greeted us when we landed had completely disappeared. The chief was so proud to have my red hair flowing in the wind on his boat that he couldn't do enough for me. And he was a perfect gentleman.

The entire group put on a remarkable performance of deep-sea, bunker fishing. They had a very good catch, which was due to my presence, or so they told Ernesto. When we returned to the other ship around two a.m. the natives were still loading. The chief issued orders and all the crews of the fishing bunkers turned out to help. The women cooked some of the catch over an open fire, and we had a lovely breakfast on the beach, watching the first colours of dawn appear in the sky.

The loading was finished by mid-morning so we went and had a few hours of sleep. Then, after being presented with every gift imaginable, and many ceremonies, we were allowed to leave for Manila.

At this point in my life, I suppose you could say I had it all. I was utterly and completely in love with my husband, I had two beautiful children, Charles was building his empire and success was in the air. It seemed too good to be true, and it was.

The maid interrupted me in the writing room to tell me I had a visitor. I told her to serve tea in the sunroom and read the note she had handed to me as I walked into the room. The switchboard operator from Charles's office sat nervously on the edge of a chair. As I entered, she jumped up and bobbed a quick bow. I smiled and asked her to please sit down. She sat with her head down and I knew she was waiting for me to ask her the problem. So I said was there anything I could do to help her.

'Oh yes, there is.' She spoke slowly at first, and then in a babble. As the speed increased, so did the accent, until it was difficult to understand most of what she was saying, indeed some parts of the monologue lapsed into Tagalog and I did not understand a word.

But slowly and surely the shiny glass of my crystal world cracked and shattered into a thousand pieces. The room became hazy around the edges as if I were looking through a hole in heavy fog. And this feeble girl who had just destroyed my life, kept saying, 'I don't know what to do, what do I do?'

So complete was the shock I was not capable of speech or movement. Eventually one of the maids came in and led her away. Still I sat. At different times during the next hour I was approached, I could hear and see people, but I just couldn't or didn't want to move. It was as if I was watching someone else and I couldn't tell her what to say or how to move.

The maids became worried and called the office. Charles was home in a flash. He knew what was wrong and he was, as later proven many times, as guilty as hell. He also knew how much I loved him, and how much control and influence he had over me.

My eyes wouldn't move even for him. He led me to our room, sat me on the bed and disappeared, then reappeared with a glass.

'Here take this, big gulp.' I did. It was straight cognac. That snapped me out of my trance. My eyes focused on Charles and the look made him gasp and step back a pace.

'Now, Darling, I can explain,' in his smoothest tone.

'Don't bother, I'm leaving you.' I was very calm. I couldn't believe I was so calm, not that I had ever given any thought to how I would act when I told my husband I was leaving him. I loved him completely. I had trusted him with my soul, my heart, my life. That was how much I loved him and I thought he loved me the same. I realised later in our marriage just how miserably wrong I was.

'You can't leave me just because I slept with her once,' he said in surprised tones.

My calm exploded into uncontrolled rage.

'You only slept with her once!' I screamed. 'Well you must have a double. Maybe he's the one who slept with her the other times. Maybe he's the father of the child she's carrying.' By this time I was screeching and my voice failed.

That was the only fact of the whole sordid story he didn't know. When she knew she was pregnant, she came to me.

The car was packed with suitcases and the children were waiting in it to go to the airport. I stood at the top of the winding staircase with Charles.

'Well, I'll call you when I reach Sydney,' I said listlessly. Apart from the cognac outburst I had spent the last few days in a trance. My heart had really broken, and every time I looked at Charles it cracked again. I was so unhappy I didn't know what I was going to do. If I hadn't had the children I'm quite sure I would have ended my life. I wouldn't now, but then, so young and so in love . . . I had to get away, not see him.

I started slowly down the stairs, trying to recover from

the 'perfectly staged kiss' which Charles had just given me. It had me crying inside, but I was not going to let him know that. I made it half way down the stairs. He said my name softly. Every fibre in my body knew I should leave this man, get as far away from him as possible, yet every fibre in my body wanted to stay.

There are major turning points in everyone's life and this was one in mine. Even to this day I have no idea if I made the right decision. You can philosophise forever and still not reach a solution. But my choice was not that straightforward, because when I turned to him, he was standing with a gun to his head.

He said, very quietly, 'When your foot touches the bottom step, I pull the trigger.' I was young, very much in love and stupid enough to believe him. When he tried that routine on me about eighteen years later, I walked out of the room and quietly closed the door, quite confident no shot would ring out.

A few months after the great winding staircase scene, I went to the office. I noticed a new switchboard operator. I asked Charles's secretary about the girl and she said she had gone back to her home town on one of the southern islands.

There were more unpleasant surprises in store. Our ships became caught up in a variety of waterfront strikes. Charles had to get the ships in and out of various ports just ahead of, or in between, the strikes. Our luck held out for quite a while as the strikes settled, but we were not to come through completely untouched. In fact, we were not to come through at all. At the very end, when everyone thought the problems were over, California waterfront started their own strike. Two of our ships were in San Francisco harbour, and there they stayed for many, many months.

It was a long drawn out affair, going broke. Charles would not give up. However, slowly but surely, his ships one by one ground to a halt. After living in luxury for six years, we were now broke.

Given the changes that were then taking place at such a

rapid pace in the Philippines, Charles decided it was not favourable to start again. So he said we would move to our cattle station and live close to nature for a while. He didn't mention how close.

'What cattle station?'

'Don't you remember? The one I described to you on our first date.'

'Oh that one?' Still none the wiser. 'When did you buy that?'

'About four years ago.'

I wasn't too upset about the prospect of living on a station. My uncle owned sheep stations near Canberra and he lived very comfortably. How wrong could I be? The Northern Territory was one hundred years behind the southern stations, and that was being conservative. I should have smelt a rat when Charles avoided all questions about the place. He just kept saying that he wanted me to judge for myself. Of course the real reason was that, if he had told me what I would find on our station, I would never have gone.

CHAPTER 8

❖

1965-1966

I flew to Sydney with the children while Charles went straight to the station. The children and I stayed in Sydney for about a month and had a very enjoyable time visiting all the family and seeing old friends again.

Mum had only seen her grandchildren on two visits to Manila, so there was a certain amount of adjustment on both sides. The children had had a full time yah-yah (amah) since birth. Bonnie was only two and a half so the shock wasn't as bad for her as for her sister. At four and a half, Marlee had her world and her yah-yah nicely organised.

We arrived home from the airport and Mum and I were enjoying a cup of tea. Marlee, with Bon in close tow, was investigating the house. After a few minutes, she returned and asked, 'Mummy, where is my yah-yah? I need her.'

'Nanny doesn't have a yah-yah, Darling.'

'What do I do? Who will dress me?'

'Well, you will have to dress yourself.'

She walked slowly to her room digesting this sobering thought. She reappeared a few minutes later with the play clothes she wished to wear in her arms and a bright smile on her face. She walked up to her grandmother and said, 'Nanny, I have decided to let you be my yah-yah.'

Mum tried very hard not to laugh, and thanked her profoundly, but declined the generous offer. Marlee was confused. She didn't even consider approaching me. In her mind, I checked her appearance when she was ready, I never dressed her. She stood there, very unsure of what to do next.

I said, 'I'll dress you, Darling,' and walked her to the bedroom. She was very relieved.

A few nights later I had a dinner engagement and Mum looked after the girls for the evening. I gave them an early dinner and bath and they helped me dress them in their pyjamas. They settled down to TV with Nanny and Poppa and promised they would be good girls and go to bed on time. Nanny said she would read them the required fairytales. The next morning Mum told me this amusing story.

Mum read the required stories and tucked them in and kissed them goodnight, but Marlee soon set her straight.

'But Nanny, Mummy always sings us a lullaby.'

This was no problem for Mum. She was a trained soprano while I wasn't anything and sang way down in my boots, just holding a tune. We were moons apart. Mum launched into song.

When Mum finished singing the lullaby, Marlee, in all the innocence of a four-and-a-half-year-old, said, 'Oh Nanny, that was awful, can't you sing like Mummy?'

Mum said maybe she could try, but Marlee said, 'That's alright Nan, you go and rest, we'll get to sleep somehow.'

Mum kept a very straight face and kissed them both and said goodnight.

After I had brought the family up to date on the madcap happenings of my life, and let the girls meet all their uncles, aunts and cousins, we departed for Darwin and the furthest point west. The station was two hundred miles southwest of Darwin by air, and a staggering five hundred by road, if you could call it a road. Our nearest neighbours were about one hundred miles away.

Charles met us in Darwin and informed me that the plan was that he would go in by road with a few necessary living requirements, and the children and I would fly in with the mail plane. At that time, the mail plane was a DC-3 en route to Perth via half the stations in the north. As we approached the landing strip on our station, the pilot asked me if I would like to see the valley—he thought it was one of the prettiest valleys he had seen. I sat there and surveyed my new home, all one million acres of it. He was right, it was indeed a beautiful valley.

The plane landed on the gravel strip, the crew and passengers waved goodbye and the plane took off. There I stood with two little girls, dressed in a white linen coat with white Garbo hat and white gloves, in the middle of nowhere. The two little girls and I should have been standing in a nice garden down south. Instead, as far as the eye could see was dust and dried landscape with heat shimmers. We had arrived in the dry season.

After the dust from the takeoff had settled, I looked around. About five hundred yards away stood a tin shed.

'I'm hot, Mummy!'

'Yes, Darling, I know. We'll go and sit in that shed over there and wait for Daddy.'

Taking the children by the hand, I started to crunch my way through the bulldust, which was ankle deep and engulfed you in a brown cloud every time you put your foot down. I'm sure it is very similar to walking on the moon.

I cleared a spot among the empty rum bottles and beer cans, sat the children on a suitcase each, and started to investigate the tin shed. It consisted of a large area in the middle with a roof and a back wall. On each end of this open section were rooms, like two little boxes. A continuation of these two rooms on one end formed a breeze-way kitchen, only two walls, and a breeze-way laundry, and on the other a bathroom and toilet. It was all tin and steel and cement and very, very ugly. But it was fairly new and well built, not the usual bush affair or lean-to.

During these explorations, I found out that although there were water pipes, there was no running water; in fact, there was no water, period. And there were light switches, but no electricity. I was yet to learn of the world of generators.

After finishing my inspection there was nothing else to do but sit and wait for Charles. He had left Darwin four days before us, supposedly in time to meet the plane. At about eight o'clock we saw headlights in the distance. I hoped it was Charles and not some landing from Mars. It was Charles, with our necessary living requirements under a few tons of bulldust.

105

The truck had bogged, otherwise, he said, he would have been there to meet the plane. He had some sandwiches, bought at a roadside store two hundred miles back, and we washed them down with hot beer. After this unbelievable meal, Charles invited me to 'make myself at home'.

'Wouldn't it be better if we went to the house now, so I can put the children to bed? They're very tired.'

'This is the house,' said Charles in a very quiet voice.

'What . . . this is an open shed!'

'This is home until we build a house.'

I sagged to my suitcase and cried. That night, hot, hungry and covered in bulldust, we went to bed on a bare mattress (Charles had thought of the mattress, but not of sheets and pillows) on a cement floor. At least we were not cold.

The months that followed were a nightmare. I cried a lot, sulked all the time, was terrified most of the time, and didn't speak to Charles any of the time. But after the first shock wave had passed over me, I started to accept the challenge that Charles had cleverly planted in my mind—to turn this horrible tin shed into a liveable house

This was the only choice open to me, short of leaving Charles. He had lost all our money trying to save the shipping company and now the station was the only asset we had left. I pleaded with him to sell and move to civilisation but to no avail. He was caught in the dream of carving a 'Charlie Kingdom' out of this hostile wilderness and, like it or not, I was to be part of it, or leave.

Leaving your husband in those days was far more difficult than today, and besides, there was one other fact which I could not ignore—I was still in love.

So I willed myself out of depression and attacked the problem.

I didn't have much to work with—apart from the dreaded tin shed, there was a caravan which the previous owner had left, and that was it.

The first and major step was to clean the place up. The shed was surrounded by empty bottles, cans, papers, tools and anything else you can imagine for a distance of about one hundred yards. This unusual landscaping had been created by the various staff over the years.

They had certainly left their mark, if not in work, then in a few thousand empty beer cans, wine flagons, and of course empty bottles which had contained that backbone of the North, rum. I spent years trying to think of a use for the above-mentioned empties, but to this day, apart from forming mountains at the rubbish dump, they have not been recycled. Just removing a few mountains of these from our potential house to the rubbish dump did wonders.

In between all this cleaning, I had to tackle the task of feeding the family, a chore which up to this point I had never had to handle. I must admit I wasn't the best in the kitchen area, but in this so-called kitchen, I was a disaster.

Its main feature was a black greasy monster, also known as a wood stove. After six weeks of scrubbing, I finally reached the enamel. It was actually cream and green, and it informed me that it was the de luxe model. I would hate to see the standard type. This fire-breathing monster sat in a black hole in one corner with a twelve-inch space around it. I have no idea what the space was for, but I do know that I lost many a meal over the side in the months to come before I had my hand in. Behind it was a most unusual rippled tin wall coated with a combination of soot and grease splashings that must have taken years to perfect.

About the only thing that looked like anything you would find in a normal kitchen was a stainless steel sink. This was suspended in mid-air, or so it seemed, on the same wall as the stove. Most sinks are surrounded by cupboards and work surfaces. Not this one. There it sat, I mean hung, on the tin wall.

That ended the first wall. The second wall, well, that was the feature wall, completely blank, unpainted, rippled tin. The third and fourth sides were the breeze-ways.

Apart from the stove and sink, the only other fixture was yours truly. Not a cupboard, shelf, table or chair could be found. Oh, I forgot the cooking utensils. They hung around the stove area on seven-inch nails and consisted of one tin frying pan with a hole dead centre (not for hanging purposes), a saucepan with half a handle, a tin cup, very chipped but whole, and one tin plate with a hole in the rim (for hanging purposes). There was also a set of knife, fork and spoon, all with holes in the handles, tied together with a dirty, greasy strip of leather. No matter how you manipulated them, there was no way you could use them for eating, except one at a time.

Somehow I managed to feed the family. It was quite a feat to make an omelette in a frying pan with a hole in the middle but after losing eighty per cent through the hole during the first week or so, I could finally gauge the heat and make a very good one without losing a drop.

I also had a brilliant teacher, a delightful bush Aborigine named Mary. She was my lifesaver. She taught me how to master the stove, tried to teach me how to bake bread, and generally how to survive in that godforsaken wilderness. The children loved 'Old Mary', as did I. She would take them tracking and hunting and it was not long before they were very good bush girls. She was our one spark of brightness in those terrible first years.

We were slowly getting some semblance of order around the place. I had installed forty-four gallon drums everywhere in place of running water. We found a hose long enough, after many joining and patching jobs, to reach from the well to the house. With this ingenious setup, we could fill all the drums when the pump was going, thus eliminating the back-breaking process of carting water all day by bucket. I had twelve forty-four gallon drums along the feature wall in the kitchen.

Of course before we arrived, this problem hadn't existed. The manager would take a weekly bath in the horse trough and wouldn't be caught dead drinking water. I installed lots of drums because it took hours to get the water pump going and when it was, we used the water up almost as fast as it was pumped. The pump would be started after breakfast, by the mechanic, and he would then disappear down to the workshop, and often we filled drums, buckets, saucepans and sometimes the house. Most times he would return at lunchtime to find us three inches under water, but it was preferable to dust.

As the months passed, the shed became cleaner, we had installed a water system of sorts, and I was actually producing meals that we could eat, except the bread. Even though we were enjoying this primitive way of life, it was apparent that we must progress. The first step was running water. When the shed was built, all the plumbing had been installed, so all we needed was a water supply. And for this we needed a tank. So we ordered one.

It took all of seven weeks to reach us but finally the big day arrived. The truck drove up and I fully expected to see one big shiny tank sitting on the back. Just quietly, so did Charles. But, no tank. My heart hit bottom.

'Oh no, not another two months?' That was how long we would have to wait for the next delivery.

'Now, Darling, I'm sure it's there, just stop worrying.'

It was there alright, in unassembled form. Pieces of curved, rippled tin and one big circle for the base.

'What do we do now?'

'Well, it has to be soldered together.'

Soldered. I knew Charles couldn't solder, I couldn't, the mechanic wouldn't, said he had too much work, and I didn't think we had a strong bet in Mary. Charles informed me he would take care of the situation, so I left it to him. We continued with our drums.

Mary knew how much I wanted my running water, so taking matters into her own hands, she found Willie and Willie assured Charles he could solder. Charles calculated how much solder would be needed to put the tank together, and ordered it to be sent on the next plane. However, in a very short space of time, it became evident that Willie could not solder.

Skilled tradesmen were hard to find and if there happened to be any, they were all employed by big established stations. And, let's face it, why would they leave good accommodation, good food, and good wages, for the privilege of working for next to nothing, living in an open tin shed, and eating food cooked in a frying pan with a hole in the middle?

To say that on our station, in the year 1965, we had not a single soul skilled in any of the trades required to operate a station, would have been one hundred per cent correct. Except of course for the 'current' mechanic. But of the mechanics we had had, a lot would fall into the non-skilled category. Charles excelled in many fields, but none of these talents was shining at this particular time. And my electronic accounting skills couldn't even be plugged in.

The mustering season was moving to a close and the wet season was approaching. Various people continued to solder the water tank, and the supply of solder regularly arrived. It was now December and the heat was becoming unbearable. The thermometer registered a steady top of the dial. I thought it was broken, but in one rainstorm it dropped to eighty-nine degrees, revealing that most of December had been one hundred and ten degrees, and it was getting hotter.

I had acquired a new look. I was covered with little red spots. I had the most complete case of prickly heat you could imagine. I spent the entire time a pretty crusty pink, permanently embalmed with calamine lotion.

During the approach of the 'wet', we also had the dust storm period of the North's delightful weather cycle. These storms have a habit of suddenly being there and everything changes to dark brown. You can't see, breathe or speak, for fear of being blinded, asphyxiated or choked. Apart from being most unpleasant, it is rather dangerous for little children. Not being able to see, they can wander into barbed-wire fences, fall down holes, walk into stock—and that's just a few possibilities.

The dust storms were not nearly as bad in the following years because I planted grass which became a reasonable lawn. But for the first year or so, the tin shed was surrounded by six inches of fine, super grade bulldust. During most of these frequent dust storms, I could be found down on all fours, with a scarf tied over my mouth and nose and welding goggles over my eyes, crawling to rescue my children from the swimming pool.

The children thought it a terrific game and would clap

their hands with glee when Mummy appeared out of the murk to save them from the dust monster. I hesitate to print what went through Mother's mind during these little daily distractions from the endless routine.

We were now well into the wet season, although the heavy rains had not yet hit. The dust storms were still around and would continue to be until we had at least five inches of rain to settle the bulldust. At this stage we were getting just enough to turn the dust into a muddy coating over everything. The heavy rains would wash everything clean.

The first heavy rain in the North is like magic. Overnight, every blade of grass and every leaf seems to turn green. In fact, all the little storms in the months before lay the groundwork, and then the first big hit puts the whole show over the hill.

With the first heavy rains, the 'wet' was officially here. It was early January and with weeks of endless rain ahead, the men departed for town to pass the time talking over some bar till it was finished. The river came up, the roads were washed out and Charles, the children and I settled down for our very first 'wet'.

Before private planes and helicopters, the entire 'top end' gradually came to a halt as one by one, each road (there weren't many) became impassable. It had changed a bit by our first wet in 1965, but not much. Visitors were very few during those months and the only way they could get in was by chartered or mail plane.

The mail could sometimes be eight weeks between each delivery. Rather than risk getting bogged down on some remote airstrip, the milk run would only land on sealed strips during the wet. So, in December and January, there were very few stops between Darwin and Perth—it was almost direct.

1965 was a lovely wet. Being new to the way of station life, we had not arranged any building supplies for the millions of things that needed to be done to transform the shed into a house. So we spent two idyllic months cut off from the world doing as we pleased. We put our caravan in the middle of the tin shed for coolness—and also so the children and I wouldn't drown running to the toilet. With our portable bedroom in the middle of our future house, we were very cosy. We had loads of good books, and a nice friend had sent us a shipment of good wine. The rain poured for days, and sometimes weeks, on end, only stopping for a few hours daily. It was a record flood year and the creek came right up to the kitchen step.

But regrettably it was over too soon. The skies cleared and the sun stayed out and everything in general prepared itself for the coming new season. The lower paddocks along the Victoria River were still very boggy and the horses and vehicles could not go everywhere, but as each week passed, they ventured further and further afield. It was not long before the whole station was declared fit for mustering.

The new stockmen arrived, mostly very quiet types, along with the most entertaining half-caste I have ever met. His name was Bob. The long line of stockmen blur in my memory, but the Aborigines are easy to remember, they were such unusual personalities. Bob was extremely talkative and very inquisitive. He was particularly interested in the fact that we were new at the station management game. Thinking I was a softy, he decided to appoint himself my chief adviser, hoping for his rewards in alcohol.

This upset Willie, who was our 'in house' character, especially when Bob offered to help with the tank. Willie would have none of it. The tank, which Willie had now spent close to eight months working on, was nearing completion. I did not dare upset the applecart, just in case Bob couldn't solder and Willie wouldn't. So for old Bob the tank was off limits. Fortunately he wasn't the least bit upset by this slight—he busied himself in the preparation of gear for the first muster of the season.

We now faced our first whole season. Would we make it? I was already wishing for the wet again.

Around this time there arrived another colourful character on the mail plane. Bill turned out to be a film director and was looking for the appropriate setting for a documentary he was planning to make. He had been in Darwin for a few weeks and had visited some of the established stations just down the track but they didn't suit him—he wanted something totally different. He had met one of our ex-employees in a bar in Darwin who had told him that if he wanted something weird and wonderful, we were it. He stayed five days, but it only took him one day to decide that we were what he was looking for.

The documentary's aim was to tell the people of the South, civilised part of Australia, just what they could expect if they were ever brave or stupid enough to tackle the wide wonderful northern Outback of Australia.

After discussing all the arrangements with Charles, Bill said he would return in a month with crew and equipment when the road was open. I quickly put in my two bob's worth and told him to include a cook in his equipment. He said his secretary was a great cook. I said that was fine, as long as he was satisfied, because he had to eat the cooking. With this excitement over, we settled back to work.

The next day was very exciting. After nine and a half months of 'solid solder', my water tank was ready. It only had to be hoisted up onto the tank stand. This was no easy feat as it was fourteen feet high. Using the back of the table top truck, along with an amazing formation of forty-four gallon drums, miles of ropes, tackle, a lot of swearing and a full day put in by every able man on the station, our 'solid solder' tank was finally put in its place. There it sat in all its glory, with a big dent outlined against the sky. It was decided that the filling ceremony would take place the next day.

Very early the next morning, the water pump was persuaded to start, the hose was attached and the water started to fill our nine-month marvel. Eventually, after getting tired of watching water pour into a tank, everyone went about their jobs. Well, not everyone. I was watching the water progress and of course Willie was still admiring his magnificent creation.

I waited for a few hours and then, with great ceremony, held a glass under the kitchen tap and announced the first glass of running water. I was wrong. In the four years that the water pipes had not been holding water, they had certainly collected a few other things. After a chorus of the most unusual squeaks, grunts, rattles and vibrations, my glass was filled with an explosion of dust and rust, followed by bugs of various descriptions, a putrefied lizard, and a large number of cockroaches. Staring at this concoction in horror, I was further shocked by the final touch, a spluttering coating of brown mud. Then, at long last, water. Still a horrible brown, but water nonetheless. I turned on all the taps to remove all the pipe inhabitants and dirty brown water, and finally the tin shed had its first operational water system.

However, as the day wore on into afternoon, the poor old water pump became very noisy and extremely smelly and hot. On inspection, it was discovered that the tank was only one quarter full. The hose was too small. This was one problem. The other problem was rather more serious. By mid-afternoon the tank and stand were surrounded by a sea of water. The tank leaked. In fact, it didn't leak, it poured! How a tank put together with so much solder could leak was impossible to comprehend, but stand under it for a few minutes and you were quickly convinced.

Willie was visibly crestfallen. I was speechless. Charles stopped the smoking pump and the tank emptied in fifteen minutes. It leaked as fast as the poor old pump could fill it. Charles decided there and then that the tank had to be lined with cement, no more solder.

Finally, after three more days, we had a solid solder, cement-lined tank that still leaked, not as much, but enough. But that was that, there were too many other things to be done. I would just have to put up with my leaky tank. Short of falling off the stand, the tank would not receive any more attention.

We had plenty of water, so I suppose the wastage was alright, though the mud around the tank was not alright. After a few days the tank stand was definitely leaning to the left. The tank and stand were sinking! The leaking problem had to be solved, and quickly, before the tank ended up at ground level again.

One of the children's horses prompted the idea that solved our sinking tank. Old Herbert would stand under the tank during the hottest period of the day. The children, having heard all the talk about the tank falling, wanted me to make Herbert come out. When I walked under the stand, I realised that smart old Herb had his own airconditioned room. The constant water running down the poles made the air as cool as could be. It was then I hit upon the idea of using it as a coolhouse for the meat (it was so hot that even our salted meat went off, not to mention vegetables and so on). Willie rigged a roof under the base of the stand, put screening around the four sides, laid a sandstone floor, and we had the best coolhouse in the North. And there was often much more than meat and vegetables in there.

Willie also built a drain around the outside of the screening with a channel to the spot where I was vainly trying to start a garden. He continued the channel in and out of my rather pathetic patches of dried plants and the change was miraculous from the next day. The ground around the tank was always moist, so I planted some grass I had taken from the bottom of the billabong. The 'experts' informed me it would die because it needed a lot of fresh water, and our bore water was a long way from that. But I reasoned that if the grass had survived the long hot months when the billabongs were dry, it surely stood a chance with water all the time, even if it was a bit brackish. I was right—before long I had a healthy green patch of lawn. I kept planting runners everywhere. Soon we had a nice little garden and a green patch of lawn.

Of course this presented another problem. We did not have a fence around the house and our two little green patches were drawing all the stock within a five-mile radius. I presented my problem to Charles and he agreed I needed a fence around the tin shed. However, the men were busy with the muster preparations, so the fence would have to wait until after the muster. I tried various arguments, but it was no good—muster before all.

'When all else fails, do it yourself' was my motto. So the next day I ventured out bright and early with pickets and an axe to hit the pickets into the ground. However, the pickets were six feet in length so I could not reach the top to hit them. Back to the shed for a chair.

When finally one crooked picket was in the ground, I knew this was not the way the fences of the Outback were built. It was then that Charles introduced me to a dolly. A dolly is a hollow steel cylinder, the required height of the fence pickets. One end is open, the other sealed, with a handle on each side. You slip it over the picket and thump it into the ground until the dolly is resting on the ground. Then the picket is the right height.

However, it's not as simple as that. Eventually, I had six pickets in the ground at the right height, but not in a straight line. And you have to have them in a straight line or you cannot strain the barbed wire tight enough. By midday I had admitted defeat and retired to the caravan too exhausted to cook lunch, which did not amuse Charles.

In fact, the need for a fence was not really that pressing. We hadn't been overly bothered by stock as most of the cattle were off in far paddocks, miles from the house, and the few horses around were for the children to ride and were very quiet. Since the introduction of the little green patch, we did have a few more visitors, but they would leave as soon as a human appeared. However, the events of the next morning changed all that. Suddenly my fence became a priority.

In readiness for departure, Old Bob and some of the men were bringing all the horses up from the river paddocks to the yards to shoe them. The house stood between the mob of horses and the yards. In typical Old Bob fashion, he didn't deviate the herd one inch and I watched in horror as one hundred and fifty horses, give or take a few, thundered down upon our wall-less kitchen. I grabbed the children and sat them on the sink, and wedged myself in the corner between the sink and wall. That left Charles with the table or the stove, and as the stove was hot, he jumped up on the table— just as the horses thundered through and out via our future living room.

After the dust had settled, Charles gave orders for the fence to be built. Judging by the time it had taken to put the tank together, I didn't think they would leave for weeks, but alas, the men knew how to build a fence and were ready to leave on muster early the next day.

'How long will you be gone?'

'Not long, and I'll check back whenever I'm near.'

'What if you're not near?'

'Don't worry, you have Mary and I'm leaving Sylvester. If you need me, he can ride out to the camp.'

'Sylvester? Are you joking? That poor boy isn't sure which foot comes next!'

'Now, Darling, don't exaggerate.'

'I'm not exaggerating, I'm flattering!'

'Just relax and play with the children, stay close to the house [as he called it] and nothing can possibly happen to you. I've had everything seen to, so you won't have to worry about a thing. Just enjoy yourself.'

He kissed us all goodbye, told Mary to look after us and rode over to join the men. They all looked very serious as they assembled in rank position, Charles, John, the manager, Old Bob and Willie side by side, the head stockman, and the young jackaroos in order of age. Orders were issued and the stockmen moved over to take the coachers (quiet cattle used to calm the wild cattle, when caught) out of the holding yard. Old Bob was in charge of the pack mules. Everyone was assembled behind the airstrip fence which separated them from the wild bush section of our station.

It was all very quiet and still. The animals seemed almost asleep. But when the order was given to open the gate, it was as if someone had fired a starting gun. All the horses, cattle and mules, especially the mules, went crazy. They shot out of the gate and once on the airstrip, began stampeding around in circles. It was mayhem. The men were racing around bumping into each other, trying to get the situation under control. Bob was yelling that the mule with the rum supply had gone bush. Trust Bob to know which mule. Eventually, after racing around the airstrip and generally kicking up a fuss and a few packs off, they finally stopped and meekly allowed themselves to be led back into position. Bob returned with the 'rum mule', John checked the rum supply and, after this quite hilarious performance, men and animals at last departed in a cloud of dust. I really think the animals looked forward to this rodeo because, in the years to follow, they did it every time the camp was ready to leave.

CHAPTER 9

❖

1966

I now faced the unnerving prospect of spending the next week or so alone—except for a few promised visits from Charles. Well, not really alone—I had the children, Mary, and of course Sylvester. I decided then and there to take a positive attitude. I would not be scared or upset. I would cope. There was no reason why I couldn't keep busy, heaven knows there was enough to do. Yes, I would think positive. I would work, swim, play with the children, and relax. I was right in the middle of my positive thinking when Mary walked in.

'No water, Missus.'

'But we must have water, the tank was filled.'

'No water, Missus.'

'They couldn't possibly have forgotten to fill the tank.'

'Sylvester, 'im clim' up, 'im empty.' She meant the tank, but she was right on both counts.

Great! The dust hadn't settled and already things were falling apart. How on earth could we manage without water? We couldn't.

Somehow we had to start that water pump. By we, I mean Mary, Sylvester and yours truly. The mechanic had gone mustering. Mary and Sylvester's knowledge of water pumps was on a par with mine. I knew when the pump was going and when it was not. And that's all. Nevertheless, we had to start the pump.

It was now approaching midday, the temperature was rising and the need for water was becoming urgent. Donning a large straw hat and sunglasses, I ventured out to the pump site with assistant engineer Mary close in tow. The children were sitting in their empty swimming pool waiting for water. There, on the ground before me, sat a small uncomplicated-looking piece of machinery. I decided that the best line of attack was to be calm and practical, so, kneeling down next to the pump, I looked for an instruction plate. I couldn't see a thing—the pump was completely covered in one inch of grime and dust. My assistant raced off and returned with a rag. After vigorous rubbing with petrol on a flat area, we uncovered the secret formula for starting the greasy machine.

I cannot remember the exact combination stated on the plate, because from that day to this, I have never ventured near another pump, but it involved moving levers to a certain position, closing some flange or other, opening another valve, and with all these moving parts in correct position, the confounded thing was supposed to start.

With roughly five moving parts, the possible combinations came to around twenty-five. In the next five hours or so, I tried about five hundred. The twenty-five deal only applied when you knew the five right parts. I didn't. And anyway, there were a lot more than five moving parts on our particular pump. Granted, a lot of them moved when they shouldn't have, for that pump had had a long service record. Too long!

After setting each combination I would wind the rope around the starting wheel, or whatever, and pull with all my strength, whereupon the horrible thing would cough, splutter, and die.

After hours of shutting this thing and opening that thing with no success, I decided to look for more instructions. More vigorous cleaning with petrol and another small plate appeared. It informed me that it was standard procedure to fill the engine with petrol and oil before starting. Having been put soundly in my place, I set about the task of trying to find the necessaries. The petrol was 'to hell and gone' down the airstrip. Because of the fire danger, the drums of various fuels sat forlornly in the middle of the paddock about a half mile from the homestead. Having exhausted myself with hours of opening and closing valves, and pulling the starter rope, I took a breather after explaining to Sylvester that I wanted a container full of standard petrol. This took quite a while because I had to make clear to him, with Mary's help, that there were three kinds of fuel in the stack of drums: petrol, diesel and aviation fuel. Each had a different colour painted on top of the drum, and after establishing the colour of the drum we wanted, Sylvester went off down the airstrip, container in hand.

The oil was located in the tin shed, all types neatly lined up against the wall in four gallon drums. The instructions told me to fill the pump with 'thirty' oil, so I did. After quite a while Sylvester returned with the container of fuel, and I filled the petrol tank.

After another half hour of the same procedure as before, opening that, closing this and so on, with no luck, I decided I would have to try another approach. I needed to eliminate each combination as I tried it. So I tagged each moving part and numbered it, then started my process of elimination. After a page of combinations, the pump started!

I was so excited I forgot to close the open gadget, and open the closed thingamajig and it stopped.

Putting a big ring around the magic combination, I then read the instruction plate again. It stated that after starting the monster, I then had to open the closed thing and close the open one. So, with the magic combination in place, I pulled the starting rope. The pump jumped into life, I quickly followed the next instructions and stood back in triumph to watch the water flow into the tank. No such luck!

Then, as we all stood watching the hose arched over the tank, waiting for the water to spurt forth, we were suddenly drenched from behind. The hose from the well into the pump had blown the fitting. The water stopped. The pump stopped. After reconnecting the hose to the pump, I found a little lever which indicated 'on' and 'off'. The lever was pointing to 'off' so I turned it to 'on' then went through the starting procedure again. The pump started, I opened the closed, closed the open, and once more turned to the tank to watch the water come forth. No water.

By this time the pump was roaring. I was just about to turn it off and try to work out what was wrong when water

121

came from everywhere! The hose from the pump joined a set of valves and the line from the pump had blown at this point and we were being drowned by a two-inch water spout!

Slipping and sliding around in water and mud, I finally made it to the pump and turned it off. I was now faced with three valves; one operated water flow to cattle troughs in nearby paddocks, the second went to troughs across the airstrip, and the third directed water to our tank. After what I had just been through, a three-way valve combination was a pushover. I tried the first valve, waited, the fitting blew. Once more I was drowned. Next valve, same result. I was now slopping around in about a foot of mud. Things slipped and slithered everywhere. The children were having a marvellous time, Mother was not.

Naturally the last valve was the tank valve. Thinking nothing else could go wong, I went through the starting operation for the hundredth time. Pump set, valve open, flange closed, water lever open, tank valve open, petrol primed, start. It did and all eyes turned to the hose over the tank. We held our breath.

At long last water sprayed forth. Boy, did it spray! Mary informed me the pump had never pumped better. I staggered through the mud and headed for the bathroom to decoat myself. I showered, washed my hair and was dressing when Mary came rushing in, eyes wide.

'Come quick Missus, flyin'!'

'Flying?'

'Quick, quick!' Mary's eyes rolled back in her head.

I ran out to the pump. There it was, hovering like the centrepiece at a seance, a few inches from the ground. I put some heavy rocks on the base and it decided to stay grounded.

I couldn't, for the life of me, work out what was wrong. Until now, the poor old pump would hardly start, and when it did, it just putted along like it was about to utter its last putt. Now here it was flying! The next shock was that the tank was overflowing. Now I knew something was wrong! Normally that poor old pump took hours to fill the tank, it had just completed the task in record time. Water was now cascading down the sides, making one big mud pool for the children.

'Plenty water now, Missus.'

Slithering through the mud to the pump, I followed the 'close the open, open the closed' routine and waited. Nothing happened. The pump continued to roar and pump water at an alarming pace. I reversed the operation, still nothing happened. I did everything. I moved, pushed, pulled, closed and opened every possible thing on that machine, but to no avail, that damn pump simply would not stop. Water continued to cascade over the side of the tank.

Mary and Sylvester ran around acting as if the end of the world was near while the children were having the time of their lives. I was covered in mud, again.

Then Mary suddenly let out an unearthly scream and pointed to the tank. I looked up fully expecting to see the tank sinking into oblivion, but instead, spouting out of the hose was brown shiny mud. We had now exhausted the water supply of our small well and were pumping liquid mud from the bottom of it. What to do? I couldn't direct the mud to the cattle trough, they would have nothing to drink. I couldn't let it continue into our tank, we would have nothing to drink. After the first wave of panic, I pulled the fittings apart at the valve connection.

This saved us from drinking mud for a week, but it was making a terrible mess of the yard. The mud was spraying all over the place and pouring back down the well. At least it was running away from the tank stand. I was just taking a breather, when Mary prompted me back into action. She was pointing at the pump which was now lurching up and down, trying to simulate vertical take-off, and belching black smoke.

The mud was getting thicker by the minute and was having great difficulty passing through the pump. The pump was protesting in the form of thick black smoke and a terrible burning smell. Oh, if only the thing would run out of petrol, I thought.

'That's it!'

I slithered over to the storeroom and found a small length of hose, skidded back to the pump and syphoned the fuel tank

123

dry. The gallant old horror gave a few sickening lurches and finally stopped. Cheers issued forth from the gallery. I was standing there basking in the applause when the muddy ground slowly disintegrated from under me and I started to slide into the well. I grabbed for the poly pipe and with feet and hands working at incredible speed, managed to stay above the mud going with me. Mary threw me a rope just in time and I crawled out to safety.

I was too exhausted to move for quite a while, so I didn't. I just sat. After about ten minutes, the sun dried the mud and I set solid. The children had a wonderful time chipping away their solid mud mother. Eventually I slopped into the bathroom and took another shower. The water was dark brown and when I had finished, I had acquired an instant suntan. I collapsed into bed and the children served me dinner.

We survived, even though the potatoes were a beige colour and the bread and milk a dirty off-white. I just hoped that our dirty water would last until the men returned. There was no combination in the world that would start that old pump again.

The next morning brought with it the promise of an extremely hot day. After breakfast I filled the children's pool with murky water, much to their distaste, told them not to swallow too much, and then decided to clean out the storeroom. This was a large room, about fifteen feet by fifteen feet, but there was only two feet of actual space. One would walk into this space and lean in the direction of the article wanted— that is, if one was fortunate enough to know where the article was.

Cleaning out the storeroom would obviously take more than one day and one pair of hands so Mary and Sylvester helped. As I sorted, Mary cleaned and Sylvester carted the rubbish out to the garbage disposal—a hole in the ground—and burnt it.

Late in the morning I came across a whole box of bullets of all descriptions. Knowing the men were short of bullets, I put the box aside then went off to settle an argument between the children. Walking back I collided with Sylvester.

I couldn't understand a word he was saying, even Mary

was having trouble, when suddenly the whole scene turned into a Chinese New Year. Our first reaction was to hit the deck and it was in that position that Mary informed me we were ducking real live bullets that Sylvester had accidentally dumped on the fire.

The children! They were around the corner from our firing rubbish dump, but what if they walked around the corner to see what all the noise was about? In the loudest voice imaginable, I called, 'Children, don't move!' and started crawling to them. The children had frozen on my command and then, following me, we all crawled to the opposite side of the house, away from the flying bullets.

The rest of the day was spent on all fours. As the kitchen was in the line of fire, not much was eaten. Around dinnertime we were all starting to feel quite hungry, but with only one sheet of tin between us and a possible bullet, there wasn't a rush on food. However, eventually, with a mattress at my side, I crawled to the fridge and took out some food.

The setting sun found us sitting on the ground up against the wall, eating cold beef and bread, and drinking brown powdered milk. As the bathroom was also in the line of fire, baths were dispensed with that night and two very dirty children crawled into bed. Mary and Sylvester made it to their camp across the flat without mishap and, behind the mattress, I made it to the caravan.

I covered the wall with the tabletop, stuffed papers and magazines between for good measure, and with the mattress on the floor, drifted off into a very fitful, nervous sleep. I could see my epitaph: 'Shot by a rubbish dump'.

It would be safe to say I was stiff, tired and completely out of sorts the next morning. I would have loved to stay right there, in bed, on the floor, for the whole day. At least that way I could be sure of nothing happening. But today was mail plane day, so I had to face the 'outside the caravan' world. I deposited the children at the back of the shed on the offside of the bullet-shooting rubbish dump, then, armed with mattress and hose, I approached and thoroughly drenched the rubbish dump. Hoping this would alleviate the risk of a stray bullet shooting down the mail plane, I went to the now back 'on limits' kitchen and cooked a healthy breakfast. Then, for the next two hours, believe it or not, nothing happened.

We were waiting for the mail plane when another plane landed. I walked out with the children in tow and Mary and Sylvester close on our heels. It was a small plane for some of the stations not on the Perth run, and there were nine passengers on board. One of the nine passengers was handed over to me. She was pregnant, too pregnant it seemed.

'You can't leave her here in that condition.'

'I can't take her with me, she's having labour pains.'

'What? Well you certainly can't leave her here. I don't even have clean water.'

'Don't worry, I've contacted the Flying Doctor and they're on their way. All you have to do is let her rest till they arrive. Alright?'

'No, it's not alright!'

I was about to continue when he closed the door, taxied out onto the airstrip and took off. My complete open-mouth daze was broken by a rather bloodcurdling labour pain scream. At this sound, Sylvester took off down the airstrip after the plane and disappeared into the bush. Mary and I helped Rosie, our newly acquired patient, into our modern tin shed hospital complete with bed and radio.

Trying hard to be calm, I made Rosie as comfortable as possible, then looked in the medical book for tips on delivering a baby. It made me feel quite ill. In a crisis, Mum always made tea, so I made tea. We drank the tea and Rosie looked miserable.

I had had two babies myself, but I'd been at the other end of the affair with a doctor who knew his job at the right end. This was a very different kettle of fish! The mother-to-be was young and after much sign language, Mary found out this was her first baby.

Mary then informed me that she had delivered 'plenty babies', bush-style that is, but still she was miles ahead of me. She said there was nothing to it. I calmed down a little, but not much.

The three of us sat there staring at each other. We felt every pain. The sitting did not last long, the poor mother-to-be was jumping all over the bed. I was trying to tell her to breathe deeply and relax, but I couldn't even follow my own instructions, so I doubted if poor Rosie could.

After what seemed like a lifetime we heard a plane engine. It was the doctor, and after he'd checked Rosie we helped her into the plane, and watched happily as it disappeared over the horizon. I skipped dinner that night and retired early along with the children. They were not the least bit tired. I was drained to the point of exhaustion.

I awoke the next morning tired but cheery. Well, let's face it, nothing else could happen. The morning passed pleasantly enough with the children playing and swimming. Then after lunch we heard a plane. Feeling quite safe from another pregnant drop-off, we awaited our visitor. It turned out to be a friend from Sydney who was taking his seventy-five-year-old mother on a trip around the North with him. He wanted his mother to stay with us for three days while he went bush on some survey work. I told him it was fine as long as she didn't mind roughing it. He assured me that it was the lap of luxury compared to where he was going.

In the cool of the afternoon, we took our guest for a walk to the billabong and showed her the wildlife. We returned home to shower and change, and then have a cold roast beef sandwich and beer while we peacefully watched the sun set. We had just settled ourselves with our dinner when we heard the drone of a plane engine again. It landed and the seven occupants informed me they were lost, and because it was a few minutes to last light (all planes must land before sunset, unless they are instrument rated), DCA had told them to proceed to the nearest airstrip, which was ours.

I now had seven more guests for dinner. They accepted roast beef sandwiches and beer, not that they had a choice, and sitting on various drums, woodstumps and the floor, they joined us to watch the sunset.

We had not been sitting for more than five minutes when we heard another engine. Everyone looked up into the sky but this time the engine was approaching on the ground. The jeep pulled up and out piled four men. They were a Department of Roads crew coming to tell us our road was open for the season. Of course they were staying the night. They had food, so it was pooled with the roast beef sandwiches and beer.

We hadn't even seated this lot when another engine could be heard, above us this time. It was now very definitely last light and whoever it was up there had to come down and be quick about it. There were six men in this plane. They weren't lost, they were the drilling engineers who were to put in our new bore, and they had come in ahead of the drill rig which was on its way in by road. More roast beef sandwiches and beer.

We now had seventeen men sitting with us watching the sun set, when, you guessed it, another engine. Out of the dust appeared a jeep with three on board. They were the people who would haul our supplies in by road that year, and having heard our road was very bad, had decided to drive in and see it for themselves. How about that, twenty men for dinner!

The problem which then faced us was bedding. It was now well into June and the nights were very cold. We average about 45 degrees Fahrenheit or 7 degrees Celsius and twenty people use a lot of blankets. The two jeep loads were equipped with bedding, but the lost load had planned hotel accommodation, so they only had clothing. The engineering team had some warm clothing, but no bedding. All their equipment was with the drill rig, somewhere on our road. As many as possible slept in the planes, and the rest on the kitchen floor in front of the wood stove. After several hours of ingenious bed-building, everyone had a place to rest his or her head.

Finally I drifted off into a well-earned sleep. But it was not to last—I was rudely awoken by a piercing scream. Racing into the guestroom, I fully expected to see my guest wrapped in a snake. I found her bed empty. Another shattering scream had me racing to the kitchen, and there I found her. It seems she was tiptoeing into the kitchen for a glass of water when she tripped and landed in the arms of a fair-haired Italian.

He was one of the trucking group. His brother owned the

semi, and he had just arrived from Italy and was to be the driver. He was big, very handsome, and couldn't speak a word of English. The more she screamed, the tighter he held her. Her Victorian upbringing was shocked to the roots.

I went to her assistance and was trying to unwind her from Rico's bear hug when he suddenly let go of her and grabbed me. She jumped to her feet and bolted out the door. I called after her to come and help me, but the only reply was the slamming of her bedroom door.

It didn't take long for me to decide to stop wriggling; apart from dislodging my nightgown, it was having a disastrous effect on Rico. I stopped wriggling, he waited. I whispered in his ear, 'Uno momento', the only Italian that came to me. He released his grip with a 'Che?' and I jumped up and bolted for the door. I was half way out the door when I ran headlong into another mountain of male flesh!

Oh no! After what I had been through the last four days, this was the last straw. I was just about to start kicking and punching when, apart from the awful smell, that big chest seemed strangely familiar. I looked up and there stood Charles. I gratefully sagged into his arms, no longer wanting to fight for my honour, and he carried me back to our caravan.

In typical male manner, he then demanded to know what I was doing in the kitchen with all those men. It took me a while to clear myself and relate the night's escapades. He finally believed me and after a shower and shave, was very loving and attentive, knowing full well that if he wasn't, Rico would be happy to oblige.

The next morning after we had dispatched all our visitors, Charles made the incredible statement that next time he went away, he would make sure that there was plenty to do to occupy my time.

'Occupy my time? Battles with water pumps, being nearly drowned in mud, shot up by a rubbish dump, a pregnant woman to deal with, twenty men for dinner, practically two rapes on my hands, one of them mine. And you are going to see that I am occupied?'

'Now Darling, don't let your imagination run away with

you, it all stems from having too much time on your hands.'

I threw a pillow at him and stormed out of the caravan and down the airstrip. I walked to the river, sat under a large tree and smouldered. After a while Charles joined me and apologised. Mary had explained to him that my wild imagination had been very much reality.

As we sat there I asked him to tell me about the muster.

'What about the muster?'

'Well I wave goodbye to you at the gate and after a lot of commotion all the animals settle down, the lot of you disappear down the road in a cloud of dust, only to reappear a week or so later with a large mob of cattle. What happens during that week?'

He made himself comfortable against the tree, lit his pipe and wove me the following picture of an outback muster.

For the horse tailer the day starts at three-thirty to four a.m. He holds a night horse in one of the small horse paddocks built along the mustering trail. The horse tailer is also usually the camp cook, so soon after he saddles his horse he stirs the fire and settles the billy on the coals so tea will be ready when he returns. He then goes looking for the mob.

All the young colts in training are left in the horse paddock. They are still green, and, like children, they learn from others' behaviour. They stand and watch the procedures and hopefully learn the right things to do. So the horse tailer goes looking for the mob on the old night horse. Now he is a special horse, he is a mate of all the stock horses, so when you let him have his head, he will immediately lead you to all the other horses, you hope.

Condamine bells are put around the mules' necks, so when they are grazing you can hear the clanging. That's in case the night horse decides not to lead the horse tailer to the mob.

Apparently the animals really are characters. They actually take turns, one mule going miles in the opposite direction to the mob, clanging furiously. The horse tailer goes off in the direction of the sound and only finds one mule, not the mob. By the time he finds the mob miles away in the other direction, a couple of hours have been lost.

Of course sometimes the old horse tailers go in the opposite direction to the noise, because they know the tricks the animals play. But some horse tailers say the horses and mules even work this move out, so every now and then the mob just happens to be grazing with the clanging condamine and the tailer has spent hours going in a wide circle in the wrong direction. Sometimes the mob varies the game for fun and, come three a.m., just before the horse tailer is about to leave camp, the clanging stops. The mules stand still and do not make a noise and it takes hours to find them. Sometimes the night horse even calls to say he is coming as soon as the horse tailer gets out of his swag, and not long after that the clanging stops, or there is a single clang that fades into the distance. At this point the horse tailer has to decide which path of action to take that morning. Deep strategy!

You never need an alarm clock to wake you, because the bells clang all night, and even though you sleep, you can hear them, then at the same time every morning, they stop, and you are immediately awake.

The horses have a pecking order. The older, experienced horses graze in a group and the younger horses in training are not allowed into the group. Eventually one of the younger horses will be allowed into the select mob. Presumably in some way he has earned his stripes, either by age or experience, probably both.

The horse tailer finds the older horses first and starts them back to the camp. The younger horses follow dutifully behind, watching the older horses' every move, and keeping up, just so they don't miss anything. If the horse tailer tried to muster up the younger horses first, there would be no end of trouble— the horses would just refuse to be led.

Finally, after all this, the horse tailer arrives back at the camp, just as dawn is showing in the sky.

The men are up now and they help yard the horses and mules. The horses spend time settling down and the men leave them and go and have breakfast, usually steak cooked on a shovel, damper or bread and black tea with lots of sugar.

Dawn in the stock camp is a really special time. There are special sights and special sounds that belong only to this scene—all the horses greeting each other, men rolling their swags, the small talk about the day to come, the smell of steak cooking and billy tea bubbling on the coals. The condamine bells clanging again as the mules move around the yard jockeying for position and the screeching of cockatoos and parrots passing over at intervals just as the dawn breaks.

With breakfast over, the men move into the horse paddock and, after more fun and games, the horses are taken out to be saddled. The men then ride over to the holding paddock and let the coachers out. The coachers are the cattle from the home yard, about fifty in all. These are quiet cattle, and the idea is to ride out into the bush and find the wild cattle, then push them into the mob of quiet cattle. The wild cattle see the coachers quietly walking along and so they join them. That's the theory anyway, but there are many variations. The bulls are the hardest to convince.

The stockmen, once they have the coachers out of the yards, move them into a close mob and off in the planned direction. They pass through a certain section and end up at an arranged place for lunch, and eventually the next holding paddock camp, for the night.

The time spent at each camp is determined by where the muster is taking place on the station. Sometimes it can be up to four days, in a heavily stocked area.

Each day the stockmen go off in a different direction. The coachers are led out in a straight line, and the stockmen ride off into the bush in long sweeps to bring any cattle back to the mob.

Lunch is a travelling affair. While the stockmen were busy all morning, chasing cattle, the horse tailer, now cook, cooked bread and lunch and arrived at the lunch camp with the meal and a mob of fresh horses. Mustering is a bit like polo, you have to change your horse about three, sometimes four, times a day. There is so much galloping in one day, one horse couldn't last the whole day.

Each man has a fifteen-minute break, one at a time, away

from the mob. Just enough time to down a couple of large tin pannikins of tea, answer the call of nature, grab a lump of bread and beef and back to the mob to let one of the other men leave.

After lunch the horse tailer takes the morning horses back to the camp and the stockmen turn the mob in a wide half circle and head back to the camp as well. On the return journey they repeat the morning operation, picking up all the wild cattle they can.

By sunset all the cattle are safely in the holding paddock for the night, the night horse is in his yard and the stock horses and mules are hobbled and left to graze.

There is so much you have to learn and know on a muster. Packing the mule correctly—if this is not done properly then you end up with a mule with a rubbed back and the next day you are down one mule. Everything you need is packed on the mules, so mules are a very important part of the overall picture.

Forward planning is essential. If the muster is on a flat and there are no trees in the immediate area, the cook has to load wood on the pack mule's load, so he can boil the billy for lunch. Some areas have no water, so the special flat-sided water cans made for the pack saddles have to be filled and taken along.

You have to plan your muster to pass through the best areas for feed and water. This is not always easy, because the cattle walk an average of ten miles a day between their feed and water. You can pass right through a grazing area when the cattle are away drinking and not find one animal. Then, six hours later, there will be hundreds of cattle grazing in that very place. Knowledge of the area is invaluable.

If the mob is restless, you can ride them over some rocky country to slow them down. They have to concentrate on walking over rocks and find it very difficult to break into a gallop. But you can't keep them there too long or they get sore feet.

If you walk cattle into the wind, they can smell what is ahead and they will be more settled. They do not like the wind behind them.

Young colts have to be trained. They make the herd restless, prancing around, so in the mornings they are tied behind the mules and led, usually against their will. But by the afternoon, they are so happy to be free they are very quiet.

If you have to walk the cattle a fair distance in one day, you cannot let them drink or they can't walk for the rest of the day. You mustn't talk or shout as it can make them restless and they could easily bolt. At the start of the day you must let them settle down into their own pace. If you push them too hard they will break. Likewise, later in the day, you must keep them in check at the pace you require. If they think they can get the upper hand you will have no end of trouble.

Finally, if all goes according to plan, the mob reaches a size that is too big for the stockmen to handle and they head for the home yard.

I sat silently, digesting all this information. It sounded very exciting.

'Well, do you understand what a muster is all about now?'

'Yes, I think I have a fair understanding, but I must learn myself.'

'You will, you will.' And he was right, I did. Years later when I finally did go on a muster it was a hundred times more exciting than just hearing about it.

Meanwhile back at the ranch, Mary and the mechanic were having a free for all. While we were down by the river, the mechanic had tried to start the water pump. He was having trouble, and at the wrong moment Mary told him that the Missus was very good at starting the pump. After the yelling and screaming had died down, I dispatched Mary to the kitchen. I then explained to him what had happened when trying to start the pump. After much investigation, he ascertained that I had filled the pump with sump oil (his fault for putting it in a drum marked 30 oil) and Sylvester had filled the fuel container with high powered aviation fuel. No wonder the poor old pump was trying to fly.

We had to be very careful with the water for the next few days while the mechanic stripped down and completely overhauled our poor ailing Pegasus pump.

The next week was spent down in the yards drafting, dipping and branding the cattle the men had mustered. This all done, the stock camp had time off with extra grog. After they had recovered from the bender, they assembled ready for the next muster, and the whole procedure started again. However, this time, the campsite would be just across the river so Charles could come home every night. At least for the next week or so, the man of the house could handle the emergencies.

There was the usual stampede of animals as they departed, and the rescue of the rum supply, but apart from that the week went off without a hitch and soon all the cattle were settled in their respective paddocks.

With the muster over the children were ready for the next challenge—every minute had to be a non-stop adventure for them. I, on the other hand, saw danger everywhere and wanted to keep them safely locked up. One day they wore me down with their pleading so we ventured into the wilderness to go fishing. This entailed walking down the airstrip and through the trees onto the river bank, about three-quarters of a mile away.

We started off down the airstrip, the children and dogs running and playing, mother in the crouched attack position, waiting for the enemy to approach. The enemy being wild cattle or any other weird creatures I was sure would explode out of the bush.

The girls ran ahead and disappeared into the tree line along the river's edge. I relaxed my grip on the branding iron I carried at all times and followed them.

The scream that strikes fear into all mothers' hearts came to me through the trees and I exploded into action. I broke out of the trees at a sprint.

Marlee's dog, Shad, was swimming for the shore. Marlee was calling frantically, Bonnie was crying. Behind Shad was a large crocodile closing in fast. Marlee was knee-deep in the water waiting to gather Shad into her arms with complete disregard for the eight-foot monster a few feet behind her dog.

I charged down the riverbank, branding iron raised. Shad

was swimming for her life, literally, into Marlee's arms. The crocodile was getting closer to both of them every second. Marlee grabbed Shad's front paws and heaved as the croc snapped at the dog's back legs. I brought the branding iron down across the croc's snout. Marlee heaved so hard, she fell over backwards and Shad was catapulted over her head to safety. This left Marlee sitting in the mud right under the crocodile's nose. I had hit him so hard, I was on my knees and we were eyeball to eyeball. No one moved for a split second. Then I let out a spine-chilling karate yell and raised the branding iron again, but the crocodile had had enough—he submerged backwards and quickly disappeared.

The girls were very disappointed I didn't want to stay and fish. I was still shaking from the ordeal hours later. The next day Charles sent one of the stockmen down to the river to shoot the crocodile. He later reported back to Charles.

'Better be nice to the missus, she broke that croc's jaw!' Charles told him not to be cheeky and walked away chuckling.

CHAPTER 10

❖

1966

Charles and the men were ready for the next muster, when we received a telegram. It told us that the film team would arrive in a few days. Charles decided to send the camp on ahead and get some work done before the film crew settled in. Unfortunately we were not highly paid actors, in fact we were not paid at all, so we had to carry on earning our living catching cattle.

The crew arrived on time and set up camp on the large sandstone area which was to be part of the house, if ever the roof was finished. It looked rather like the ruins of Pompeii with all the posts silhouetted against the landscape—very beautiful by moonlight but a trifle hot by day.

There were eight people in the film crew and with Charles supervising and the mechanic helping, they set up camp on the Pompeii terrace, a sort of indoor-outdoor deal. I retired to the kitchen.

I was busy preparing lunch when the entire film crew went through the kitchen at forty miles an hour with the mechanic a good twenty yards in the lead. I didn't have time to ponder this strange behaviour because Charles charged into the kitchen, hurled the two children at me and yelled, 'Run!'

One look at him told me enough not to ask questions. I went out the wall-less side of the kitchen with a child under each arm, just slightly under the speed of sound. I overtook the film crew in the middle of the airstrip. When we had all caught our breath I asked, 'What happened?'

They all started talking at once. It seemed the oxygen cylinder gauge arrow had been pointing to the word 'danger'. I turned to ask Charles what was the . . . Charles! He had stayed behind! I let out a blood-curdling 'Charles!' and all eyes turned towards the house. There was silence.

I left the children and headed for the shed. Charles appeared as I reached the corner. He had managed to release the malfunctioning safety valve and all was now clear.

Everyone let out a deep sigh.

'Welcome to the Outback!' I said.

With all the excitement over and the tents rigged, I escorted the secretary into the kitchen to show her around. She didn't seem to get the point, so I made the point clearer.

'You will be cooking for your group.'

She looked at me in shock. What she expected out in the middle of nowhere, I have no idea—perhaps a Chinese cook. Whatever, she went out the door with a will and was heading for Bill. She didn't have to ask who had put her in.

Bill appeared with hat in hand and I said a firm, 'No! No way in the world I'm cooking for another eight people. I already have nine to cook for. No!'

He explained to me that she couldn't cook. He thought all women could cook. We came to a compromise—she would help prepare, I would cook, and she would organise everyone in the cleaning up after. They slipped a few times, but I would not start cooking till things were in order, so we settled down to a reasonable routine.

The filming progressed but they had their problems. The heat was playing havoc with the film and the glare outside made inside shooting impossible without lights—the backgrounds were too different when spliced together. This last problem could be overcome with special lights but they had not brought them with them. So Bill wired his office down south asking for the special lights and shooting of all indoor scenes was put off until they arrived. This took place a few days later, by chartered plane. Bill got quite a shock when he opened the box.

'They're unusual lights,' I said, peering into the box.

'Damn, I forgot!'

138

'What?'

'Well, when filming is not going as well as it should, I have my secretary send some champagne and after a night of relaxation, things usually get back on track. I always use the word "lights" as a code name for champagne.'

The 'lights' certainly put everyone in a great mood, but without the real lights, no indoor work could be done so all this good effect was going to waste. Another telegram and finally the lights arrived.

During the waiting period, Bill decided to shoot a bull-catching operation. One of the Toyotas was to be the platform for the camera so it could follow the chasing of the bull at close quarters. I went along as guide. We arrived at the campsite to find everyone busy. Cattle were being moved in all directions. Some of the ringers were further in the bush, bull-catching, so with the camera mounted on the back of the Toyota, we drove towards the billowing dust clouds in search of action.

The art of bull-catching from a horse is now a dying art and, even in the sixties, I believe the North was the only place left in the world where wild bulls were still caught and thrown by the tail. It worked something like this: the ringer, riding a horse, chases the bull in a zig-zag or straight line, depending on the bull. After a fair chase and when the ringer decides that the bull is tired, he gallops up to the bull about level with its tail, and still at a fair gallop jumps off, grabbing the tail at the same time. He then has to hang on and run to keep up with the bull. His life literally depends on this, because if he lets go of the tail, the bull can immediately turn and gore him to death. As long as he keeps hold of the tail, whenever the bull turns to gore him, he swings wide of the attack with the force of the bull's turn. Finally, the bull stops running and decides to really rid himself of the pest on his tail. The ringer, after regaining his wind, waits till the bull turns to gore him and then, just as he does, gives a sharp tug on the tail. The bull, being in an off-balance position, falls over. The other ringers then close in to help. Leather straps are quickly wrapped around the hind legs, front legs and horns and when the bull is trussed up like a chicken, he is then dehorned.

After this the bull is allowed to sit for a while to calm down and regain his composure, before being released and pushed in with the quiet cattle, or coachers. If he stays in the mob and behaves, the job is over. If he charges out of the mob and heads for the bush, the ringers set off in mad pursuit and the whole procedure is repeated.

As you can see, it is very demanding, takes a long time, and is very taxing on man, horse and bull. Some bulls are so stubborn that after many hours of this gruelling work, they have to be let go or they would die from exhaustion or over-heating. On many properties the bush bulls were just shot. But being a small family operation, we couldn't afford to shoot and ignore our bulls. We had to catch them and sell them for the income.

On this particular day one of the ringers was in full pursuit of a very large wild bull. He kept appearing and disappearing in and out of the scrub with the thrower close behind on his horse. This old fellow was a smart scrub bull who knew his business. He spent his time running into the low scrub so the horse and ringer could not follow. Bill decided that all he would get on film from this distance was dust, so he gave the order for the Toyota to 'follow that bull'! The soundman was driving, Bill was hanging on outside my door shouting light meter readings to the cameraman, and the cameraman was trying to stand up in the back of the Toyota with the camera. The soundman was a mad driver and we were soon abreast of the galloping ringer and bull.

Every time we came to rough scrub, Bill would dive into the cabin, but being on the rather heavy side he would only make it up to the waist, so his behind took a hell of a beating. We were close on the hooves of the horse when the bull swerved sharply to the left and the horse and rider veered around the thick scrub to catch the bull on the other side. Our soundman was all for following the bull, but Bill, thinking of his rear end, called out, 'No.'

At this point, things started to happen rather quickly. The bull met the horse and ringer on the other side of the scrub and immediately turned to retrace his tracks. Bill and the driver were still debating the pros and cons of driving into the thick of it, when suddenly a mad bull charged straight for the Toyota. The soundman threw the gears into reverse, and stalled. The bull was now charging straight for Bill's behind. I screamed a warning to him and he vaulted onto the cabin top just as two enormous horns embedded themselves in the door, right under my nose!

Bill was beside himself with excitement and kept shouting instructions and meter readings to all within earshot. To him, this was a director's dream. And all the while, he hung off the side of the Toyota, trying to keep his balance, like a crewman on an eighteen-footer. The ringer galloped up, leapt off his horse, tied a rope around the bull's horns and ran the rope around the nearest tree. The bull wrenched himself free of the door and started running around, charging everything that moved or didn't move. The ringer was behind the tree and every time the bull allowed the rope to develop slack, he would tighten it around the tree. Eventually, instead of racing around on sixty feet of rope, the bull found himself tied to a tree by the horns with only enough slack to sit comfortably. So he did.

Bill was jumping up and down yelling to the cameraman, 'Did you get it all, did you get it all?' No answer. All eyes turned to the cameraman, or rather, where the cameraman used to be. No cameraman! The tripod and camera were bolted to the floor of the Toyota, but unfortunately the cameraman had no such fittings. We went back along the track and found him unconscious. No bones were broken and with no rocks handy, it was hoped no head injuries. Bill was concerned about the man but, being a true director, he was more interested in how much footage had been shot. When Bill found out none, we had two patients on our hands. He knew he would never get another chance at a bull sequence like the one we had just experienced.

Having completely fouled up the day's muster and with not one foot of film to show for it, we returned to the house a very dejected lot. To cheer us up Bill decided to bring out the champagne, and I cooked a special meal of sweet and sour fish with the big barra one of the stockmen had caught. Because the evening was hot we decided to eat dinner on Pompeii terrace under the full moon. The men picked up the table fully laden with food and everyone else followed with chairs and boxes and champagne.

Just as the procession turned the corner, something moved on the ground. The lead guy let out one unearthly scream, shouted, 'Snake', and dropped his end of the table. The chap at the other end just froze, still holding his end. The result was that our entire dinner slid to the floor with a loud crash.

All eyes turned to where the shaking finger pointed to see a shaky-paw lizard with his head on one side looking at us, shaking his paw. So we had cold roast beef sandwiches and champagne. The champagne didn't help—no one could forget the sweet and sour fish. We all retired early hoping the morning would bring a brighter day.

Bill was still determined to have his bull-throwing scene and approached Charles for help. Bill's idea was to shoot the bull with a tranquilliser gun, using just enough dope to make the bull manageable, but still have fight.

We had experimented with a tranquilliser gun as a way to catch bulls, hoping to eliminate wear and tear on bull, horse, man and equipment. But the result was a lot of wear and tear. To tranquillise an animal at close quarters, caged or standing still, is a lot different from trying to tranquillise a wild bull at full gallop in the middle of the bush. The serum is dangerous: if too much is used it can be lethal; if too little, it has no effect at all. If the animal is too hot, the effect is this; if the animal is not hot, the effect is that. But our director wouldn't take 'no' for an answer, so off we went.

We arrived at the camp, and after driving around found the ringers. They had five big to enormous bulls cornered in the rocky ravine. The plan was that one of the ringers would go after the bull, then a stockman would ride close by with the tranquilliser gun, fire a dose into the rump of the bull, and, after a few minutes, the camera would start filming the throwing. The overall effect would be very exciting, explained Bill.

The first of many problems was that the bulls were all different weights, which meant they needed different doses of serum. The next problem was that the Toyota couldn't follow the action—the country was too rough for fast driving. This problem was overcome by Bill himself riding a horse and taking the shots with a hand camera.

So the scene was set. Five bulls faced the ringers, Charles had the tranquilliser gun, the director had the camera, and the Toyota followed behind with me in the back with details of the serum, and the serum in a cooler. Another small problem was the serum—over a certain temperature it was useless.

The plan of action was to be as follows: the head ringer would pick out his bull, shout the estimated weight to Charles, who, in turn, would scream it to me. I would quickly look up the table for the amount of serum required, fill the capsule with the recommended dose, hand it to Charles, who would gallop back to the scene of action, and wham, shoot the bull in the rear. Why in a million years they thought it would work in practice when it sounded impossible in theory was beyond me. But they were sure they had everything under control.

For a few seconds silence hung suspended over this comedy scene. The ringer moved away from the group of horsemen and cut out a bull. He galloped him a while and then shouted the estimated weight to Charles. But while Charles was over with me fitting the capsule to the tranquilliser gun, the ringer changed bulls. His thousand-pounder went bush so he switched to a fourteen-hundred-pounder. The serum would not have the same effect on the bigger animal but the ringer, not being aware of this, failed to mention the change in weight.

Charles galloped in with the dart and shot the bull right on target. Everyone waited the prescribed few minutes while the bull did a war dance, trying to dislodge the dart. He then paused, looking at the ring of horses and humans closing in on him, and the over-anxious director gave the order, 'let 'em roll'.

The ringer jumped off his horse and raced in for the bull's tail. The bull, seeing his enemy at close quarters, snapped out of his trance, turned towards the ringer and charged with all

143

the alertness and determination that only a mad, wild bull with a dart in his rear can achieve. The ringer, realising too late that he had a very awake, mad bull on his hands, did a nifty sidestep leaving his hat for the bull to pulverise, and shouted to the other ringers still on horseback to surround the bull. They did, and the ringer dived to safety.

The bull, really mad now, charged at random, and his next target was our director. Beside himself with excitement, Bill was so busy filming he did not realise that the face of the charging bull he was filming just happened to be charging at him. However, his horse, having a better grip on the situation, promptly turned and let fly with several short rapid kicks, which successfully discouraged the bull but dislodged our director over the horse's head.

Eventually, the bull was directed away from the scene, the dust cleared and Bill was found to be in one piece. Then, after a long discussion, it was discovered why the bull hadn't behaved as planned. The ringer was informed of the importance of giving the right weight. And, believe it or not, they were going to try it again! With one change—this time Charles would carry the serum in a small cooler around his neck.

I stood on top of the cabin and watched. As impossible as it all seemed, the ringer did his job and cut out a bull. Charles somehow managed to measure and load the serum at a gallop, Bill actually made it to the scene with camera rolling, and everything was going beautifully, when the bull propped! Bill's horse went flying past the bull just at the moment Charles fired the dart, and copped the dart. Luckily the dart fell out before the poor horse received the full dose, thus saving its life. However, it still collapsed like a house of cards and poor old Bill was catapulted once more over its head and into a creek. Bill was alright but the camera was waterlogged and all the film was ruined.

It was decided that night, over many more bottles of champagne, by everyone but Bill, that he would have to be satisfied with the footage he already had on bull-catching.

We said goodbye on Monday morning and watched them drive down the road. After the dust had cleared, we started to assemble what was left of our employees and station and once more set our minds to normal operations. By mid-afternoon this was going along nicely, when a cloud of dust appeared in the sky. They were back.

It seemed that a semi-load of supplies, with bear-hugging Rico at the wheel, was bogged in three feet of bulldust on a slight rise where the road was carved into a twenty-foot ridge of sandstone. The truck was stopped right in the pass, making it impossible for any vehicle to pass. Obviously Rico's driving skills were about as good as his English. Bill said the truck was right down to the axles in bulldust and needed a tow. He and the crew left an hour later in the Toyota with winch attached.

Bill was back again after dinner. The winch could not do the job, the truck was too heavy. We now also had the stock inspector on the other side of the truck waiting to come in, so out went the tractor and stockmen to help. Next morning, Bill returned once more! To Rico, the stock inspector, the head stockman, and a few more stockmen, had been added a very dangerous item, namely, a six-month supply of grog. It had been casually discovered when someone lifted the tarp. Bill reported that everyone on the scene of 'operation move truck' was well and truly plastered.

Charles departed with Bill, they unloaded the grog and left the men to sober up. The film crew also returned to the house to await the clearing of the road. Two days later the truck was finally moved and the road was cleared. A very miserable group turned up, all with massive hangovers.

The film crew departed again, the stock inspector arrived, and we tried once more to settle down to station routine.

The stock inspector worked with the stockmen in the yards for a few days and then departed, saying he would see us at the races. I questioned Mary on the subject of the races and was told that everyone goes to their local race weekend, and they also go to every other race meeting within two hundred miles. I put the thought of races aside to discuss with Charles at a more convenient time. The work and mustering were progressing and the season was drawing to a close. It was approaching the end of September and it would soon be too hot to work cattle.

Before I had a chance to bring up the subject, Charles announced we were going to the races the following weekend to celebrate our surviving one year in the Outback. He also had another surprise. He had bought a little four-seater plane so we could go in style. About mid-week, the entire staff left for the races by truck. It seemed the system was you arrived days before the weekend to get in the right mood, drinking mood, as far as I could see, and then spent several days after the event winding up the weekend. And this was not counting the days it took to get over the whole thing once you finally arrived back at the station. If it was a distant race meeting, you had to add time for travel, and this in turn was determined by how many hotels were between the races and the station.

We arrived at the races on Saturday morning to find everyone well in the mood. Having only ever been to southern country race meets, I turned up in hat and gloves, expecting to stroll the lawns. I was in for a rude shock. The racetrack was set in a red bulldust gully, just off a red bulldust highway, and the highway was the only road in town. Every time a vehicle of any sort drove down the road, the whole racecourse area was drowned in a layer of thick red dust. The track itself was the same high grade bulldust. There was only an inside rail, and that only extended the length of the straight. The rest of the track was open. What there was of the inside rail was made of extremely crooked paperbark saplings tied together with wire. The outside rail of the straight depended on how excited the crowd became and fluctuated during the race, according to how wide the horses swung at the home turn.

The members' stand was a continuation of the inside rail, more crooked paperbark saplings. These saplings were a little stouter and held up the roof, which consisted of chicken wire covered by dead branches. A few tables formed a square and an unbelievable array of sun umbrellas tried in vain to keep the sun off the dried-up, fly-covered sandwiches and cold hotdogs.

Bar? That consisted of an endless row of kegs that reached

all the way back to the pub. The system was really quite ingenious. There were plug-in drawing guns and these gadgets were attached to the first few kegs in line. A table was placed in front of the operating kegs and the bar was open for business. This procedure continued down the long line of kegs until the bar ended up back at the hotel, along with the race-goers. At the point of no return, that is when it was too far to walk back to place a bet, the races were officially over and the crowd would settle down in earnest to a steady night of drinking.

In complete shock, Charles and I wandered around being gawked at. Most of our fellow race-goers were barefoot. The best-dressed wore singlets, while the casually attired wore only a pair of dirty, wrinkled footy shorts.

We wandered over to the betting ring hoping to be lost in the crowd, and also to place a bet on a horse that someone in Darwin had said would win by a mile. The horse was in the second race and was a rank outsider. I had visions of winning a mint. Charles wasn't the least bit interested in racing and I was not enjoying myself, but thinking I was about to win a fortune, I managed to momentarily ignore the heat, the bulldust and drunks.

The first race had just finished with only two horses crossing the line, and one of them without a jockey. Two bolted through the inside rail coming down the straight and went bush and another hit a deep hole of bulldust and fell over. It was quite a sideshow watching the intoxicated stewards trying to deal with the protests and announce the results.

The second race was not long away and I anxiously awaited the prices. The names went up, the favourite was six to one on, the second favourite was two to one on, and my rank outsider was even money!

Disgusted with the prices, I didn't even bet. We went back to our airconditioned motel. Charles ordered some cold beer and snacks, and we settled down to a few good books. The rest of Saturday passed most pleasantly.

Saturday was to be 'finished off' with a ball and this was to be held, believe it or not, in the meatworks. Not on the killing floor, thank heavens, as Charles had led me to believe. We really didn't want to go, we were too comfortable where we were, but we had been invited by our neighbours to join them at their table so we had to put in an appearance.

We arrived late and the ball was in full swing. Most of the men had come straight from the keg line. Why they called it a ball I have no idea—no one was dancing. Inside the hall, along with a few decorations, was the musical entertainment for the evening. This consisted of piano, bass, drums and violin. To say they were 'old time' is a compliment.

Charles joined the men and had the required rounds of welcoming drinks. He then excused himself and took me in to dance. This shamed a few at our table to do the same, but none of the old diehards! The six of us had the floor to ourselves. This would have been great if we could have danced to the music, but the group had its own time and it was a secret to the dancers. One of the men went home and returned with a record player, and we finally had dance music. The group played along.

As soon as we could we slipped away, back to our airconditioning. Having learned our lesson twice the hard way, we decided not to leave the room again until we went home. There were knocks on our door all day Sunday but we just ignored them. We flew home Monday morning after Charles had found our very sad and sorrowful-looking head stockman and told him to 'round up' the camp, plus a new man Charles had hired.

We had a smooth flight home and enjoyed a few days alone before the truck arrived back, loaded down with supplies and people. What a dejected lot! I handed out an enormous supply of headache tablets, indigestion tablets, diarrhoea tablets and sent them down to the camp to sleep off medication and alcohol until the next morning.

Still sitting on the truck was a load of people, mostly children, with a few women and two men. I told Charles about them and he said, 'Must be the new man.'

'What do you mean "new man"? There must be at least twelve people on that truck.'

Here I am, about six years old, in the garden at Halcyon with our pet cockatoo, who had the very original name of Cocko.

With my dog Lucky. Lucky was born under the house away from the rest of her litter and we did not find her for two days; the vet said she was lucky to be alive.

*At Central Station, Sydney, the day I was picked for the Schoolgirl
Under-Fifteen NSW State Team. With friends, Glennis and
Pauline, aged fourteen.*

ABOVE: *With Mum and Dad the night of my twenty-first birthday at the Barclay Lounge, Bexley, 1957.*

BELOW: *With Bob Pennell, dancing at my twenty-first.*

*A quiet moment sailing on Sydney Harbour, the same day
that I met Charles, 1959.*

Charlie was named 'Yank of the Week' during World War II; here he is speaking on radio for the USA war-bond drive.

October 27, 1945

My dear Mr. Henderson:

I have addressed this letter to reach you after all the formalities of your separation from active service are completed. I have done so because, without formality but as clearly as I know how to say it, I want the Navy's pride in you, which it is my privilege to express, to reach into your civil life and to remain with you always.

You have served in the greatest Navy in the world.

It crushed two enemy fleets at once, receiving their surrenders only four months apart.

It brought our land-based airpower within bombing range of the enemy, and set our ground armies on the beachheads of final victory.

It performed the multitude of tasks necessary to support these military operations.

No other Navy at any time has done so much. For your part in these achievements you deserve to be proud as long as you live. The Nation which you served at a time of crisis will remember you with gratitude.

The best wishes of the Navy go with you into civilian life. Good luck!

Sincerely yours,

James Forrestal

James Forrestal

Mr. Charles English Henderson, III
Gibson Island
Maryland

A letter from the Secretary of the Navy to Charlie after the war was over and Charles had returned to civilian life.
I think the letter says it all.

ABOVE: *Our wedding day in Hong Kong. Dick Kirby, Charlie, me, Peg and Jack Cater, on the steps of the Hong Kong Cathedral.*

BELOW: *Telegrams being read by Jack Cater at the reception at the Repulse Bay Hotel, 4th July 1960.*

ABOVE: *The fifty-seven-foot yawl, the* Lady B – *the boat we sailed through the typhoon in the China Sea.*

BELOW: *Expecting Bonnie. With Charles at the Manila Polo Club, close to April 1963.*

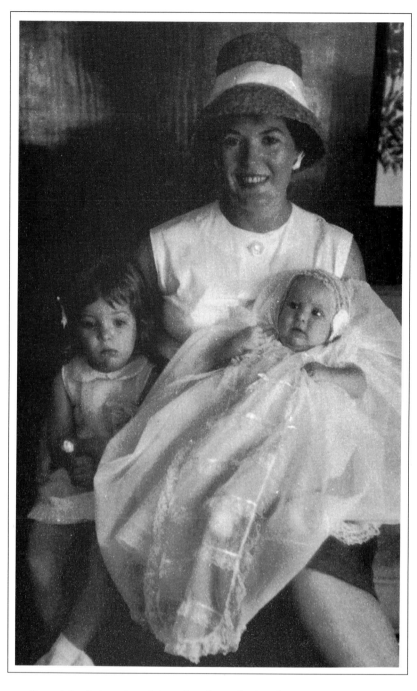

Bonnie's christening. Mum hand-made the christening gown for Marlee, and Bon wore it too.

ABOVE: *My first home on Bullo – what more can I say!*

BELOW: *Marlee and Bonnie helping me care for baby emus.*

ABOVE: *School Bullo River style. 1965 – Marlee is four and a half.*

BELOW: *Marlee and Bonnie making bread under Mary's watchful eye.*

ABOVE: *Our palatial caravan in the middle of the equipment shed –
the first step in my long journey to turn the equipment shed
into a home.*

BELOW: *The herd of horses Old Bob galloped through the breezeway
kitchen and out of the future living room, continuing
on to the yards.*

ABOVE: *Laying sandstone. Charles and two stockmen – the next step in home improvement.*

BELOW: *Me, sitting in the beginnings of the living room. The caravan has been removed and there is a bedroom to the left of me. Early 1970s.*

Mum with Marlee; Bonnie's christening. Mum made Marlee's dress and bonnet.

ABOVE: *Sending a message on our old radio in 1970. With me is Lieutenant Commander Tim Anderson, RAN.*

BELOW: *Bullo River Airport – USA Ambassador Phillip Alston visited Bullo in 1980. Planes in order of size: US Ambassador's plane; Bertha, Charlie's town plane or as we called her the flying butcher shop; and WOO the super cub, Charlie's runabout.*

Charles went outside to investigate. He came back bewildered. The man he had hired was there, but so were his wife and ten children!

'Who are the other two?'

'They just tagged along.'

'What do you mean "just tagged along"?'

'Well, it seems that the guy I hired lost his eldest daughter in a card game to Billie, the guy tagging along. Jason hasn't yet handed the girl over to Billie, so he just follows him around until he does.'

'What? You can't be serious?'

'I'm afraid it's the truth, and you can't do anything about it, so don't start trying!'

'Who's the other woman?'

'Oh, that's Billie's wife.'

'Typical. He already has a wife and is looking for another!'

'Well, there's a lesson to be learnt—don't get fat or I'll trade you.'

The next day was busy with preparations for the last muster of the season. Departure was to be at dawn the following day. That night, Charles informed me that he needed my help with the mustering.

'Me? Not on your life! What I saw while filming was enough for me! Sorry, but I'd like my children to grow up knowing their mother!'

Charles explained that he didn't want me mustering on a horse, he wanted me in the plane with him. He was going to try to muster the cattle with the plane. That way, he could move a lot of cattle, which would otherwise be impossible to get within reach of the horsemen. All I had to do was pull the trigger on the shotgun whenever Charles told me to. Because it was such an insignificant job, they did not want to waste a man on it.

Apparently this method of mustering had been tried successfully in America, except that they used a helicopter. We were going to use a plane. However Charles was sure that the high lift wing of his small plane made it almost as manoeuvrable as a helicopter. It was the 'almost' that worried me. But Charles reckoned that with the horses and men on the ground, and his skill as a pilot, we could achieve nearly the same effect at one-twentieth the cost. Or so it worked out on paper. I reluctantly agreed to go.

We had to take off early in the morning when the air was cool. Low flying is dangerous at any time, so you have to make use of any factor in your favour. The men on the ground were in position, so with a waggle of the wings we were off. Charles was a superb pilot and this day he excelled himself— a helicopter couldn't have done the job as well. He moved mob after mob into the coachers held by the men. The men didn't have to move and I didn't have to fire a shot.

We continued through the morning until it was too hot for low flying, but on our way back to the airstrip, Charles saw a large mob of about twenty animals in a ravine under some trees. They weren't far from the herd, but impossible to get to from the ground. Charles decided to move them into the approaching herd, which was just to the left but over the ridge.

We approached at extremely low altitude. I was to fire a round into the trees above the cattle and this would scatter them. Then Charles would pull the plane up sharply to miss the rock wall in front of us, do a slow turn, and put the cattle through a narrow break in the ridge just in time to meet the herd on the other side.

He told me to get ready as he started the approach run. I was on the straps, leaning out the hole where the door had been, gun at the ready. He was coming up on the rock wall fast.

'Fire!' he shouted.

I hesitated. Charles pulled up to avoid crashing into the cliff and my shot hit about one hundred feet up the cliff face. Charles executed a perfect roll and brought the twenty head of cattle straight into the narrow break in the ridge. At the other end they walked into the mob just as quiet as lambs. My one shot, which hit halfway up the cliff face, had had no bearing on the operation at all. Charles just wanted me along so he could show off his new mustering skills in a plane.

So that finished the mustering for the season. The cattle were drafted through the yards and put out in the paddocks and the maintenance was started immediately. The supplies were now coming in weekly so that there would be enough to last the seven months that the road was out. There would only be the family and possibly one or two stockmen to feed during the wet, but that still totalled six, and six people can eat a lot in seven months.

As it was the end of the season, our road was badly cut up and some of the semi drivers would not risk coming in for fear of being stuck for the entire wet. They would bring the load as far as they dared, and then we would have to run back and forth with our four-ton truck until we had carried it all back to the station. The last truck was caught in heavy early season rain and would not come in any further than four miles, so the driver left the load just off the highway and went to the next station house, which was on the highway, and told them to inform us on the next radio session.

Charles suggested that we all go to pick up some of the load. That way we would see a lot more of the station, and also our front gate, which was something I had never seen. When your front gate is fifty miles away and over a mountain range, you don't exactly go tripping out to it every day to collect the mail.

The trip would take the best part of a day because it was a good four hours each way. I arranged the children and Mary in the back with mattresses and pillows and a shade cover to keep the sun off them. The boys tied a pole across the truck so they had something to hold onto going over bumps. Charles had the steering wheel to hold, but I had nothing and never stopped going up and down the entire trip. That road was a nightmare. We lurched and bumped all the way till I thought my head would drop off. Charles could see I was not faring too well, so he decided we would camp for the night and go back in the morning.

We stopped at a beautiful part of the river, with lovely shade trees, pure white sand and crystal water. There were birds everywhere. Mary gathered wood and made fishing poles for the girls and herself. They caught five fish among them. There was great excitement cooking them over the fire, and along with the food I had packed, we had a magnificent meal.

Charles had slipped a bottle of rum into the glove box, so we mixed it with the children's orange cordial and sat under a tree watching the girls and Mary and just talked. It was one of those days that just happen, but are the best.

Early the next morning, in much better condition, I made it to our front gate. I put a pile of stones on each side of our entrance to mark it, as there was no gate or fence, then helped Charles load timber and cement onto the truck. Mary and the children sat on top of the flat load and we started the return journey. I made it home, but only just. A few more miles and my teeth would have been where my eyes are.

One night Charles was late returning home. The girls and I were out watching the skies and listening for the noise of the engine. We were also watching a black wall of weather approaching from the northeast. Charles finally appeared in the north. He and the storm were neck and neck. He made it to the end of the airstrip in front of the storm, but not the wind. Every time he put the little Supercub down, the wind would lift it up again before he could cut the motor and tie it down.

The children and I were watching this 'round and round the mulberry bush' when Charles beckoned to me to come onto the airstrip. During his next brief landing he shouted, 'Jump on the struts!' I just stared as he swooped into the air again.

He needed more weight to keep the plane on the ground until he could tie it down. If he turned off the engine and a gust of wind hit, it could flip the plane over. With my extra weight, he could taxi to the tie-downs, cut the engines and tie the plane down in between gusts.

Charles and the storm approached the strip again. He landed the plane, taxied towards the tie-downs, and screamed at me to jump. I did and along came a gust of wind and off we went, Charles comfortably in the cockpit and me wrapped around the struts. He had the window open and we were only a few feet apart.

'Hold on, we'll try again.'

The 'hold on' part of the instructions was superfluous. He banked gently and came in again. We landed, and he taxied at high speed to the tie-downs and cut the engine. Charles and I quickly tied each wing, then the tail, and she was safe. Not a moment too soon—as we ran to the homestead heavy rain lashed the valley.

Along with the approaching wet season came poor radio contact. Apart from our plane, the two-way radio was our only contact with the outside world. By 1965, the Flying Doctor base had done wonders with the system which provided help to all the isolated people in the North but nevertheless, come sunset, and the last radio session at five-thirty, we had no contact with the base until eight the next morning. If any medical treatment was required after five-thirty, it just had to wait. The Royal Flying Doctor (RFD) was in the process of rectifying this situation by installing an emergency alarm system at the hospital. The station needing help would set off the alarm in the hospital and a doctor would be available to talk to them over the radio.

The alarm was a sensitive mechanism, set off only by an oddly-shaped, two-sided whistle. Because of the skill required to set off the alarm, we had to engage in what became known as whistle practice. This was very important because if we had to use it, it would be in an emergency, but the whistle practices over the radio were really something. The base controller took it very seriously and demanded that we all (every station on that particular network) attend whistle practice. Suddenly all the men who used the radio all the time were not available, so it was up to us women.

Our base controller tried, really tried, and we really tried too, but it was no good. As each woman collapsed in uncontrollable fits of laughter, unable to speak or blow, he would move on to the next one, only to have the same thing happen.

Just imagine someone directing you over a two-way radio, 'Blow ten seconds on the long whistle and six seconds on the short whistle. Now, dearies, good healthy blows! No beeps, nice long boops!'

153

One day I was in such hysterics listening to the others that I dropped the whistle down the back of the filing cabinet and when it came to my turn, I had to explain that my whistle was temporarily out of commission. I was told to put it on a string and attach it to the radio.

Another time I was rolling around in the radio room in stitches when Charles walked in. He was immediately alarmed, thinking I was in pain. I couldn't stop laughing long enough to tell him that I was alright. He picked me up and whisked me off to the bedroom in a panic. By the time I finally stopped laughing long enough to explain the situation and got back to the radio, I had missed my turn. I was reprimanded during the next whistle session.

After some weeks our controller gave up in disgust. I am happy to say that when an emergency did occur, there was no giggling or laughing and the whistle blowers set off the alarm admirably. In fact, one even blew a fuse.

So with a reliable twenty-four-hour medical service and our own plane, we settled in for our second wet. This time we had lots of building materials, so during that wet Pompeii finally turned into part of the house. Just putting on the roof made an amazing difference. All the plants I had put in that year turned into live, healthy green things and the big tin shed finally started to look as if someone cared about it.

CHAPTER 11

❖

1966-1971

In typical fashion, Charles suddenly announced one day that we were going to America! He wanted to spend a few years with his mother and he wanted the children to see his home in Maryland.

Our manager, John Nicolson, was now our partner, so with John to take care of the station during our absence I was instructed to prepare for our departure.

We were about to go from the tropical heat of December in the north of Australia to mid-winter in the northern States of America. The last we had heard was that they were snowed in by blizzards and we had no winter clothes whatsoever.

So I took the children with me to Sydney, to visit my family and to get some warm clothes together. Charles was to follow in a few weeks when all was running smoothly at the station and we would then leave for America and be with his mother in time for Christmas.

While in Sydney, our director called and said he wanted to take me to lunch. He told me to meet him at the studio. I arrived and was shown into a small viewing room and there on the screen was our movie! It was really quite good. Charles, who in person was as confident as hell, showed up on film as nervous as a kitten, and I, who was so nervous that I had to sit during filming, looked as if I had been before cameras all my life. Bill declared me the star of the show. I was a little pleased. He also said the film would be shown nationwide, so I went home and told Mum she would see her daughter on television. Of course Mum told half of Australia to watch.

I had already left for America when it was finally shown, but Mum proudly informed me by letter that everyone thought it was terrific.

As usual our departure was not without incident. The day before we were due to leave Sydney the airline went on strike. Luckily our travel agent was able to rebook us before the rush, but we had to go almost right around the world to get there. It took so long I nearly completed a sweater for Charles.

We finally made it to London, but boy, were they in a mess. Three major airlines on strike and Heathrow almost closed in with fog. Our New York flight took off three hours behind schedule and we only made it by five minutes as we were lost in the fog at the airport. We arrived in New York and went from heavy fog to complete blizzard. In fact, we were the second-last plane to land—the rest were rerouted to Detroit. When we went to collect our luggage, it was discovered that it was on a different flight, and that the airline had no idea which flight.

After four hours of running around we found all but two suitcases. The airline people promised to find them and deliver them to our door. They were, but not before they went all around America. We had a two-hour stopover in New York before our flight to Baltimore, so Charles arranged a madcap taxi ride around the city. The driver was marvellous. We saw everything possible, including the Empire State Building, and rounded off the tour with lunch at a fabulous little oyster bar.

After one more flight and an eighty-mile drive we were finally there. Fortunately a snowstorm set in for the first six days so we had time to recover before facing all the family and friends.

After too many years in the tropics, our first winter in Maryland was delightful. Charles's mother lives on the eastern shore of Maryland, on the Choptank River, surrounded by natural woods, wheat and cornfields. It was a place you could stay forever. The children had a pony and would ride into the woods to watch deer and other wild animals. After Christmas they started at the little country school and made many new friends, and Charles saw a lot of his old friends.

In the summers we did a lot of sailing and I finally mastered the art. I even graduated to racing. We had some funny times when I would forget the correct sailing terminology or pull the wrong halyard, but Charles still managed to win a few cups, and he had to admit he couldn't have done it without me. I was pretty nifty whipping the jib around on a tack.

My biggest faux pas was trying to set my first spinnaker. We were under full sail and Charles was directing me on how to bag the terrible thing. We were about to round the mark, so as well as the 'on the spot lesson', I was working against time.

I raced up on deck, holding all the ends, praying I did not forget which were the bottom ropes, otherwise I would hoist the sail upside down. The entire time Charles was shouting directions.

I attached the sail to the various lines that went back to the winches and attached the halyard to the last hole left in the sail, with fingers crossed it was the correct hole.

'Stand by, we're coming up to the mark, now don't mess this up, we're in the lead, and don't lose the spinnaker bag overboard when you hoist the sail!' Charles yelled from the cockpit.

We were neck and neck with the other boat, but we were on the inside closest to the mark, with the wind. If we went around without a hitch and broke out the spinnaker we would take the other boat's wind and gain a very large lead—it all depended on my first spinnaker hoist!

Charles was first boat around the mark, perfectly timed. 'Drop the jib! Now!' I sprang into action, dropped the jib and quickly dragged it in before it hit the water.

While I was still occupied with this task, Charles started screaming, 'Break out the spinnaker!'

Fine for him, standing in the cockpit holding the tiller and smoking a cigar, while I was running around the foredeck like a demented chicken.

'Hurry, we're losing speed!' I had a few remarks I wanted to shout back, but I needed all my wind to hoist the spinnaker.

Up she went and cracked right on the wind, what a beautiful sight, I sagged to the deck in relief.

'What's that!' he screamed.

'It's the spinnaker, you bloody nitwit! What do you think it is? You just told me to hoist it!'

I looked further up the mast to where his finger was pointing and there at the top of the mast was the spinnaker bag. In my haste I had tied it to the top of the halyard, so we were flying the spinnaker and bag, not done in sailing circles.

While I was still looking at the flying spinnaker bag Charles screamed, 'You forgot the pole!'

'What on earth are you talking about? You didn't mention any pole!'

'On the deck, on the deck!' At my feet was a ten-foot pole. I looked up at the fitting on the mast. That was within my reach and capabilities, but the other end, Charles informed me, had to be attached to the corner of the spinnaker flying about ten feet above the deck.

That day, apart from hoisting my first spinnaker, I also introduced the loose-footed spinnaker and spinnaker bag flying. Most of the leg home I was ten feet above the deck airborne on the spinnaker ropes, trying to hook the lines under the two cleats on the deck. Then I sat and played the spinnaker so it did not spill.

We won, but the second boat protested that we were carrying extra sail. The sailing committee could not find anything in the rule book about a spinnaker bag, so they gave us the race.

My sailing career was put on temporary hold when, in the middle of the winter of 1969, a beautiful baby girl arrived, our number three. She was that one in a million pill baby. This time I made Charles stay with me right up to the last breath. I think it did the trick because he didn't bring up the subject of having children again.

We all enjoyed our new little doll and life settled into a very pleasant pattern for the next year or so, but alas it was not to last.

I drove into Easton, the nearest town, to have my hair set

for a dinner party. I had not made an appointment so I just walked into one of the many hairdressing salons and asked if they could fit me in. The response was typically American and friendly.

'Come in, now you just sit yourself down and rest a while, I'll be with you before you know.' She had a big broad smile, all teeth, was blonde and fitted her job image perfectly.

I didn't feel like talking so when she asked, 'Are you travelling, just passing through?' I replied, 'Yes.' I thought this would stop any conversation, but I was wrong. There were endless questions, where, when, how long, why. She started to wash my hair but excused herself when the phone rang. It was then that the chatter of the two women next to me started to filter through.

'. . . the latest, his name is Charles . . . ' My heart started to sink. My first reaction was, 'Don't listen,' but it would have been like saying, 'Don't breathe'. They were talking about another woman so at least I wasn't sitting next to his latest affair. I suppose I had known deep down in my heart that there must have been women since the 'great winding stair affair', but I had taken the 'head in the sand' approach. But here it was presented to me on a platter. The heartache started all over again.

The conversation came to me in waves. She had met him in Washington; they laughed as one said 'she' had worn out four sets of tyres since the affair began. My mind went back over the past months, all the times Charles had finished too late to drive back from Washington, calls at nine-thirty at night to say he'd just finished a very important meeting and was very tired, there were more important meetings in the morning as they didn't finish, so he'd stay overnight and come home early. Or, the weather was so bad the roads were impassable. And so on.

'. . . from overseas . . . but American . . . married of course.'

I stopped the hairdresser, saying I had forgotten another appointment, could I come back in an hour.

I fled to my car and burst into tears. I sat there going

over and over my life with Charles—sadness, revenge, hate, I experienced all these emotions and many more. But revenge surfaced the winner. I decided to fight fire with fire.

Men regularly made advances towards me, but being completely in love with my husband, I'd never been interested. That was about to change.

Having made this momentous decision, I gathered myself together and dried my eyes. If I was about to play the 'femme fatale' I had to look the part, and wet hair and red puffy eyes would not be appropriate. Having conquered the hair, I went home and, with a permanent smile to hide my sorrow, I chatted and dressed with my cad of a husband. It is an interesting scenario, watching your husband dress, knowing he is about to meet his 'current'. No, now I would consider it interesting; then, it was heart-wrenching.

It was a large dinner party, about forty people, but it didn't take me long to single her out. I just watched Charles. I had to admit he was smooth. He cruised around the room charming every girl on the way, but finally lingered with one a little longer. And even though I was on the other side of the room, I could follow his lines almost word for word. They were so familiar.

There were a few men there who had, over the months, given me the 'eye'. One my eyes rested on had recently finalised his divorce. I decided he was the least complicated, so I took a deep breath, a large gulp of gin and tonic and headed into the fray. I'd certainly read the signals right. All I did was smile and he nearly carried me off to the bedroom.

Human nature never ceases to amaze me. There was Charles, showering attention on this female on the other side of the room, but the moment I started laughing and talking to another man, he was at my elbow in the flash of an eye, enquiring what I was doing.

'I'm playing your game.' I had consumed a few gin and tonics for Dutch courage, but I was certainly a long way from being intoxicated.

Charles grabbed my arm and said quietly in my ear, through clenched teeth, 'You're drunk, we're going home!' I wrenched my arm free, and told him I was not drunk, and I was not going home. I was going to have a good time and why didn't he just go back to his new interest on the other side of the room and leave me alone.

'Don't you like it when the shoe is on the other foot, Charlie boy?' It was then that I learned I couldn't play serious games with Charles. When I refused to leave, he went quite crazy. I turned my back on him, saying I would have someone drive me home when I was ready. He grabbed me around the neck in a half-nelson grip, twisted my arm up my back and propelled me out of the house. Then he threw me into the car and skidded out of the driveway in a shower of gravel.

I was in shock. I had just seen a side of my husband I did not know existed. Would this happen every time I crossed him? Charles was a great actor and he was always positioning, as if life was a game of chess—all his moves had a purpose. But looking back now I realise he was just a spoilt boy having a tantrum.

He drove home like a maniac, I think to scare me, but it was in vain. I couldn't generate any emotion at all. Neither of us said a word.

However, by the time the car finally screeched to a halt I was fuming. I jumped out and slammed the door. How dare he treat me like that? As far as I was concerned that was it. Love or no love, his unfaithfulness was bad enough, but this was more than I was prepared to tolerate. Good heavens, I'd only smiled at the man, what would he have done if I'd kissed him? I went upstairs and locked myself in the children's room.

He knocked on the door several times, saying he wanted to speak to me. I told him there was nothing to talk about. He said if I didn't open the door he would be forced to do something.

'What will it be this time, Charlie? The gun to the head? Maybe you can shoot the door down. I'm sure you'd like the children to see you shoot your way in and then drag me away in a half-nelson. Go ahead, Charles, they're awake, strut your stuff.' There was silence. I kissed the girls and told them to go back to sleep. I said everything was alright but mummy was not speaking to daddy tonight and I would sleep there with them. They settled down and were asleep again within minutes. Not so mummy.

I didn't speak to him for weeks and I was still sleeping in the children's room. I knew this couldn't continue, but I had no solution. Every night when I thought the children were asleep I cried. But one day Marlee came to me and said, 'Mummy, do mummies cry all the time?' I burst into tears.

'No, darling, not all the time.'

'When will you stop crying?'

'I don't know, darling, I don't know.'

Finally Charles came to me.

'I don't know how to prove to you that I love you.'

'I would think it would be easy—just don't chase other women.'

'They don't mean anything to me.'

'Then you shouldn't have too much trouble giving them up. But really, I don't think it matters any more. I don't care what you do. I knew in my heart this wasn't true, but part of me did hope that he would finish it so that I could start putting some sort of life together again.

'To prove how much I love you I'm willing to go back to the station—it'll be just you and me in the wilderness.'

Like a fool I believed him. I reckoned that if he was willing to go back into the wilderness, he must love me. Then as proof of just 'how much he loved me', he said he would sign the station over to me.

'Now would I do that if I didn't love you?'

My trust in Charles had changed over the years. I no longer believed everything he told me—but I had to admit that handing the station over seemed a fantastic gesture and certainly put a lot of power in my hands. However, years later, it was revealed that his gift had an anchor and chain attached to it, and he could haul it in whenever he liked. It seems that he had altered the Articles of Memorandum of the company, and if I ever had told him to get out, I would not have ended up with the station.

A few weeks after I returned to the station, I likewise found out that his declaration of love in the wilderness had also been a statement of convenience. Just after the fateful party, he had received a letter from John saying that things were not too good on the station and he had better return quickly. The deciding factor was that John could not send any more funds from cattle sales. Because there weren't any more. Funds or cattle sales.

Our departure was much the same as our arrival—trouble prone! We had a shocking drive to the airport through a blizzard, and were down to five miles per hour most of the way. We checked in late and were rushed on board. We had just settled down after all the tears and farewells, when I noticed that the hostesses were doing a lot of running back and forth. It turned out there had been a telephone call to say the plane had a bomb hidden on board. All the passengers disembarked and an army of detectors went over the plane from tip to tail. No bomb. It was a very nervous group of passengers that quietly filed back on board after going through the detector screen. And there were quite a few empty seats. Even with dinner, wine and a movie I could not relax, and was very relieved to leave the plane in Los Angeles.

On arrival we walked for miles through the tunnels that connect local with overseas airlines. After many wrong tunnels we found our flight and handed over our luggage, passports and papers. It was while the attendant was checking our papers that I saw the mistake. I went as white as a sheet and Charles immediately wanted to know what was wrong. I managed to put him off and the clerk handed back our passports and told us our flight would leave in two hours.

I quickly dragged Charles and the children to the coffee lounge, where he demanded to know why I was acting so strangely. I took out our passports and showed him. The travel agent had attached all the necessary travel papers to our outdated passports. Fortunately the checking clerk had missed the expiry date on our passports. After many cups of coffee, we decided to worry about the passports when we reached Sydney. Somewhere in our luggage was a bundle of passports marked 'out-of-date'. At least I hoped so.

It was January 1971 and we discovered at boarding time that we were on the first Jumbo flight to Sydney, and of course the whole plane was booked! There was very tight security, so more luggage-searching and detector screens. This is all part of air travel now, but twenty years ago it was very new and quite unnerving.

By this time it was two a.m. east coast time and we were getting extremely tired, especially the children. We were standing in line waiting to file through the screen when a man in front of us set off the alarm system. There he stood on the raised platform, with red lights flashing and bells clanging! All three hundred plus passengers were looking at him. He was a small man with glasses and looked as if he wouldn't hurt a fly.

The officer in charge of security stepped up to the little guy. 'Do you have anything to declare?' he asked in a deep, dramatic voice.

'No,' the little guy croaked out.

They asked him to step down and they put his briefcase on the stand—no alarms. They put him back—alarms! With red lights flashing and awful clanging noises everywhere, the security man asked again, 'Do you have anything to declare?'

'I want to go home!'

They took his coat, he stepped onto the stand—alarms! They took his shirt—alarms! They took his shoes and socks— more alarms! By this time the poor man was shaking from head to toe. They took off his belt and, clutching his pants, he once more headed for the screen. He slowly went up the ramp, took a deep breath, and stepped onto the platform. Silence. He nearly collapsed with relief. Apparently the metal in the buckle on his belt was the same metal used in bullet and bomb casings. The man never did board the plane. He grabbed all his clothes and while the security guard was trying to apologise, ran from the building with clothes flying in all directions.

We eventually made the plane and were all seated waiting for takeoff when the air was once more shattered by alarms. Oh no, not again! Everyone was jumping up and down in their seats when the captain announced that everything was fine. Because there were so many doors on the Jumbo, the hostesses had to go through a door drill, and if any of them didn't follow the steps in order, it set off an alarm. By the colour of the hostess's face next to us, I would say she missed a step.

When we got to Sydney the airport was in chaos. Along with the first Jumbo was one 707 from Europe and another from the Far East, all at the same time. By the time we reached the customs officer, he was fit to be tied and not the least bit sympathetic to our problem. He just kept shouting, 'Back to America!'

I then asked if I could open our luggage and produce our current passports. Finally, after much arguing, I was allowed into the customs baggage area. There, with customs men peering over my shoulder, I tried as calmly as possible to remember where I had packed the passports. I found them, but the next problem was that we hadn't even checked out of America on the right passports. Five hours and twenty pages of red tape later, they combined old checkout passports and new check-in passports and we were free to go.

After a brief holiday with my parents and family, I once more headed for the Outback, this time loaded down with all the requirements for living—sheets, towels, furniture and so on. Our first stay had been strictly camping with a few bare essentials. This time around I made sure I had all the trimmings.

Charles had a friend send a shipment of rattan furniture to us from the Philippines and this went a long way towards making the tin shed look as if someone lived there. Linen and non-breakables were no problem to bring in by road, but there were some things I had to wait many years for. Large mirrors could not come by road, the trip was just too rough.

I finally received my first mirror by plane. Many hands carefully unloaded it, but when Dick was attaching it to the wall one of his assistants slipped and dropped one end and we then had lots of odd-shaped small mirrors.

It was another few years before I got my next large mirror,

so we survived on hand mirrors. I didn't realise how much weight I had gained until the full length mirror arrived.

Uncle Dick made a lot of steel furniture and I created many coffee tables out of very large slabs of sandstone with lumps of tree trunks for legs.

With endless boxes of 'relief' packages sent by Mum and my sister over the years, the finishing touches started to appear in the rooms and the tin shed slowly turned into a homestead.

CHAPTER 12

❖

1971-1974

Drought had spread across most of America. Crops failed, the price of corn skyrocketed, and feed lots, closed right across the country. The profit margin between buying store cattle, feeding them corn, and selling the finished produce as table beef, disappeared.

The American range cattle, which had traditionally gone into the feed lots, were now used for the industrial beef market: small goods, hotdogs, tinned beef, spam and so on. America had imported only two per cent of its beef requirements from Australia, so it was just a short sneeze, but as it was the complete market for the north of Australia, we now had no market at all. So the prices plummeted. The meatworks paid us less for our cattle than it cost to get them there. This cattle depression lasted for seven years.

We struggled through the first year, but it was evident, even at the beginning of the season, that if the drought in America continued, we were in big trouble. There was no time to discuss private problems. Survival took up all our waking moments. So our private life was put on hold.

We started supplying Port Keats Aboriginal mission with beef. Port Keats was our next door neighbour, so to speak, across the Victoria River and north a bit. It had a large settlement of Aborigines, around three to four hundred people, and it was run by the Catholic church. The road into it was long, and almost non-existent, so it had difficulty getting supplies. Charles arranged to supply their beef by air, and so the Bullo River Family Abattoir was born.

Around this time, Charles and John decided they were not suited as partners. John was very hardworking and extremely careful with his money, so being a partner to Charles must have given him constant heart attacks. Charles had no regard for money, his or anyone else's. In Charles's eyes, money was to be used, and this he could do very efficiently, much to the horror of any poor person whose money he happened to have his hands on. At this stage, what was worrying John was the debts that Charles was accumulating against the partnership. They settled on splitting the station in half and John moved to a part of the station known as Sandy Creek. Sandy Creek was the southwestern half of Bullo, bordering on the Ord River Irrigation Scheme valley, quite close to the town of Kununurra in Western Australia. Charles kept the Bullo River valley, a stretch of land surrounded on three sides by mountain ranges and on the fourth side by the Victoria River.

At that stage, Charles and I were not on regular speaking terms, so I was not privy to the events that followed. But letters on file suggest that the running up of debts was a planned exercise, and at the right time Gus offered to buy John out. Around 1972–73 John, after spending months and months in negotiation with Charles and Gus, departed for Queensland.

Gus then renamed Sandy Creek Spirit Hills and Charles and Gus set about building their empire.

Charles called it 'The Victoria Project', and it involved many stations, an abattoir, a sea port on the Victoria River, ships carrying produce to the Far East—heady dreams for the Outback in the seventies.

Charles and Gus were unusual business partners. They spent most of their time arguing. However, they also worked very hard and if work had been the only criteria, perhaps their grand scheme would have succeeded. But as it was, the station just kept gobbling up money. The only bright spot was that at least Gus was able to draw tax losses against Bullo for his other companies.

Of course all these empire-building plans spread over some years. The abattoir was the first step.

Charles designed and supervised the building of the abattoir and what with the planning, discussions, official visits, permits and forms that went on, I suppose I expected to see something rather large and impressive. For months, trucks lumbered past the homestead loaded down with supplies, depositing tons of bulldust into my tin shed. And, even though this so-called abattoir was apparently going to rescue us from poverty, seeing all that building material go by for another building when the children and I were living in an open tin shed did not sit well with me. I refused to have anything to do with the abattoir construction, and in any case, I would not have had the time. The abattoir was being constructed about a quarter of a mile from the tin shed, and I was fully occupied from five-thirty in the morning until ten at night.

At that stage I was cook for the staff and family (about twenty), teacher to the three little girls, secretary/telephonist, first aid officer/nurse, gardener, requisition/purchasing officer and hostess all rolled into one. The answer to all problems was, 'Go ask the Missus.'

So when I finally did venture down the road on the opening day of the Bullo River Family Abattoir, I was not prepared for the vision that met my eyes. Charles had insisted I come down to officially open it, press the button, throw the switch or whatever one does to open an abattoir. I had to close my eyes until we stopped in front of the abattoir.

'Okay, we're there, open your eyes.' Charles was very excited. I opened my eyes and just stared, speechless.

'Well?' he asked.

'Is that it?' I asked incredulously.

'What do you mean, "Is that it?"?'

'All those months to build that?'

Before me stood a new but forlorn corrugated tin shed. It was very tall to accommodate the electric hoist which lifted the carcasses off the floor, in fact twice the normal height. Silhouetted against the vast natural landscape it looked ridiculous, just an ugly, skinny building.

I suppose I should not condemn it completely—it did make it possible for us to survive the next six years. Only just—

169

each year we slipped further into debt—but it created a cash flow, and that was what the bank was interested in. The fact that cash flowed out a lot faster than it trickled in was not ideal, but at least it flowed.

Starting an abattoir changed the entire routine of the station. There was now no sleepy rainy season. It was full steam ahead, all day, all year round. And we had a full staff for twelve months of the year.

We supplied Port Keats Aboriginal mission with quarters of beef. We had no chillers or refrigeration, just the tin shed, so the animals would be slaughtered late afternoon, hung overnight, and at first light Charles would fly the meat to Port Keats. The mission grew and so did our orders. Then Bathurst Island mission was included. The missions had their own butcher's room where the carcass was boned out, but as butchers became harder to find, we were requested to bone out the quarters, so a boning room was added to the skinny tin shed.

We were now supplying about twelve carcasses per week, so the necessity for refrigeration became obvious and a walk-in chiller was added.

As the missions' populations increased their 'stores' were expanded, and we were now requested to package the meat in cuts to be sold in the store. So the boning room was extended to incorporate a packing section and a snap-freeze to freeze the packets. Another extension was required for boxing the cuts, and another holding freezer to stock-pile the finished products.

By now we were supplying Port Keats, Bathurst Island, Snake Bay, Garden Point, Delissaville, Maningrida, Wave Hill and Hooker Creek. We had started with a little four-seater Tri-pacer plane but when Bathurst Island became a regular customer, the flight was too far for such a small plane so we bought a Piper Cherokee. Well, not one, but many, a long line of them.

Charles finally said, 'This is no good, we need a work horse, something rugged, a small freight plane built for rough handling.' And that was how we ended up with Bertha, our Beaver De Havilland.

I am sure that stories told to Aboriginal children in the future will include Bertha in them. Sister Fred at Port Keats said that on meat delivery days she could never get the children to settle down, they would be too busy listening for Bertha's very distinctive sound, the Beaver De Havilland big radial engine.

When they heard it the children would run en masse from the schoolroom and wait for Charles to put on a display for them. He never disappointed them. They would squeal in delight and hide behind Sister Fred as he dive-bombed them, and then rush out again as he climbed into the sky, only to dive again.

For ten years Bertha flew the northern skies and she became something of a legend, or I should say Charles and Bertha. The other pilots called the BR/PK/BI/DWN/BR track—Bullo River to Port Keats to Bathurst Island to Darwin with a return back to Bullo River—the Henderson Highway. Everyone knew when Charles was in the air. 'Charlie's up,' they'd say, and that was enough, everyone on the ground would track him, and everyone in the air would avoid him—he had a disconcerting habit of reading a book while flying and if it was a particularly exciting one, he would often stray off course.

But although Charles could appear dangerous in the air, he was world-class. One time he took off on a bush strip, a rather dangerous strip, with a telephone wire across one end. Charles always tested fate to the extreme, and this day he had a heavy cargo plus seven children on board. On takeoff the wing struck a sapling growing on the strip and the blow wrenched the wing back from the fuselage, jamming the flaps. He could not bank or land as the pressure of this manoeuvre would rip the wing off completely. He had to fly straight ahead, with no sudden movements, for Kununurra Airport forty miles away. Somehow he kept the plane in the air and lined it up with the airstrip. When he landed, the tip of the wing was almost scraping the ground. Part of the damaged wing had separated about twelve inches from the plane's body.

Of course, during those ten years, Bertha also faithfully delivered Charles to all his females around half of the Territory, and dutifully broke down whenever he wanted to stay overnight.

For me, those were nightmare years—three little girls, a

171

property going broke and a marriage that was floundering. I often wonder, now, how I stayed sane, although when I look back, I realise I was probably on the verge of a nervous breakdown many times. I guess my life had been panic, chaos and unhappiness for so long I didn't know the difference.

And into all this was thrown the added pressure of Charles's four sons from his first marriage. The boys had visited and lived with us in the Philippines and America, and Hugh and Fraser had gone to school in Manila for a period. They were nice enough boys but just their presence added yet another complication to an already impossible undertaking.

One by one they left the station to live their own lives. Life on Bullo in those days was extremely hard, and it was normal for a young person to want more than just plain hard work, sleep and more hard work. They all left during the failing, debt-ridden years. The place was in a miserable mess and if you didn't have to stay you didn't.

I lost count of the number of times I packed up and left. Sometimes for months on end. It didn't faze Charles, he would just move in a few females until I returned, and he was always confident I would.

We were now well and truly into the abattoir business. The ugly tin shed had turned into a large spread with all the additions. We had an abattoir manager, boners, slaughterers, wrappers, slicers, packers, and along with all these people went all the usual problems.

The abattoir had been built from scratch with never enough money or time to do things properly. And everything that happened there was always a panic, a panic to get the cattle into the yard, a panic to get the meat packed, a panic to get the meat onto the plane, a panic to fuel the plane, you name it, and it was a panic.

One very funny incident occurred in only the second year of operation. Every year there had to be an inspection of the building before the licence was extended for a further twelve months. At this time, we had a very good head butcher but he was definitely not management material. However, he was all Charles had, so he was put in charge of the spring-cleaning for the inspection. Charles went over the abattoir the day before the inspectors were to arrive and he said it was really quite good, all neat and tidy with everything in place.

The next morning, the inspectors, Charles and I marched down the flat and into the building. The staff were all very busy and our butcher was boning out.

Then one of the inspectors looked over in the corner and said, 'What is that?'

We all looked in the direction of the accusing finger and there sat the butcher's fourteen-month-old son in a two-hundred-pound tub of mince. Everyone was horrified and speechless, except the butcher, who replied, 'That's me kid.'

'I know it's a kid, but what's it doing in a tub of mince?'

'Oh, the missus didn't feel well today, so I had to look after it. Only place I could find to keep it quiet.'

Of course the inspector started pencilling furiously. No children allowed in abattoir, one black mark, a naked baby in a tub of mince, goodness knows how many black marks.

We went back to the house and Charles said the butcher had only been with us for two months and he had never had the baby in the abattoir before. I don't think they believed him, but it was soon confirmed when the butcher came charging into the house with his son screaming at the top of his lungs.

It seemed the chemical used to preserve the mince and keep it a bright pink had had a terrible effect on the poor baby's skin—his legs and behind were red raw and getting worse by the minute. I quickly bathed him and rubbed on some soothing cream, but he had to be taken to hospital. Charles later found out that the mother's incapacitation was due to a bottle of brandy for breakfast.

We received our twelve-month extension, but only on the condition that the butcher and his family were never in close proximity to the abattoir again. Of course the two hundred pounds of mince were condemned. All in all, the only ones to profit from that day were the dogs. They ate in style for many weeks and were sad to see the butcher and his mince-playing son leave.

At this stage in the abattoir business, we had branched

out into pigs. We had a new, very opinionated 'pig man', and his ambition was to manage Bullo River Station. He would arrive at the kitchen door every morning at five-thirty to discuss the pig schedule for the day. Of course Charles handed him over to me. I did my best to ignore him after the few regular questions, but he would stand there for the next hour or so, expounding on how he would run a cattle station.

As the weeks progressed, it became obvious that ignoring him was not enough. Charles, with pressure from the abattoir manager, Uncle Dick and a few others, was about to give him his marching orders when the 'pig man' took matters into his own hands.

He appeared in the kitchen one morning very early, while Charles was drinking his coffee.

'Don't rush your coffee, the plane won't be loaded today, the staff have gone on strike.'

Now, the word 'union' upset Charles enough, but if you really wanted to see fireworks, tell him his staff was on strike!

'Strike!' The 'pig man' looked a little shocked. He hadn't expected this violent reaction. 'I'll show them what happens to strikers!' He stormed out of the kitchen towards the bedroom.

'What's he going to do?' asked the now very worried 'pig man'.

'I've no idea.'

'But I'm supposed to handle this.'

'Handle what?' I asked.

'I'm supposed to handle this for him.'

I started to smell a rat. Charles reappeared loading his pistol. The 'pig man' sank to his knees and grabbed Charles's trouser leg.

'Please, let me handle it. I know I can get them back to work!'

Charles ignored him and started out the door. The 'pig man', still pleading, followed close behind.

Our abattoir manager told me the rest of the story.

'We could see Charlie charging down the flat with the "pig man" in hot pursuit. I looked at my watch and knew we were not late for the six-thirty loading, so I wondered what the commotion was about. Charlie came barrelling through the door shouting, "Strike will you, eh, strike?! I'll show you strike!" and started firing pistol shots around the room. It all happened so fast, no one even ducked for cover. We just froze in various stages of eating and drinking, and stared at him. When all the chaos had died down I asked Charles who was on strike.

'"You are!"'

'"No we're not!"'

So that was the end of the pig man.

Another entertaining type was working as general rouse-about. One morning Charles told him to fuel the plane and pointed to the drums of fuel in the paddock nearby.

Charles then came into the house to get the invoice book and other papers he required for his day in town. Our mechanic, Dick, came into the kitchen with the information for a spare part he required and he and Charles walked out to the plane. A few minutes later Charles was back, hopping mad. Ian had filled the plane with diesel fuel. Luckily he was still pumping it into the tanks when Charles and Dick walked up and they had both immediately noticed the smell of diesel instead of avgas. Charles left Dick out at the plane to supervise the emptying and cleaning of the fuel tanks. All this would take hours, so Charles had to call Darwin and cancel various appointments for the first three hours or so.

Dick appeared and said the tanks had been emptied and washed through many times and were now ready to be refilled. He had left Ian to do it. After spending all that time helping to empty and clean the tanks, Ian proceeded to fill the plane with diesel again!

When Charles found out, he was ready to murder him but he could not afford the luxury because he had to stop Dick from doing just that. Dick once more emptied and cleaned the tanks and three hours later he fuelled the plan himself. Charles had a one-way passenger to Darwin. I don't think Ian ever realised what he had done.

One day Charles came home with a surprise for me, my first station cook. I thought, how wonderful, a cook. Now I'll be able to do all the things I never get time for. Boy, was I in for a shock. Until then, I had only been associated with legitimate cooks, by that I mean people who were what they claimed to be. All the cooks I had employed in the Philippines could cook. In the Northern Territory things worked differently.

My first cook was tall, big, rough and of German origin. However, she had not inherited any typical German traits such as love of work, or devotion to order and cleanliness. She was lazy, dirty, and the worst food mutilator this side of the black stump. She covered everything with instant gravy. Each morning she would make ten gallons of this gluck and pour it over whatever she served for breakfast, lunch or dinner. You couldn't tell what was underneath, but maybe that was just as well. The men complained bitterly but I enjoyed not being in the kitchen, so I tried to encourage her to improve her cooking.

However, after a few weeks it was evident that her heart was not in her cooking. When she wasn't chasing one of the stockmen or trying to steal their grog, she could be found at the kitchen table cleaning her fingernails (my orders) with a can opener (not my orders). She had to go.

The next time Charles decided he would steer clear of the local talent and try his luck in the South. The result was certainly something different. After her first night on the rum of the North (which is about four times stronger than regular rum), she informed everyone that she was a striptease artist. The men encouraged her to perform but she said she couldn't because she didn't have all her props. This statement caused great amazement because as far as I was concerned, and indeed everyone else, she was one big performance from sunrise to sunset. The only part of the act that was missing was the music.

She never used the buttons on a blouse above the navel, and the cheeks that made the men walk into closed doors weren't the ones she put her make-up on. Of course the last thing she could do was cook. In fact, she had a mental seizure trying to boil water. I asked her why she applied for the job when she couldn't cook, and she said she'd wanted a change, she thought it would be fun.

Next came a fiery character! We were back with cooks from the North, and she was a very nice person when sober, but wow, when she was drunk . . . When we met her in town for the interview, she was neatly dressed and very well-mannered.

Of course I was not experienced in spotting the signs of an alcoholic. Up to that point in my life I had not met any, or at least lived in close proximity with any.

We discovered she was an alcoholic about two hours after she arrived at the station. It turned out she couldn't survive three hours without a drink.

She had one thing in her favour—she could cook, that is if you could keep her sober long enough. So I persevered.

To make sure the grog was out of temptation's way, I moved it into our caravan and hid it under one of the bunks. The next night, drunk on grog she'd stolen from the men, she came screaming into the caravan and attacked Charles, demanding a drink. We couldn't calm her down, so we locked her in her room. After smashing everything possible, she fell asleep.

The next morning she was as meek as a kitten, but I told Charles she had to go. I didn't want the children to grow up thinking this was normal night-time behaviour.

The following evening, when I was tucking the children in, the youngest asked, 'Is Auntie Joan going to put on another show tonight?'

The long line of cooks continued, almost all hopeless at cooking. I grew very tired of paying these people to cook, while still doing a lot of it myself, either because they were drunk, or because the staff refused to eat what they produced.

There were only two good cooks in that endless parade. Both were young, friendly and cheerful, and best of all they could cook. Everyone regretted their departure but both were travelling around the world and could only stay a limited time. One stayed seven months, the other nearly six.

Two other cooks stand out in my mind, but not because of their cooking. The first of these had a hang-up about knives. She would hide all the knives in her room and every time I wanted to cut something, I would have to ask her for a

177

knife. She would then ask endless questions as to why I needed it.

She would take the knives when I was in the office or talking on the phone. I would tell her to put the knives back, and eventually they would all be returned to the kitchen, only to have them disappear again the moment I turned my back.

She was a hopeless cook, so I didn't put up with this for long. I moved back into the kitchen to cook and she became dishwasher and domestic. This did not sit well with her and she became even more troublesome. As well as stealing all the knives, she started turning off the stove. I would put a roast in the oven and go to do other work, then come back an hour later to find the oven off and the meat still raw. She finally wouldn't talk to me at all, only to Charles, which of course made it impossible for me to get her to do anything.

I told Charles to take her out on the plane as I couldn't stand it any more. He said he would look for another cook, but maybe she would be alright in the abattoir. We always needed more people in the meat-wrapping section. I didn't care where she went as long as it was out of my sight.

Two days later, our abattoir manager came to Charles and said, 'Either she goes, or I go!' Her knife-hiding caper was causing havoc in the abattoir, not to mention the effect on production. She'd hidden all the knives on her very first morning while the staff were at morning tea. Charles finally took her to Darwin.

The next one was a wonderful cook—good down-to-earth country fare. She was everyone's idea of what a grandma should be, at least on the surface.

Each morning after breakfast we would sit down with a cup of tea to plan lunch and dinner for that day and breakfast for the next morning. At first things went smoothly, but then one day . . . Well, it went something like this:

We sat down as usual with our cup of tea.

'What meals do you want today?'

'Well, let's see. Maybe lunch, hamburgers, onions, potatoes, vegies and custard and jelly for dessert.'

'Right,' came her brisk reply. This was out of character

for a start. She was usually very chatty and had some comment or suggestions, but I thought maybe she was not feeling well and did not attach too much importance to the change.

After I had discussed the day's meals I went into my office. About an hour or so later, I looked up from the accounts to find her standing beside me. The expression on her face was one of annoyance.

'Something wrong?' I ventured.

'I would like to know what I'm expected to cook today,' came the terse reply.

'But I told you,' I said in disbelief.

'You did not!'

Something in her voice told me it was a waste of time following this line of conversation, so I said, 'Oh, I'm sorry, I forgot to come to the kitchen this morning to discuss it with you.'

'That's right, that's why I'm here,' she said in very emphatic tones.

'Right,' I said slowly, desperately searching for an answer to this weird and wonderful exchange.

'Right,' I said again. We then repeated the conversation we had had an hour before, in the kitchen, over a cup of tea.

'Good,' came the brisk reply, 'as long as I know the plan I can keep to a schedule.' She then turned sharply in military style and marched out of the room.

Shaking my head and sighing deeply, I returned to my bookwork. About an hour later I was on the phone when she burst into the room. I told the person on the phone I would call back, put the phone down and gave her a withering look. It had no effect.

'I can't be expected to serve meals on time if you don't discuss them with me!'

By this time I was getting annoyed.

'I've told you what I want cooked!'

'Then why would I be here now?'

I had a few choice answers to that, but refrained. I decided to change tack.

'What do you suggest we have?' I then sat there and listened

179

while she repeated exactly what I had told her twice that morning.

'That sounds wonderful,' I said.

She smiled and left the room mumbling about how she was expected to do everything.

For the rest of the day I was left in peace, and I began to think it was just a one-off event. I was wrong. The next day we went through the normal routine of meal planning, I went to my office, and, right on cue, an hour later, she appeared.

'I'm still waiting for you to tell me the meals for the day,' she said, with her arms folded and a look of annoyance on her face. Realising this was now an ongoing problem, and likely to be repeated daily, I thought I would shortcut the routine.

'Well, what do you think we should have?' I asked.

She looked at me for a few seconds, then said, 'I'm here to cook the food, not to decide what to cook! I'm not paid to do the thinkin'!'

Again I had a good answer to that remark but I held my tongue. We started to repeat the whole procedure but eventually I lost my temper.

'I don't care what you cook, just go away!' I said.

She departed, saying, 'Well, if you can't make up your mind over a few simple meals, I suppose it's up to me.'

She walked out of the office and proceeded to cook exactly what we had discussed at breakfast. The next day I typed out the meals and left the menu on the kitchen table. Every time she appeared to tell me she had not seen any typed instructions, I silently handed her a copy.

The following day I went one step further. I left the menu on the kitchen table, then locked the office door.

That night she spoke to Charles. She said she had noticed I was acting most peculiarly and maybe he should get some medical advice. In the meantime, however, she didn't really want to work around anyone with mental problems, it made her nervous. So she left.

The background to our two slightly off-beat cooks was later revealed when the employment agency sent us an extraordinary expense bill for hiring them. After many discussions, a casual remark revealed the truth.

'It's impossible to believe we would get two people in a row with serious mental problems, you must be near an institution.'

I was joking, but the pause was too long. The agency was indeed a few blocks away from a rehabilitation centre for patients recovering from nervous breakdowns. Both our cooks had been out on six-week trial periods. We changed our employment agency. In fact, to be on the safe side, we went interstate.

The rate of staff turnover at Bullo was unbelievable. In the first year alone about 160 were hired, and some were fired, departed or just plain walked away. We only needed a staff of about twenty so that was an almost complete turnover of staff every five weeks. There were many reasons for this. It was very isolated, beer was rationed, food was mostly beef, cooks were mostly lousy, work was endless, weather was very hot, there was nowhere to go and, of course, there was Charlie. Some employees might have put up with all the rest, but Charles was another problem altogether.

Charles ran the station along the lines of a battleship. He told them how long they could have their hair, what clothes they had to wear, when to go to bed, how much grog they could have to drink, what they could do with their time off, and so on.

He also managed to instil the 'fear of God' into most of them. This was illustrated one day when we were loading the plane with the meat cartons. He usually taxied the plane down to the abattoir for loading, but Homestead Creek had flooded overnight and washed away part of the plane's taxiing ramp. So we had to form a human chain across the fast-flowing section of the creek and pass the cartons of meat along till they reached the plane on the other side. Charles supervised this operation from the plane, and shouted directions to everyone within hearing distance.

'Hurry up, don't drop the cartons, don't wet the cartons!' he bellowed.

One chap in the middle of the current was reaching to hand the carton to the next person, when he stepped into a hole and went underwater. He uttered a terrible gurgling sound as he went under, but held the carton up in the air at full arm's length. Everyone stopped and watched the meat carton teetering and then steady.

'Oh, well done, you didn't drop the carton!' said Charles.

'Charles, he's underwater, he can't hear you and if someone doesn't take that forty-pound weight off him, he'll drown!'

Hands from all directions grabbed the carton and dragged the poor fellow out of the hole. He came up coughing and spluttering. When he'd finally recovered, the first thing he said was, 'Did the carton get wet?'

I know if I had applied for a job, I would not have been there long. But unfortunately I was the wife, so I just had to keep working.

Many pilots came to Bullo to build up their hours so that they could go into jets. Often, when flying Ansett or Australian Airlines, I hear the name of a pilot who cut his teeth delivering meat for the Bullo River Family Abattoir to some remote mission in the north of Australia in the seventies. I am sometimes tempted to ask the hostess to tell him I am on board, but refrain for fear the name Henderson might make him throw the plane into a nosedive.

One top-class pilot we were fortunate enough to have with us for a while was Les Wright. On his first day on Bullo, Charles introduced him to Bertha, our Beaver De Havilland aircraft. She was sadly overloaded with boxes of meat and Les politely pointed out this fact.

'Now, boy, just get in and fly the thing. Leave everything else up to me.'

Boy, if I had a dollar for every time I heard that 'Leave everything up to me', I would be a multi-millionaire. Being his first day on the job, Les followed orders.

Charles had told him to circle the mission and buzz the store and the store manager would then drive out to the airstrip and unload the cartons of meat. Les did this and flew on to the airstrip, which was about six miles from the store. He lined up the plane and, remembering the heavy load, made a careful touch-down. He stopped the engine, got out of the plane and turned to watch for the store manager. Just then a large spear embedded itself in the closed door of the plane right under his nose. For a few seconds he stared at the spear in disbelief, then as another whistled over, he jumped into the plane, gunned the engine and flew out as fast as overloaded Bertha could manage.

While he was on the two-hour flight back to Bullo from Hooker Creek, the irate store manager got on the phone to Charles wanting to know why the plane buzzed the store and then took off with the meat as he was driving to the airstrip.

When Les arrived back, Charlie was on the airstrip waiting. 'What's your problem, son?'

Les explained what had happened and pointed to the spear still firmly embedded in the door of the plane. To Les's amazement, Charlie said, 'Now, boy, that's nothing to do with us, they're just warring, you should have gone about your business and ignored them.'

'How could I? The plane was in the middle of the war zone. And if that spear had been a foot to the right, it would be sticking through me, not the door!'

'Now, the store manager is upset. You just go back and park the plane down the south end and the spears won't bother you. He's waiting for the meat.'

So Les took off from Bullo, buzzed the store two hours later, landed at the south end of the Hooker Creek strip, unloaded the boxes in record time and jumped into the plane and took off.

He always maintained that after that first day, everything else that happened to him at Bullo seemed ordinary.

In the early days Gus would come to Bullo for Christmas and usually stay for the Christmas week until New Year. The first Christmas he brought with him a beautiful white and gold portable Christmas tree in an old brown suitcase. This beautiful sparkling tree would be assembled in the middle of our bare tin shed. The temperature would be in the high forties with heat waves shimmering across the flat, and yet this small glittering tree would cast its Christmas magic over that harsh and drab Outback setting.

At night we would light candles around it and sit and sing carols. Our abattoir stockmen in those days came from Port Keats, and our first Christmas they amazed me when they sang Ave Maria in Latin, accompanied by guitars.

Each year Gus would arrive by plane with Charles just before Christmas day with the brown suitcase and presents. I don't know who had more fun, Charles and Gus or the children.

The tin shed slowly, very slowly, improved so that the little tree did not look so ridiculously out of place. Despite the children being as careful as they could, each year the tree became a little more worse for wear. Finally it reached the stage where it was allowed to reside at Bullo permanently instead of travelling back and forth to Darwin. But it became quite forlorn and there came a time when a new tree had to be thought of.

The children told their dad there were some real trees in the camp paddock that looked just like fir trees, so he said they would cut one down. There was great excitement as they set forth on the first Christmas tree expedition. Horses, rope, packed lunch, billy for tea. They departed into the wilderness, Charles leading. It was a great adventure and they arrived back very proudly with a rather scraggly tree. But after much cutting and manoeuvring, tying and flower arranging, and lots and lots of streamers and hand-made decorations, it looked, well, festive.

The children thought it was the most beautiful thing they had ever seen and sat staring at it for hours. It was quite tall, about seven or eight feet, so what it lacked in style, it made up for in size. I stood the little gold and white tree under the spreading green limbs and it looked strangely out of place. The big spindly, rambling green tree actually suited our tin shed.

That year Gus could not spend Christmas with us and indeed never did again. Each year the Christmas tree improved in size and appearance to where it now is about twelve feet high and ten feet in width, with decorations that would rival the Rockefeller Center tree.

Over the years the little white and gold tree has been reduced to nothing more than three tattered and almost bare branches. The gold silk on the balls is all fuzzy and broken, the steel branches almost bare of white artificial snow. But to me that little tree will always be special. It brings the memories of the past years flooding back, right from that first year in the bare shed, when it seemed to be the centre of the universe, the only evidence of beauty.

In the long years that followed, the shed became a homestead, the whole valley turned from a vast hostile wilderness into something of beauty. I suppose it is correctly called progress and development, but I would like to still think it was Uncle Gus's little gold and white Christmas tree that spread its magic each year.

'What's this crap?' These words brought me back to the present. One of the boys was picking up my three little branches I had put on the tree when a hand stopped him.

'Don't touch, Mrs Henderson put them there.' He turned to me and said, 'Oh, sorry, I didn't think it was anything special, it looked like rubbish.'

I smiled. I suppose they did look like something you would throw on a rubbish heap and not decorate with red satin bows, but twenty years ago it was a very different story. To me, they were the only touch of beauty in a hostile wilderness, and they will continue to be a part of our every Christmas on Bullo.

CHAPTER 13

❖

1974

The year was 1974. It was a year of many ups and downs, more downs than ups, but by far the most devastating event was the sudden death of my dad.

To receive the message over a two-way radio that your dad, or indeed anyone you love, has died, is the most gut-wrenching feeling. It is as if something just reaches in and pulls all your innards out. I found myself doubled over gasping for breath, the microphone swinging over the side of the desk and and the speaker saying, 'SLI, Sierra Lima India, are you receiving? Over.'

I wandered from the radio room out across the paddock, and found myself next to the creek behind the tin shed. I sat beside the fast-flowing rainwater creek and watched images form in the water.

Poppa's face came to me and I smiled. I had only seen him a few times over the last fourteen years. Since my marriage, you could count the times on two hands. He and Mum had visited us twice in the Philippines, but he had never been to the station, or to America, so apart from a few holidays in Sydney during the first years of the seventies, that was it.

I sat for many hours by the shady creek going back over all the wonderful things that were my father, or as we fondly called him, Poppa.

Aubrey George Whelan Barton was born on the 23rd of February 1896 at 'Walton Cottage', Marlborough Street, Leichhardt. His dad, George Robert Barton, was a civil servant and his mother, Emma May Whelan, was from Turrawan Sheep

Station near Narrabri, New South Wales.

As a young man he was a great athlete and played against the All Blacks at the age of sixteen when at De La Salle. He also played Maher Cup football all through the west of New South Wales.

His dad went into hotels and by the time Poppa had married my mother, they were moving from hotel to hotel in western New South Wales as owners, checking on the general running of each hotel and building trade. Over the years the hotels stretched from Cootamundra in the southwest, to Coffs Harbour in the north. I remember names like Krumbach, Lake Cargelligo, Bungendore, Gunnedah, Coonabarabran, and many more.

Dad was the most eligible bachelor in town when Mum married him and, according to her, every girl in town was after him, except Mum, so naturally she was the one he wanted. Mum had been raised in the normal way ladies were in the twenties. She played the piano, had a lovely trained singing voice, did exquisite needlework, was a good cook, a skilled milliner, and wasn't too bad at sketching. No wonder Poppa wanted her!

Mum said he would stand across the street from her house, chewing gum. This was considered a disgusting habit and Mum didn't want anything to do with him. He would walk next to her on her way to church and chatter all the way. He told her he was a football player and loved boxing. That's why he chewed gum all the time, to strengthen his jaw. Apart from football and boxing he helped his father in their hotel, but the only part of the hotel business he liked was throwing out the rowdy types as he would then have the chance to get himself into a good fight. Mum would run into church very quickly.

But it seems Poppa had made up his mind that this quiet refined talented girl was going to be his. So he just kept walking her to and from church. Mum was Church of England and Poppa was Catholic, so he waited outside the church. He would visit her at home and sit and talk to her in the parlour. Mum said he would bring her a bag of grapes or sometimes chocolates, but would usually eat them all on the way to the house.

He finally proposed, and Mum accepted. They were married

in St Mary's Cathedral on the 11th of January 1922.

The priest told Mum that because she was not Catholic, they could not be married at the main altar. She was also told that all the children had to be raised as Catholics, and that she had to become a Catholic too.

Mum waited patiently until the priest had finished, and then politely told him that she would only be married at the front altar, would not become a Catholic and that all the boys could be Catholic, but all the girls would be Church of England. 'If this is not to your liking, please say so and I will make arrangements for the wedding to take place in my church.'

Poppa was not a churchgoer; he was a great Christian in his everyday life, but not a churchgoer. Mum on the other hand was very religious and attended church regularly. So Poppa left all the arrangements to Mum.

The priest, no doubt realising that he could lose all, including Poppa, agreed to her terms.

The life that followed is a book in itself. Stories of the town running out of water and Mum giving my brother beer when he was thirsty and receiving a letter from the schoolteacher requesting her not to send her child to school smelling of liquor, colourful tales of remittance men who lived permanently in the hotels with their bills paid from England, of floods, bushfires, droughts, of balls in shearing sheds, cross-country horse events, and on and on.

Poppa was a good father, but his life revolved around Mum. The first thing he always said when he walked in the door was, 'Where's Mummy?'

I was thankful for at least one thing, that Mum did not go first. Poppa would have died of a broken heart and I would have lost them both.

'There you are, darling.' Charles sat down and wrapped his arms around me and I cried and cried. That day I really felt his love for me.

We walked back to our tin shed with black menacing clouds spitting lightning and thunder all around the valley. It was an appropriate setting for my mood. It was also the edge of a low depression which moved in swiftly that night. When

Charles checked with flight service the next morning, the front was all along the coast and Darwin airport was closed to all small aircraft. After three days, Charles couldn't stand looking at my misery and I was going to miss Poppa's funeral, so he flew me to Darwin anyway. The weather was so low the only thing Charles could do was fly very low and follow the road. He flew out our road, along the Victoria Highway and turned left at Katherine and up the Stuart Highway. At one stage we were so low he scared a semi driver out of his skin— we were about twenty feet above him as we passed. I looked back to see the truck weaving all over the road. Charles dared not go any higher or we would have been in the clouds and unable to see the highway or the hills. If we lost that white line, we were goners.

I took the jet to Sydney while Charles went to face an inquiry as to why he had landed at a closed airport, and what he was doing in the air, period, as all small aircraft had been grounded.

Mum was like a little girl. She had collapsed. Gone was the strong woman I had known all my life. Poppa's death had devastated her. I was at a loss as to how to handle her. I remembered her solution in a crisis: have a cup of tea.

I opened the curtains and, ignoring her wails of protest, gently sat her up in bed, washed her face and hands with a hot facecloth, put on her robe and led her downstairs.

We had many cups of tea and after hours of crying, reminiscing and laughing at memories, we went to bed exhausted. A week of this got her back on the road to living. Everything was, 'What do you think your dad would do?' After another few weeks of talking through the third person, we were ready to step back into the world again.

I decided to move her out of the two-storey house, into an ocean-side unit. I called an agent and told him what I wanted.

'Do you have a few million to spare?' he asked.

The family told him to do the best he could for a lot less. I left Mum at home and did the rounds with him. Some places I wouldn't even get out of the car.

'You call that waterfront?'

'Lady, if there's water within a mile, that's waterfront.

After three days of saying 'Drive on' the man finally accepted that it was waterfront I wanted. After a few units actually on the waterfront, I said, 'Okay, we're now on the water, but two problems, the rooms are too small, and the price is too big.'

He looked at me for a while and I could see him making a decision. He finally said, 'I think I have just what you want, but there are complications.'

'Let me see it first. If it's what we want, then tell me the complications.'

We stopped in a lovely cul-de-sac and stepped up to an intercom-controlled door. Two out of two. We walked into a carpeted foyer with a winding staircase and two lifts. Four out of four. We went up to the second floor. Five out of five. Mum had to be above the ground so she couldn't be burgled, but not so high that she couldn't run down the stairs in case of fire. We walked into the living room. It was a big room with ocean views from all the windows, even the kitchen had ocean views, in fact, every room had ocean views.

'Okay, so what's the problem?'

'The owner.'

'Oh?'

The unit had been on the market for five years. This was hard to believe, but he told me to believe it.

'My partner and I have given up showing the place, the owner is just so difficult.'

'In what way?'

'Apparently he was one of the foundation members of the body corporate and felt very responsible about who he handed his unit on to. They couldn't have any children, they had to make a lump sum payment to the body corporate and, most difficult of all, they had to pass his personal evaluation.'

'Well, when can I meet him? My mother has no young children, she can pay the full amount of money and, as for his personal evaluation, I can tell you my mother's the biggest snob you could ever meet, apart from being very nice.' I arranged to meet the owner at the apartment in two days' time. I explained that because my mother was still so distressed, I would like to meet him first, and if there was any chance, then I would bring her along.

I was quite nervous when I walked up the stairs two days later. The apartment was perfect for Mum, and I knew I wouldn't find anything else like it, well not in our price bracket. The agent had confirmed that. It all depended on an eccentric old man.

I pressed the bell, took a deep breath and waited. The door opened and a man of about seventy-five stood before me. He was stooped, but had agile, piercing eyes and looked very aggressive.

'What do you want?'

'How do you do, I'm here about the unit. My . . .'

'You're too young.' Slam!

I stood facing the closed door. My only thought was, Wow! I took a deep breath and pressed again. The door opened and he let fly with both barrels.

'I told you already, I'm . . .'

I fired back. 'I am not buying, my mother is, and she is seventy-seven.'

We stood there glaring at each other, breathing fast. I saw a small twinkle in his eye.

'Come in.' He turned abruptly and walked ahead of me.

'Tea?'

'Thank you.'

'Get it over there.' He waved his hand towards the kitchen, the twinkling eyes watching me. I decided to let him win this round. We drank the tea in silence. I wasn't going to put my foot in it now. He broke the silence.

'Who are you?' I gave him a quick outline on Mum. Widow, President of the Red Cross, State Champion Bowler, model citizen and so on.

When I had finished, he said, 'I'll give you an answer in a month.' His eyes were dull. I knew I had lost him.

'Oh, please, I must go home. I live in the Northern Territory and I can't leave before I settle Mum.' On the words 'Northern Territory' the twinkle returned.

'What part of the Territory?' I could tell by the way he said 'Territory', it was in his blood. I was back in the race. I chose my words carefully.

'Oh, not in any town. I live on a cattle station, very remote.' The eyes were young again, looking into the past.

'Anywhere near Auvergne?'

'Why, Auvergne is our next door neighbour over the mountain range. In fact, our station was part of Auvergne until 1959 when a million acres was taken from Auvergne's five million, and called Bullo River. We bought it a few years later, no improvements whatsoever, just an airstrip and a road.'

'What's the road like into Bullo?'

I paused. I don't know whether it was intuition or what, but when he asked that question I detected a subtle change in his expression, and instead of telling him exactly what I thought of our fifty-mile nightmare, I found myself saying, 'What a marvellous example of engineering knowhow. How the engineer ever managed to get a road into that valley is beyond me.'

He sat up very straight, and his chest expanded. My intuition had been spot on.

'I built that road.'

'No!' We spent the rest of the day going over every rock in that road and in a number of other roads as well. His road-building career in the Northern Territory had spanned forty years.

'Tell the agent to send the papers over first thing in the morning and I'll sign them.'

'Thank you very much.'

'Nonsense, have to get you back to your family on the station.' And for the first time he smiled. I raced down the stairs and out of sight before he changed his mind.

After moving Mum into her new home, I decided it was time to get back to the station. All my brothers and my sister lived in Sydney, so I was leaving her in good hands.

My return to the station obviously took Charles by surprise. He had a female there. She had arrived just a few hours ahead of me.

There were no hysterics, I didn't even ask any questions. Losing Poppa and looking after Mum for two months had drained me clean of any emotion. I felt nothing.

They presented me with some stupid story. I just looked at her with contempt—I didn't bother to look at Charles—and moved into Marlee's room. This was now a regular occurrence, so it went unremarked by the children.

I slept in, and Charles came into the room wanting to know why I wasn't cooking breakfast.

'Let your lady friend whip up a few meals.'

'But she's not here to cook.'

I glared at him and he backed out of the room. A few days in the kitchen soon dispelled any fancy ideas she may have had about life with Charlie. She packed her bags and left. I stayed in Marlee's room for a few more weeks.

My birthday was approaching, so to put the 'show back on the road' Charles made an effort to do something special.

The year before he had made a big mistake on my birthday. His gift to me was a beer-making kit!

'A beer-making kit!' I said, horrified. 'Why would you think I'd be interested in a beer-making kit?'

'Well, we are always running out of beer.'

'Charles, we would need a factory, not a kit, to keep up with the amount of beer consumed here! Besides, I hardly touch the stuff, you're the one who drinks it non-stop.'

He didn't reply. I would make it, he would drink it. He couldn't understand why this wasn't acceptable to me.

However I did manage to get my revenge, a few months later at Christmas. Of course I never made any beer, but the kit remained in my mind.

He opened his gift on Christmas morning.

'What on earth is this?' he said, as yards of black lace and silk tumbled from the box.

'It's a black negligee, don't you like it?'

'Don't be ridiculous, I wouldn't wear that!'

'Oh good, then I'll have it.'

He smiled. 'Touché.'

So this time he had to come up with a winner, and he did.

193

The children had baked a cake and with great ceremony they lit the candles and sang happy birthday, as I blew them out. Then a large carton was placed in front of me. I opened the top and it was full of money, all scrunched up.

'Is it all money?' I asked in disbelief.

'Yes,' said Charles smugly.

It was one thousand dollars in one-dollar bills. It took hours to count it, but it was great fun. He was forgiven for the beer-making kit, but only the beer-making kit!

At the end of that year we all went to Darwin for a few days to do the Christmas shopping. Usually Charles did it all by himself, so it was a special treat for the children. We stayed with Gus at Fannie Bay.

The shopping for the presents and food all done, we started packing up our mountain of purchases ready to take to the plane early the next morning. However, when we got out to the airport, radio trouble. So we unpacked all the perishables and went back to Fannie Bay while Charles looked for a man to repair the radio. It was Christmas Eve, and as the hours passed, we discussed the option of spending Christmas with Gus. However, I was tired and wanted to get back to the station and also, we had Christmas dinner and all the presents for the people back there.

So at around two-thirty p.m. we took off, about twelve hours ahead of Cyclone Tracy. We were flying southwest and the weather deteriorated as we moved along the coastline. It reminded me of typhoon weather in the Philippines.

By the time we reached the Victoria River, Charles was flying at around forty feet. We flew up the river, low over the water and did a right turn into the Bullo Valley. It was raining as we landed. Grey-black clouds swirled around over the hills, then slowly descended and blocked out the world. It stayed that way for about two weeks. A few times the sun peeped through, but not often.

We found out on Christmas morning that Cyclone Tracy had hit Darwin during the night and that Darwin had been virtually destroyed. Charles tried to contact Gus and other friends, but our communication was still by radio, and this was difficult at the best of times, let alone with Darwin in chaos.

Early on Boxing Day Charles flew into Kununurra to try and contact Gus. While in the air, he was contacted by flight service and asked if he would fly to Darwin and start aerial spraying for disease control. Of course Charles wanted to go straight to the rescue. He returned to Bullo and I packed the plane full of food, water, clothes and bedding. According to the reports, there was nothing in Darwin—there had been no power or water since Christmas night, and everything in refrigeration was now rotten. After receiving strict instructions from me about how he was not to drink the water, and only to eat tinned food and so on, he took off for Darwin. I had no idea when I would see him again.

While he was flying from Bullo to Darwin, a two-hour trip in our dear old Beaver, Darwin was declared in a state of emergency and suddenly new laws were in force. The first of these was that Darwin was closed to all air traffic except military.

When Charles finally reached Darwin and called in, he was told to go away. Darwin was now a restricted area. Charles was furious but no amount of explaining could convince the control tower of his authorised mission. So, needing fuel, and being Charles, he just landed and was promptly arrested.

Eventually the mess was sorted out and Charles was given a pass, so he went to find Gus. The house was almost gone. The front bedroom on the second floor no longer existed and the one remaining wall of the second bedroom was leaning dangerously. The roof was gone. The front wall of the living room had blown in, the laundry and bathroom downstairs were still standing, but all the plants were gone and the trees that remained had no leaves on them. However Gus was okay, as were other family members and friends.

Charles arrived back at Bullo with a plane full of pets. People were being moved out of Darwin in their hundreds, and no provision had been made for all the pets. Charles never described the trip back, but I am sure it was interesting. He had canaries, cats, dogs, budgerigars . . . When we opened the doors of the plane chaos reigned. Charles just walked away with his hands in the air.

Months later I went to Darwin with Charles and, even after all that time, the place still had a look of devastation. Cleaning up was in progress, hotels were in operation, some shops were open and leaves were appearing on some of the trees, but there was a long way to go.

Darwin was never really the same again. Out of the old Darwin rose a new Darwin, with many more people. The unsophisticated town we had known was gradually replaced by a city.

CHAPTER 14

❖

1975-1980

According to our old telegram book, on the 25th of February 1975, Wyndham Radio, the Royal Flying Doctors' base, was closed and all the traffic it had normally handled was now to be handled by Derby. Because we were in the Northern Territory, we were directed to Darwin, and so our old call sign of S.O.V., which had been our call sign since 1963, was laid to rest. I cannot remember how many times I screamed 'Sierra Oscar Victor' into that antiquated Treager Radio amidst crackle and static.

In the telegram book is written: 'End of S.O.V. and Wyndham Radio'. Just one line, written by one of the staff helping me in the office at that time. She did not know of the long months during the wet season when it was our only link with the outside world. As the rains increased and we became isolated in our own little world, Radio Wyndham would reach in daily, and assure us the world was still there.

Many times the operators talked people through a medical emergency until the plane arrived with a doctor, or spoke to the part of the family in the civilised world on our behalf during a family problem or crisis. I am sure anyone who lived in this area in the fifties, sixties or seventies, and who relied on Radio Wyndham as their lifeline, carries Radio Wyndham in a little corner of their heart.

The next page of the telegram book reads:

27/2/75
VJY Darwin—New radio call sign
S.L.I. 'Sierra Lima India'

We were in the big league now. No more chatting and swapping cooking recipes. VJY covered a big area, with a big switchboard and many operators. Over the years they all became friends and were as essential to our lifestyle as Wyndham Radio.

With VJY Darwin came a new radio. Our old Treager did not have the strength to reach 200 miles to Darwin, so it was also 'laid to rest' and in its place we purchased a sleek small Codan two-way radio with a press-button microphone. On our old Treager, you flipped a switch and shouted at the middle of the machine. With the two-way radio, we could hear the news at 6.45 each morning as it was broadcast by VJY. This brought us up-to-date with the news of the world on a twenty-four hour basis. Until then, we had relied on a twice-monthly delivery of *Newsweek* magazine by mail plane. Of course during the rainy season it was back to *Newsweek* as we couldn't hear a thing.

The next invention that came our way was a radio telephone. Now we were in the super league. To have a private conversation on a phone and a reply then and there, instead of waiting days for a telegram, was magical. However there was a catch. We had to work through the switchboard in Darwin, and to get an operator it was not unusual to have to wait hours for a free line.

As the network expanded, it was decided to regulate calls. We could call in on the hour to book calls, then the operators would spend the rest of the hour handling incoming calls and calling our booked calls. The operators did a sterling job but there were never enough lines.

Of course Charles did not think the system applied to him. He looked upon the operators as his personal assistants and would call in and book twenty or thirty calls at a time, to be put through at specific times during the day. When the operator refused, he would scream, 'Put on your supervisor!' and when the supervisor refused, he would scream, 'Put on your supervisor!' and so on, until one day he was speaking to a Managing Director for Telecom in Melbourne. There was a long conversation, a lot of shouting by Charles, but the next day, he was back to square one, speaking to the operator.

198

Charles always considered himself 'Admiral of the fleet' not mere 'Captain of the ship', and until we moved to Bullo he had never answered a phone—he had always had a secretary to screen the calls, and if he didn't want to talk he would dictate a message for her to pass on. When we moved to the Outback Charles tried to maintain this system, so along with the titles of cook, schoolteacher and so on, I acquired that of substitute secretary.

The office was a good twenty-five-yard dash from the kitchen and schoolroom where I would be busy cooking or teaching. The phone had an amplifier on the ring tone, so it made quite a loud noise. I would run to answer it only to find Charles sitting right next to it, reading a book.

'Why in heaven's name didn't you answer the phone? I had to run all this way!'

'I mightn't want to speak to them,' he would calmly reply.

'Well I *know* I don't, it's probably someone asking for money.'

I would answer the phone, ask who was calling and hand him the phone. If he didn't want to speak, he would say, 'Tell them this', or 'Tell them that'. I would listen to the person, then ask them to wait, tell Charles what they said, listen to Charles's reply, and so on.

One particularly frenetic day when nothing was going right and the phone was ringing constantly, I decided I'd had enough. Charlie was sitting at the phone desk reading his pirate story and drinking a beer. The phone rang for the twentieth time and I sprinted in to answer it.

'Hello . . . No sorry, he's not here.' I put the phone down and started to walk out of the room.

'Who was that for?'

'You.'

'Me? You said I wasn't here!'

'Did I? I wonder why I'd do a thing like that.'

'Who was it?' he shouted as I disappeared in the direction of the kitchen.

'Gus,' I replied.

I stopped just out of sight and listened.

'Hello operator, get me Gus.' There was a pause and then he said, 'Hello, Gus, just came in from the yards. Sara said you'd called.'

I walked back to the kitchen with a smile on my face. Half an hour later when the phone rang, Charles called, 'I'll get it, Darling.'

After sitting at the phone desk most of the morning, he would then move into the bedroom and recline on the bed for the afternoon. For this effort he would require constant replenishment of cold beer, cheese and crackers. He would bellow orders all the way to the kitchen, usually to the children, and they would spend their time running backwards and forwards doing his bidding. Eventually I told him that this room service was taking up too much schooltime, and he would just have to walk to the kitchen and do it himself. He then had the bright idea that if Dick could set up a buzzer system, it would save time, and he wouldn't have to shout.

A Machiavellian scheme began to form in my mind. For Father's Day we gave him a buzzer next to his bed. He was overjoyed. What we didn't tell him was that Uncle Dick hadn't wired it!

The first day he pressed the buzzer and patiently waited. Finally, when no one appeared, he came to the kitchen to tell us he was buzzing. Hadn't we heard? We all looked at him wide-eyed. He then told us to stand by and he would test the buzzer.

'Sure, but since you're here now, why don't you make your own snack and take it with you.'

It didn't take him long to realise he was being duped, and the next week found him quietly preparing his own snacks.

A few days later, when we were having a Sunday sleep-in, Charlie said, 'I'd like breakfast in bed.'

'Press the buzzer, you never know your luck.' I couldn't keep the smile off my face.

By late 1975 it had become evident that Charles was suffering from some kind of health problem. He was definitely not his usual robust self. We went to Darwin to see a doctor. I say 'we' because Charles was absolutely convinced that there was nothing wrong with him, and if I had not taken him there in person, he would not have gone at all.

We were finally told that a virus had lodged in his lungs, and so he embarked on the endless road of pill-taking. I am sure that if, at that point, he had stopped drinking and done some exercise, it could have been beaten. But he continued to drink, he gained a tremendous amount of weight and he refused to do any physical exercise at all. He later had two close bouts of viral pneumonia and from then on his health steadily deteriorated.

In early 1976 a friend of a friend arrived at Bullo on holidays and just happened to be a doctor. He examined Charles and said he would like to do further tests, could he come to Sydney? He showed me how to drain the lungs so that Charles didn't exhaust himself coughing up the muck. He also told Charles lots of things he could do for himself, but apart from letting me pound his back and ribs four or five times a day to loosen all the phlegm, he would do nothing.

We finally went to Sydney the next year. Even Charles had now realised it was not something to be taken lightly. The coughing would not stop, hours in the morning and again at sunset—sometimes he would cough until he dropped.

We made an appointment with Bill Foulsham, the doctor who had visited us at Bullo. Bill Foulsham was a wonderful person and doctor.

We arrived at his surgery and after catching up on events since we had last seen him, he examined Charles and arranged for the many tests he wished to carry out. He then turned to me.

'I want to examine you,' he said.

'Oh, I'm alright, just tired.'

'I think you're more than tired.'

'No, no, just overworked. Anyway, I can't afford to get sick, and that's that.'

'Well you are, nothing about "getting", you're there.'

He now had me scared. I really couldn't be sick. Debts were increasing by the day and it was only the fact that there was a cash flow which stopped the bank from finishing us off.

I suppose we all tend to think we are indispensable, and in those days I was no different. I was about to find out that life goes on, regardless.

'How long have you been feeling tired?' the doctor asked.

'Oh gosh, I suppose when I stop and think about it, years. Ever since we've been on the station.'

'Any other symptoms?'

'Like what?'

'Temperatures? Fevers?'

I sat and thought. It no doubt would seem strange to some people that I had to actually stop and think if I had been sick, but our days on the station were so full you didn't have time to think, and when you did, you were so tired you only wanted to sleep.

'Well, this past year I've been getting fevers. I'm always tired when I get up. I can live with that, but some days around mid-morning I'm so tired my limbs just refuse to move. It's been so bad of late that I have to make sure lunch is ready the day before, because when these attacks happen I sometimes fall asleep for hours. The children love it. They wait for me to fall asleep and then sneak out of the schoolroom.'

Dr Bill smiled, 'You know you can't keep up this pace. Your body is already telling you that.'

'Oh, I'm young, I'll be alright.'

'You're not alright, and if the tests confirm my diagnosis, you'll have to have an operation. How old was your mother when she had her gall bladder out?'

'Oh, I guess about thirty-one.'

'Well, you lasted longer. Now let's not go on about this. When you get your first attack you'll be in here begging to have the operation. I've never yet had to convince a patient to have their gall bladder out, after the first attack that is. I want you to have an x-ray, and that will give us the answer.'

The x-rays were done and I went back to Dr Bill's surgery to hear the verdict. The gall bladder was a mess. He said he was surprised it was still together—it was literally pumping

202

poison into my body. He was amazed I was still walking around.

I had to have the operation as soon as possible. I said maybe at the end of the year. Bill looked very stern and said I was not listening. If I had a first attack and was not close to a hospital and surgeon, I would die in a matter of hours. I could not go back to the station.

The surgeon Bill wanted was number one on gall bladders, but he was overseas lecturing, so I had to wait. Charles went back to the station and I spent four blissful weeks in Sydney doing exactly what I liked. Then I had the operation and it was not so blissful. I was quite sure I would never raise my arms above my head again. For weeks I walked around holding my hands over the scar, quite sure if I removed them, everything inside me would fall out. It was a horrible sensation.

After another few months, I was declared fit enough to face the wilderness again. Charles came to Sydney to take me home. It was our wedding anniversary so he arranged for us to have dinner at the Chelsea Restaurant, the restaurant we had gone to on our first date.

Charles always spoke in a loud commanding voice, as if he were issuing orders from the bridge, so when he lowered his voice to say something intimate, only the surrounding room could hear.

During dinner he was sharing various personal incidents from our married life with the rest of the restaurant, when I looked across the room and saw Alfred Hitchcock.

'Isn't that Alfred Hitchcock over there?'

In his usual booming whisper, Charles asked, 'Who is Alfred Hitchcock?'

Mr Hitchcock stood up, turned towards Charles and bowed.

'I am, sir,' he said, then sat down and completely ignored us.

As we were leaving, a couple at a table near the door congratulated us on our wedding anniversary.

'I wonder who told them it was our anniversary,' Charles commented when we were outside.

He was serious.

I had expected a mess, but what greeted me on my return to the station almost made me want to end it all. Months of mail piled up, dirt and mess everywhere, no schoolwork done. As far as I could see, the only thing they had done regularly was eat—the state of the kitchen testified to this.

Just as well I had some extra energy after my rest in Sydney, because it was needed. It took me months to get the house, office and school into running order again.

Charles was so pleased I was home, he actually gave me a compliment. He said he had needed three girls to get through my workload. Of course now that I was back, they could go. The loving, caring Charles who had come to Sydney to wine and dine me disappeared somewhere along the way.

To top it all off, I found out that he had taken advantage of my absence to entertain a few of his women friends. It saddened me that he would behave in this way in our home, and in front of the children. But when I took him to task, I was told in no uncertain terms that it was not my place to criticise. I realised then that he really didn't care what I thought or felt. I also realised, to my surprise, that I didn't care quite as much as I once would have. I think my love for him was finally starting to die.

The long stay in Sydney had also brought something else home to me. For years now, I had worked long and hard to save money being spent on extra wages, but no matter how long or how hard I worked, Charles would always find extra work for me. So I slowed down. The operation helped in this— it was a good six months before I was really strong again and the doctor had told me not to lift anything heavy during that time. But after that period, I just continued to require help. To add to the continuous line of so-called cooks, I now had a domestic and someone to help in the office. Of course, Charles complained but I stood firm.

In the latter part of 1976, Charles arrived home one day and said, 'Gus and I are going to buy Montejinni Station.'

And they did. Charles, the girls and I moved to the station to live for the next few months. The plan was to move as many meatworks cattle as possible off the station before the wet season. They had bought the property for a very good price but, as usual, money was tight and as much as possible had to be made before the wet started, as that represented six months of no income.

We mustered cattle non-stop for weeks. By October, which was usually the end of the cattle season, the weather was very hot so we mustered the cattle at sunrise, and then put them in large holding areas near the yards during the heat of the day.

The yards were made of steel and during the day the heat off the rails could be felt from a distance of three feet, so the cattle could not be yarded until just before sunset. We would draft until it was dark and then load by headlights. The loaded trucks would be away around midnight and it would all start again at four a.m.

Montejinni had not been mustered for around three years and cattle were virtually leaning up against trees. For us it was an amazing sight. On Bullo, if we had a muster all day and ended up with four hundred in the yards, it was cause for celebration. On Montejinni, after the helicopter had mustered for two hours, there were two thousand in the yards with cattle still streaming down the wings and nowhere to go. Of course at that time we had about 5000 head on Bullo and Montejinni was running 20 to 25,000 head.

Katherine meatworks agreed to stay open past the usual closing date as long as Montejinni could supply enough cattle to get up a full day's production. This was done well into November.

We moved back to Bullo for Christmas and the mountain of problems that had accumulated there while we were at Montejinni. Christmas was the only bright spot in a troublesome year. The following year saw the prospect of a recovery in the price of cattle, but not much, just enough to make you hold on by your fingernails hoping you would manage a toe hold.

Charles and Gus continued to argue, if not face to face, then over the radio, mostly over Montejinni, but I am sure

205

if it had not been Montejinni, it would have been something else. They seemed very at home arguing. They even argued about how much time each one was allowed to argue. The radio telephone was really a private line two-way radio in as much as you had to release a button in order to hear the other person. Gus in Darwin, on a normal phone, could not interrupt Charles until Charles released the button. The phone calls were limited to twelve minutes because of the overload on the system and it was not unusual for them to spend the entire twelve minutes arguing over how much time each one could have, only to have the operator say, 'Twelve minutes are up, please finish.'

I came into the office one day to find Charles holding the phone in one hand and a timer in the other. The timer was ringing furiously and Charles was saying, 'Gus, I know my time is up, but just let me make this point.' Click. 'Gus?' Click. 'Are you there, Gus?' Click.

He looked up at me. 'Now why do you suppose he hung up?'

'Maybe he doesn't like you going into his time.'

'Bloody hell! Now it will take me ten minutes to get him back and I'll forget what I was saying. Don't talk, don't talk while I write it down.'

As I walked away, I could hear him saying, 'Operator, I was talking to Gus and the line was disconnected.' Pause. 'No, no, he wouldn't do that. It's most important we finish the conversation.' Pause. 'I told you, he wouldn't hang up!'

I know what the operator was thinking, the same as me, 'Like bloody hell he wouldn't!'

Around this time they bought a ten-thousand-acre irrigated farm complex with its own dam called Kingston Rest. It had been built by an American and it was not a piece-by-piece lean-to affair as most of the North was in those days. It was a well-built, first-class project. With this purchase, the Victoria Project was starting to take shape. They had Bullo River, Spirit Hill, Montejinni for growing cattle and Kingston Rest for finishing and fattening. Montejinni Abattoir for processing was on the drawing board, just waiting for approval.

206

So all they needed now were the ships to move the meat to the Far East. They had kept a finger on the pulse of the shipping market and were just waiting for the right moment. It never came.

❖

CHAPTER 15

1980-1981

By 1980 cattle prices were back to the price of seven years before, or a bit higher. We had survived, but back loans and interest had been mounting and our debt was staggering.

The best thing to happen in those seven miserable years ' was that we closed the abattoir. I know having the abattoir made it possible for us to survive during the bad years, but it was one of the happiest days of my life when we closed those doors. We were now back to just a muster camp and when the rainy season started, we had our wonderful quiet period. Not the magic of the first wet—too much water under the bridge for that, and of course there was a lot to do, schoolwork, office work and so on—but we would be down to just a few people and that was bliss.

With the abattoir closed and the meat not flying out in kilo packs, we were faced with the old system or the normal system of moving the cattle out in trucks. There was only one problem, our road. It meandered over twenty miles of rock, then thirty miles of sand and bulldust. No trucker in his right mind would contemplate putting one wheel off the highway onto the dreaded Bullo River road.

So began our long asociation with the Department of Roads in the Northern Territory. I am sure they have a whole filing cabinet on the 'Bullo River Road', and of course on Charlie. If he had carried out even half the threats he screamed at those unfortunate people over the years, most of the North would have been eliminated.

Despite Charles, our road did slowly improve with the years, but in the meantime we still had to get the cattle to the highway. Charles's solution was simple.

'We'll walk the cattle to the highway,' he said, something we did before the opening of the abattoir. Of course it was simple for him, he only had to say it, but it was up to the girls and the Aboriginal stockmen to achieve it.

In those days our cattle were very wild and to walk them fifty miles through trees and over rocks and mountains was no mean feat. I told Charles I would not let the girls go on the road for a week by themselves with the stockmen. He said he couldn't go, so of course I went.

It took four to five days to walk the cattle to the highway. On our first journey, Charles arranged for us to walk out meatworks cattle and bring in breeders and some breeding bulls.

By chance I saw Charles's plan for the operation:

'Walk 350 m/w [meat workers] to highway, meet trucks, unload breeders, load m/w, walk back 400 breeders.'

Two lines. It took about twenty hours a day of everyone's time for ten days to achieve this small notation in his notebook. It entailed rodeo bucking, mad charging steers, mad charging cows, mad charging stockmen and a mad cook. At one stage, everyone had diarrhoea from the cook's atrocious cooking, and trying to keep a herd of wild cattle together with the entire stockcamp going bush every five minutes was quite an achievement. Somehow we blundered through and arrived at the yards. The small feat of unloading the cows off the trucks, holding them and loading the steers onto the trucks saw another rodeo of cows and steers racing around the flat.

The big boss, Charlie, then arrived to make sure everything was going according to his plan. His timing was perfect. He landed the plane on the road that is the Victoria Highway and taxied over to the yard just after we had settled the cattle down.

The plan now was to let the cows rest in the yards for the remainder of the day and then leave early in the morning to get them across the Auvergne flat and up our road and over the pass into Bullo before the sun was up. We didn't want to walk them over the rocks during the heat of the day.

209

But before we could settle down to the first peaceful full night's sleep in four days, we had to see Charles off. This meant we had to block off half a mile of the Victoria Highway so he could use it as a runway for take off.

Two of us went and stopped a few cars at one end. The people got out with their cameras and asked if we were crossing cattle.

I told them not right now, a plane was taking off. They looked down the road and saw the Beaver barrelling towards them. Letting out a yelp, they headed for the bush as Charlie roared overhead.

Early the next morning we started back with our mob of cows under a full moon across the Auvergne flat. For ten miles there was not even a bump, then it was hundreds of feet almost straight up on a two-wheel donkey track carved into the side of a sandstone cliff. This was a new mob just on the road, so there was a lot of mooing and battling for position.

Cattle are very methodical animals and if anything seems out of place, even in the slightest, they all stop and stare. The steers were bad enough, but the cows were hilarious. We had four hundred of the most inquisitive sticky-beaks on four legs. If one of the riders even changed position, they became suspicious. I was the worst rider, so I was the lead. The second morning I changed my shirt and they would not follow.

It was one of the Aboriginals who told me about the different shirt. 'Them got a picture of you, Missus, if you change you clothes, 'em don't know ya!'

Anything to keep the peace and get the cows home, so I washed the shirt each night and wore it all the way. It was fit for the ragbag when we finally made it home, but 'lead cow' was happy and faithfully followed the back of my shirt for fifty miles.

Sometimes she would walk beside me and I would chat to her or sing. She would look up at me with those warm chocolate-brown eyes as if she understood every word I said. That first hundred miles of droving developed my love for cattle and for cattle droving. We walked cattle for about four to five years before the first cattle truck ventured down our

210

road. I couldn't go on every drove, but I still managed quite a few in the early years.

Around this time we had with us a delightful character called Diesel Don. Charles christened him this because he worked in the workshop, and also because we already had two Dons. Don was Yugoslav, a marvellous chess player, very intelligent and thoughtful, not a bad mechanic's assistant, and a very willing worker. His one big problem was that he could not speak English very well. In fact, it would be safe to say that he could not speak English at all.

One day Charles was complaining to Uncle Dick our mechanic that Don could never understand his instructions. Dick said he never had any trouble explaining to Don what he wanted done. He withdrew this statement the very next day.

Because Charles had put our fuel order in too late we were running out of fuel for the generators, so Dick was syphoning diesel out of tractors, Toyotas, water pumps, anything he could find. He was down to a quarter of a forty-four gallon drum when he remembered that there was a drum of diesel at the six-mile muster campsite. He decided to dispatch Diesel Don to get it.

'Don.'

'Eh?'

'You go six-mile.' Pause. 'Okay?'

The less words you used with Don, the better.

'Six-mile, okay.'

'Good. Six-mile muster camp.' Repetition was also important.

'Muster camp, okay.'

'Good, six-mile muster camp, gate.'

'Gate?'

Dick knew he had hit a snag. He walked Don over to the gate nearby. 'Gate,' he repeated, patting the gate.

'Ah, door.'

'Okay, okay, the bloody door at six-mile!'

'No, is gate, yes?'

'I don't care what you bloody call it!'

'Call gate,' said Don, in very definite tones.
'Go gate, next to gate, drum of diesel, okay?'
'Okay, you say so.'
'Yes, I say so. Bring here.'
'Here?'
'Yes, here!' Dick was now losing his temper.
'Okay, okay, bring here.'
Dick went back to the workshop. After some time Don finally returned.
'Where I put?'
'Where do you bloody well think? In the generator shed.'
'Not here?'
'No, what good is it here? In the bloody generator shed!'
'Okay, put generator shed.'
Don walked off muttering to himself and shaking his head. Some time later, when Dick went to the generator shed, instead of a drum of diesel, he found the six-mile gate!

Another time it was Charles's turn. I came into the kitchen just as Charles was giving Don instructions to go and pick up Marlee at the gate a few miles past the twenty-two-mile camp. When he had finished, I told him Don would not have understood and would go to twenty-two-mile camp. Charles said Don understood perfectly and I was not to say anything or it would confuse him. So Don departed. This was at three o'clock in the afternoon. At nine o'clock that night, and two trips later, Marlee was still sitting at the gate a few miles past the twenty-two-mile camp.

By now Don was so upset he was lapsing into Yugoslav. He was worried about Marlee sitting out on the road, and he could not get across to Charlie that 'Cap-a-tan' was not where he said she was. 'Cap-a-tan' was his name for Marlee—he would salute her whenever she asked him to do something and say, 'Yes Cap-a-tan!'

'I drive twenty-two-mile, no Cap-a-tan. I stand on hill and I go "cooeeii" this way, and "cooeeii" that way.' This was all done with actions including standing on the breakfast stools which represented the hills and the full volume of his voice to show how far the sound had travelled. 'No Cap-a-tan! I climb next hill, I go cooeeii this way . . .' We couldn't have stopped him even if we'd tried.

I was thoroughly enjoying this exchange. Charles was amazed, he had never seen Don angry and shouting.

'Don.' He paused and looked at me. I took a sheet of paper, drew a line and said, 'Road.' I put an 'X' and said, 'Twenty-two-mile camp.' I drew the line past the 'X' representing twenty-two-mile camp, and put a gate across the line. I put another 'X' and said, 'Cap-a-tan.' His eyes lit up and a big smile came over his face.

'I here.' He pointed to the twenty-two-mile 'X'. 'Cap-a-tan, here.' He pointed to the second 'X'.

He then launched into rapid Yugoslav—I think he was telling Charles what he thought of his directions. He finally lapsed back into his version of English.

'Missus tell good. Now I go get Cap-a-tan!'

Marlee arrived home with Don at eleven-thirty p.m. Apparently she had got the whole routine all the way home, including the 'cooeeiis'.

Diesel Don was with us the last time we took cattle out to the road before the truck era. On this occasion we again walked steers out, and cows in. Charles was sick with pneumonia and, as it was late in the season, most of the stockcamp had gone. So we were down to the girls, two Aboriginal stockmen, myself and Diesel Don following up in the Toyota.

It was early December so we had to walk the cattle in the very early morning and rest them in the shade for the hot part of the day. On the way back to Bullo the cattle were difficult—the last thing they wanted to do was walk fifty miles. I had been told by the 'old timers' that cattle always prefer to walk in a northerly direction. However, I think this particular mob of cattle must have missed the geography lesson on north, because although we were travelling in a northerly direction, it was like trying to push jelly through a keyhole. They just kept spilling out at the sides. The only time they behaved was going up the road over the pass into Bullo. They had no choice— it was up the road or over the side—so they marched like little soldiers.

I was lead again, due to my lack of riding skills and most of the time that was it, just the cattle and me. The poor little girls and two Aboriginal stockmen were constantly up mountains and down dales, chasing the bolters and bringing them back to the mob. The cattle hated walking over the rocky country, and they performed the whole twenty miles. Then when we reached the grass country, we couldn't move them at all— all they wanted to do was graze. All this had put us two days behind schedule.

About fifteen miles in from our front gate, the road crossed the Bullo River. Marlee told me that, as lead, I had to keep them from rushing the water. We had to stop them drinking water in the heat of the day or they would not be able to walk long distances. The plan was to keep the mob tight and get them across the water as fast as possible before they could drink too much. That was the plan.

About half a mile away the cattle smelt the water. They became noticeably restless and started to increase the pace. At that point the road was a cut-away along the side of a hill, with a steep drop on one side and a rock face on the other. The cattle were strung out quite a way, with the girls and stockmen right back at the tail.

I held them back as long as possible. I kept weaving back and forth across the road in front of them; however, slowly but surely the pace increased. I turned and shouted, hoping it would balk them, but they ignored me. I stayed just ahead of them until the last hundred yards. At that point, you round a bend in the road at a high spot and can see the river running along quietly at your feet.

My horse was also very thirsty, and, completely ignoring my protests, suddenly took off at flat speed. So, horse, cattle and dust barrelled towards the quiet waters of Bullo Crossing. Somewhere in the midst of all this dust and commotion, I was holding on for dear life. Horns, hair, tails and hooves went flying past me at an alarming rate. Then, without warning, I was airborne. My horse had reached the river's edge and slammed on the brakes to lower his head and drink. I was deposited plunk in the water. I came up spurting water, with cattle milling all around me.

'Are you alright, Mummy?' I looked up into the concerned faces of the girls and the stockmen on horses. Diesel Don was standing with them, hat in hand, shaking his head and rolling his eyes.

'Well, I think so. I haven't tried to move yet.' With wild cattle starting to sniff my hair, I thought it might be a good idea to try.

By the time the cattle were out of the river and under control again, they had all consumed far too much water to travel. We had to rest them for most of the afternoon and, as a result, had to walk well into the night to reach our next yarding. We yarded them at around ten p.m. by the light of the moon.

Diesel Don had gone on ahead to set up the camp. He had a lovely campfire and a nice hot cup of tea waiting. However, the two days' delay on the road had caused him a few problems with the food. He was running out, and what he had left meatwise was off. So he marinated the steak in, well, I don't know what, and then cooked it on the steel plate. It was a sight to see, but it tasted worse. I couldn't even swallow it and threw it in the bushes mouthful by mouthful when he wasn't looking. He would ask after each mouthful, 'How Missus like?'

After dinner we all settled down for a short night's sleep. We woke at 4 a.m. to the sound of the Toyota returning from somewhere and the smell of breakfast and coffee simmering on the side of the campfire. I asked if anyone knew where Don had been. No one did.

The Toyota, like most vehicles on the place, should have been in the rubbish dump. It was held together with baling wire and glue. Whenever Dick, our mechanic, asked for any spare parts, Charles would go into such a tirade that Dick found it easier to improvise than ask. He had bypassed the starter motor in the Toyota and, although the vehicle worked alright, it had to be roll-started each morning. This had been no problem through the twenty miles of hills, but now we were on the flat it was presenting big problems. So Don had driven to a hill, parked, walked back to the camp to cook dinner, then walked back to the vehicle in the morning and brought it back to camp. He had walked ten miles during the night.

By the end of the return journey, my poor old gammy leg was really playing up. The extra days were just too much for it. After four hours in the saddle it would be numb and by the end of the day I could not dismount as I could not stand on my left leg to swing out of the saddle. My dear old horse would patiently stand there while I wriggled and squirmed until I could slide down and put both feet on the ground together. The last day, even that wasn't enough. The leg just collapsed and I ended up underneath my horse. He didn't move, just turned his head around and sniffed my head to see if I was alright. Having satisfied himself of this, he stood there, resting one leg, waiting for me to get the saddle off so he could have his rest. I crawled out and removed the saddle, washed him down, gave him a Weet-Bix, his favourite, and he trotted off to join his mates.

We had ten miles to go—I kept saying to myself over and over, 'Nearly there'. My whole side was aching and I hadn't felt my leg since mid-morning. The girls realised I was having trouble and at lunchtime, they sent one of the stockmen ahead to get Charles to come out and meet me. They knew I wouldn't give in and go home with Diesel Don, so they correctly decided to send for Daddy.

As we approached the four-mile gate, we saw the other Toyota waiting by the side of the road with the lights off. I had to admit I was finished. The cattle slowed as Charles got out of one door with a bottle of champagne, cheese and crackers, and Uncle Dick the other side with a bunch of wild flowers. They clapped. I was near tears as Charles gently eased me down from my patient horse and helped me to the Toyota. It was one of those moments that Charles was a master at creating.

'Don't make all this fuss over me. The children and the boys did all the hard work, I was just there.'

'But they do it every day, it's nothing for them.'

'True, but they still like to be appreciated and told, and they really did a marvellous job.

216

He paused. 'You're right.'

He went back and turned his charm on the children. They glowed. He gave them each a sip of champagne, said 'Well done', to the stockmen and shook Diesel Don's hand and congratulated him on bringing the whole operation home safely. Don didn't understand a word of Charles's elaborate speech, but the smile and handshake said it all.

The first cattle roadtrain into Bullo was a big step. It held none of the magic of droving, but it only took four hours to get the cattle to the front gate, not four days. I listened in silence to the driver's complaints.

'Four bloody hours to get over that flaming road!'

We loaded the cattle and listened as the roar of the big engine going through its paces filled the valley. The driver slowly worked up through the gears and we watched the cattle adjust their stance with each gear change until they disappeared in a cloud of bulldust.

'Well, that's progress for you!' stated Charlie.

'Is it?' I couldn't help feeling sad that the droving days were over.

CHAPTER 16

❖

Uncle Dick

I think it is time I told you a bit about this 'Uncle Dick' character who keeps popping up. Actually, to do him justice, I would need a whole book, but I will just have to settle for a chapter.

Uncle Dick is a salt of the earth, fair dinkum, hard-drinking Aussie battler. Talented in many trades and certified in more than a few, he is also well-read and polite, the Fred Astaire of the Outback, and now, in his later years, a wise philosopher on the subject of the roads in life you should not take. I know this for a fact, because there are very few roads that Uncle Dick has not taken.

I know he sounds too good to be true, but Uncle Dick was not perfect—he had the curse of the demon drink as the levelling factor. And oh boy, in the early years did that demon level.

Dick came into our lives in 1973. We were all in Darwin staying with Gus at his house in Fannie Bay. One of Charles's sons, Fraser, was soon to leave for America but his father, in his usual brash way, told him before he could leave he had to find a mechanic for the station.

Charles, Gus and I were sitting on the patio talking and watching the sun set when a taxi stopped in front of the house. Two people emerged, one of whom we recognised as Fraser. After a lot of stumbling and mumbling, they arrived on the patio and Fraser introduced us to Richard Peter Wicks.

He was well and truly under the weather but that didn't seem to bother anyone but me. He sat down on a stool and

Charles asked him about his experience. He certainly seemed to have the knowledge required for a wide field of station work. He was neatly dressed and quietly spoken—he seemed to be exactly what we needed. Except for one thing. I took Charles inside the house.

'What about his condition?'

'Well, no cook or mechanic in the North is going to be a teetotaller. You just have to put up with it.'

I went back and sat down. Gus was telling a story about one of the old characters of the North and Uncle Dick leant back in his chair laughing. Only it wasn't a chair, and he went 'head over turkey' backwards. His feet came up under the coffee table sending glass, flowers and peanuts everywhere. Charles roared with laughter, Fraser just stared and Gus carefully picked up all the peanuts.

When everything was back in order, they all sat down and the questioning and yarning continued while they munched on the recycled peanuts. But the peanuts were not to escape that easily, as Uncle Dick started to use them as an ashtray. Gus ignored this and still offered the peanuts around but Uncle Dick was the only taker.

Charles hired Dick, and a few days later with a still red-eyed, very under-the-weather Uncle Dick, we flew to the station. I think Charles's remark that there was no alcohol on the station could have had something to do with Dick's condition. He was making up for the drought to come.

I will always remember my first conversation with Uncle Dick. Charles, as usual, had given his directions for the day, and I had dutifully written them all down and delivered them to everyone concerned. Dick appeared and I read out Charles's instructions for the day. His reply was as follows:

'She's jake. Tell his nibs I'll grab crib, have a bit of a kip, whizz the head off the u/s bastard, slap him in the eye with the part numbers, in a flash of a nod, and Bob's your uncle.' And he walked out the door. I was still digesting this when Charles came into the kitchen and asked if I had given Dick his orders. I said yes and he asked what his answer was.

'I really don't know.'

'What do you mean you don't know? Did he give you an answer or not?'

'Yes, he gave me an answer, but I don't know what it means!'

Charles spoke very slowly as if he was dealing with someone who was a bit simple. 'Tell-me-his-answer.'

This treatment immediately got my back up so I rattled off what I could remember of Dick's answer at break-neck speed, and then sat and stared at him.

'What?'

'What's the matter Charlie, can't you understand plain English?'

He went down to the workshop and spoke to Dick himself. I have never forgotten that conversation, and later, when I knew Dick better, I asked him to translate it into English. He told me that he had said, 'That's okay. Tell Charlie I will have my lunch, have a short sleep, take the head off the broken-down motor, get the serial numbers to him as soon as possible, and he can take it from there!'

Dick's first workshop was just a canvas awning under a big gum tree. Because there was never any time or money, he had to wait years for something more substantial. Eventually, one was built out of bush timber and secondhand iron. One day, he tried to hoist an engine up, and the roof came down with the engine, so he graduated to steel trusses. And after that the workshop stayed that way for the next fifteen years, one bay, thirty feet wide.

Back in the early days, it was unbelievably hard. Dick and Charles argued endlessly about the reconditioning of old machinery. Charles had the philosophy that 'the older the better'. He maintained that any vehicle or machine could be reconditioned and brought back to its original condition. Dick's view was that this might be true if you were working with quality handmade machines, but to put it in his own words, 'When you're working with robot machine-made junk off assembly lines that has been thrown together, forget it, not practical.'

Of course Charles won, and Dick started the restoration

of an old vehicle that we had actually taken out of the dump at Montejinni when Charles and Gus bought the station. Dick said the compression was so weak, she couldn't drive out of a pig wallow.

This was the vehicle that was going to prove Charles right. Thousands of dollars and a book of spare parts later, Dick had finished, and he told Charles he still had exactly what he had started with, a pile of shit.

Charles wouldn't have a bar of it. He said we now had a one hundred per cent reconditioned vehicle which was the same as new.

Dick said, 'No, maybe ninety-eight per cent,' and that's what the vehicle became known as, 'Ninety-eight'.

One day, when one of our younger, less knowledgeable employees asked why the vehicle was called Ninety-eight, Dick said, 'Because she was built in 1898.'

'Gee, she's in good condition!'

Dick didn't answer.

Danielle was only four and a half at this time and, up to that point in her life, had received at least ten bedtime stories every night. However, since living on the station, she had been having trouble getting her quota as Mummy was always cooking. So from bathtime to bedtime, she would be on the prowl for a 'bedtime story reader'. Uncle Dick was a complete softy where Danielle was concerned, so it didn't take her long to rope him into this extra duty.

Every evening she would swing on the back gate waiting for him to wander up the flat from the workshop. She would call to him to hurry as she had to go to bed in two hours, then wait for him to get his clean clothes out of his caravan, walk him to the shower, and stand patiently outside the bathroom door. As soon as he had savoured his first beer she would put the open book on his lap, and then lean back with her hands clasped behind her head to listen.

I soon found out that Uncle Dick's version of the accepted fairy tales was vastly different from the printed words. One evening he had to work late on a breakdown and Danielle waited faithfully on the gate, but soon realised if she was to get her quota of stories that night, it would have to be with someone other than Uncle Dick.

Now I prided myself on being a 'top of the ladder' storyteller. I estimated that over the years I must have read around 50,000 stories. However, apparently I wasn't in Uncle Dick's league.

'Once upon a time there was a little girl called Red Riding Hood . . .'

'That's not right!'

'What do you mean "That's not right"? Of course it is.'

'That's not the story Uncle Dick told me.'

'Oh, isn't it? Well suppose you tell me what is right.'

'Once upon "the flip of a dime" there was this slick chick called Big Red, and she had this groovy dude called Wolfgang. He was one mean dude, but he was a great "hoof and prancer". That's a dancer,' she informed me, looking up at my shocked expression with delight. I tucked her into bed and went off to find Uncle Dick.

I have been asked many times by visitors and new employees why everyone calls Dick 'Uncle Dick'. Who is he related to? Of course he's not related to anyone, but when the children were young I told them to call him 'Uncle Dick', rather than just 'Dick'.

One year it was Dick's birthday and apart from a cake I was making I did not have anything to give him. I was trying to think of something when I remembered he had asked me to mend a tear in the knee of his white overalls. He was going into Katherine with Charlie in the plane to celebrate his birthday, so as well as mending the tear, I embroidered on the back in big blue block letters 'Happy Birthday Uncle Dick'.

He put the overalls on without seeing the message on the back and went off to town. Of course he went on a drinking 'bender' for a few days and wandered around Katherine in a very happy state.

When Charles went to pick him up, Dick remarked what a great town Katherine was—everyone was so friendly, and he was amazed at how many people had known it was his birthday. Charles said he didn't think it was too amazing considering he had it printed on his back.

Dick took the overalls off right there at the airport and looked at the advertisement he had been wearing on his back. According to Charles he sat down on the wheel of the plane and laughed and laughed.

It was the middle of the season and we were very busy. Dick knew there was not enough time to spare for him to go to town and get 'spaced out' for four or five days, but he really was feeling the urge of a 'bender' coming on—'skin's cracking' is the term he used. So Dick and Charles came to a compromise. On a Friday night Charles gave him two cases of beer and took him about ten miles out into the bush, and said he would pick him up on Sunday afternoon.

I was horrified by this arrangement. 'What's he going to eat?'

'He doesn't want to eat, he wants to drink.'

'But he can't go two days without eating.'

'He can, and does go a week without eating.'

'Where will he sleep?'

'Under a tree, it doesn't matter, he just has to get this bender over with and he'll be alright for another six weeks. Don't worry, he'll be fine.'

Of course this didn't stop me worrying.

Sunday, about lunchtime, we had visitors—a delightful girl called Lyn Collins, who was our district nurse, plus a new recruit. Lyn was stationed in Timber Creek and drove around the district, about a two-hundred mile radius, tending to the medical needs of everyone in the area. The new recruit was a fully qualified nurse, but was green to the Outback, fresh from Melbourne. When they arrived, she was very upset. Lyn sat her down and I gave them a cup of tea.

'I had my head down sorting out medical cards . . .' began Lyn.

'When suddenly this thing . . .' put in the new recruit.

'You said it was a man,' said Lyn patiently.

'Thing, man, whatever, came staggering out of the bushes

and across the road in front of the car. I nearly hit him! I had to swerve to miss him.'

'I can vouch for the swerve, my entire file of cards is on the floor of the car.'

'What else could I do? He was naked!'

'Oh you found Uncle Dick!' I said, happy to know he had survived.

'See, I told you Sara would have an explanation,' put in Lyn.

'Uncle Dick? Uncle Dick?' The girl's voice got higher and higher. 'That's your uncle?'

'No, he's our mechanic, everyone just calls him Uncle Dick.'

'But he was naked! What's he doing running around the bush naked?'

'He was probably going down to the river to wash,' I offered lamely. No doubt there were many reasons why Dick was staggering around the bush naked, but I didn't know them, and didn't want to know them.

'Why does he go ten miles to wash in the river?'

'No, no, he's out there camping, a break away from the workshop. A few beers and a lot of fishing.'

'I would say a lot of beers and nothing else.'

This was her first Outback patrol. What a start. Two months later, Lyn arrived at Bullo alone.

'Where's your driver?'

'Gone back to Melbourne. Uncle Dick and the Bullo road tipped the scale, I think.'

On one occasion it was necessary for the whole family to be away from the station for five days. This left Uncle Dick alone, which in itself was not a problem, as he could take care of everything. The problem was five days' supply of beer. If we gave it all to him when we left, he would drink the lot the first day and then there would be no end of trouble.

It was only safe to give him a day's supply at a time. I finally hit upon the scheme of hiding each day's ration in a different place and at 5.30 Dick was to be by the phone and I would call and say where it was.

Before we left, Marlee hid the five days' supply. The first night the static was so bad on the radio phone that Dick could not hear me. So I gave the operator the message to pass on.

'Is this a joke of some kind?' she asked.

I assured her I was serious and that Uncle Dick was very serious. So she passed it on.

'Uncle Dick, the beer is in a plastic bag hanging in the deep end of the swimming pool attached to the skimmer box.' There was a pause and she said to me. 'He's going to see if he can find it.' Another pause. 'He's got it! Is that it?'

'Yes, till same time, same station, tomorrow evening.'

'Okay.'

It was the talk of the VJY switchboard and by 5.30 the next evening they had a competition going: 'Guess where Uncle Dick's beer is!'

'Where is it?' was the eager greeting when I asked for the station.

'Under the white marker on the airstrip, third from the gate.'

'Oh, no one guessed that!' She was disappointed. 'I said it was in the toilet cistern.'

'Good heavens, that's the first place he'd look!' I couldn't believe I was having this conversation.

Everyone on the switchboard was sad when it was the last day. They'd been having such fun.

In 1987, my first year in control, I decided Uncle Dick should have a small reward for all his years of hard work. He had always wanted to go on a cruise ship for a holiday, so I booked him on the *Fairstar* for a Pacific cruise. We planned it with military precision. We had to get him past all his favourite haunts, or watering holes, and onto the ship in time, or it would sail without him. I enlisted the help of friends all the way from Bullo River to Circular Quay.

He flew into Kununurra in a charter four-seater and the pilot, a friend, promised to put him safely on the jet to Darwin. Another long-suffering friend sat at the airport for two hours and slowed down the drinking so he was able to walk onto the jet to Sydney. I made sure the flight was direct as we had, over the years, lost him on many a flight during fuelling.

He arrived in Sydney, having been constantly drinking in flight. Nicky Whorrod, our abattoir manager in the seventies, had courageously accepted the unenviable task of getting Uncle Dick onto the *Fairstar*. He did it and when he called to say Uncle Dick had sailed with the ship, he said the last two days had not been too bad. But he let slip that he had taken a week off work—no doubt to recover.

Nicky said the first day he kept him busy buying clothes for the cruise and that night was heavy drinking and reminiscing, so he slept late. The next morning Nick took him shopping again but that was soon exhausted and it was into the nearest bar for more solid drinking. He got him home about midnight and a friend and Nicky got him to bed, but he said the next morning was the hardest. Dick wanted to go straight off to the nearest pub for more of 'the hair of the dog' and wasn't the least bit interested in sailing time. But somehow Nick got him on board and kept him there until the gangplank was hauled ashore.

Nick was pleased to hear the cruise lasted for two weeks. He needed that amount of time to get himself in the right frame of mind to do it all over again, in reverse. He was also pleased to hear that I had arranged for another friend to help him get Dick off the ship and onto the jet to Darwin.

It must have been some cruise. It would be safe to say Dick did not draw a sober breath the whole two weeks, but by all accounts he had a marvellous time and met some wonderful people. We received regular ship-to-shore phone calls at about ten dollars per minute just to talk about the weather, postcards from every port saying he was jumping ship and one letter saying he was jumping overboard! But he did arrive back in Sydney, he and the *Fairstar*, I would say, a little worse for wear.

Nick and Peter Roberts went to meet the ship and no Dick! Not in his cabin, not anywhere. They finally had to admit he had slipped the noose.

About three days later I received a phone call.

'This is the business office of the *Fairstar*.' I waited. 'I'm trying to locate a Mr Wicks, can you help me?'

I wanted to say 'So are we lady, so are we,' but instead I said, 'Dick does work for me, and he's on his way back to the station from Sydney. Can I take a message?'

'Well, he left his false teeth in his cabin and we're wondering where to send them.'

I gave her our postal address. Ten days later we had Dick's teeth, but that's all. As we looked at them in the little box I said to Marlee, 'Maybe that's all we'll ever see of Dick again.'

After two weeks I was really starting to worry. No reverse charge calls, no bank managers calling for funds, nothing of the usual routine. I called our local police to see if they could help. They ran a check on the gaols and hospitals in Sydney, but that was all they could do. The problem was, he could have been anywhere in Australia, if he was still alive.

About one month to the day, Bluey Lewis our stock inspector from Timber Creek called.

'Guess who just rolled up at our front door?' he said.

'Uncle Dick.'

'Yeah, boy is he a mess. Annie made him stay downstairs till he cleaned up. He's certainly been through the mill. He came in on the bus. No luggage, no money, lost his passport, dressed in just a pair of Stubbies, thongs and a singlet. Lost his glasses and teeth.'

'His teeth were mailed to me. He left them on the ship.'

'That should make him happy, says he can't eat. He's pretty crook, so I'll give him a few days rest and then drive him in, okay?'

'Thank you, Blue.'

A few days later a very battered Uncle Dick gingerly stepped out of the Toyota, glad to be home. Blue was right, he had suffered. But according to Dick it was worth it, although he hasn't mentioned going on a cruise again.

Dick and his teeth were reunited and another pair of glasses was ordered from Mr Sloley in Darwin. This is a yearly event as he loses his glasses every holiday.

The very first time I called I was told, 'Oh goodness, I

couldn't supply a pair of prescription glasses without testing his eyes.'

I patiently explained Dick was never in town and on the few occasions he did make Darwin, he was in no condition to keep appointments. In the meantime, he needed glasses to do his job. Dick gave me an old prescription for the lenses in his lost glasses and said that he could see much better with Charlie's glasses. With this information, Mr Sloley was able to send a pair of glasses that suited Dick perfectly, and every year since then, the strength has been increased in line with the verbal report.

A few years back when I called to order the yearly glasses, I was told Mr Sloley had retired. I immediately thought, Oh dear, I will have to explain this all over again! I took a deep breath.

'My name is Mrs Henderson, and I need a pair of glasses for an employee of mine, a Mr Wicks.'

The voice on the other end interrupted.

'Oh, hullo Mrs Henderson. Has Mr Wicks been on holidays again?'

'Why yes, but how . . . ?'

'Oh, Mr Sloley left special instructions in regard to Mr Wicks. Now, we just have to strengthen them a tad, don't we? Any particular style?'

Uncle Dick has now been at Bullo River with us on and off for eighteen years. His loyalty, love and friendship are shared by all the family, and he has been an integral part of Bullo's growth and its struggle to survive. Without that extra effort and concern of Uncle Dick's, I doubt that we would have scraped through.

I have told him many times over the last five years that both of us will have to die in the field, the amount of work we still have to complete. He has picked out his resting place under a four-hundred-year-old bottle tree.

'You won't find me sitting in an old men's home bludging for my tucker and waiting to die. I'll do a fair day's work till the the day I drop!'

And he will.

CHAPTER 17

❖

1981-1986

It was New Year's Eve 1981. Charles had left for America in early December to visit his mother. All the staff had left and we were down to Uncle Dick and Stumpy, the stock camp cook. Under Charles's direction New Year had always been a serious official event. We all had to prepare resolutions, and he would expect us to take those commitments seriously and achieve them over the coming year. Of course he would only conduct the proceedings, never participate in them. And if we couldn't find enough things wrong with ourselves, he would cheerfully supply each of us with a long list. Especially me!

This year we were at a bit of a loss with all the military procedure missing, so we decided, 'What the hell, let's do something different, why don't we just have a party? So, New Year's Eve found us busily cooking and preparing for our party. All except Danielle.

'Where's Danielle?' I had noticed she was a bit quiet the day before and now she was not joining us in the cooking. I found her in her room and she was not a well girl.

I called Wal Tracey, our doctor in Darwin, and put Danielle on the line so he could ask all the questions needed for a diagnosis. She felt sick, wanted to vomit, had a dull pain in her right side. Wal asked to speak to me.

'I think she has appendicitis. If you carry out a little test, we can be sure.'

With the phone in one hand, and Danielle flat on the floor, I had to run my finger out from her belly button three inches, down about the same, and when I reached this spot, press firmly with the tips of my fingers, hold a few seconds and then lift quickly.

'What did she do?'

'Elevated about ten inches off the floor.'

'Get her here, pronto.'

The charter plane landed within the hour. She was so bad by then she couldn't even bear the seat belt across her tummy. We flew into Kununurra and just made the jet to Darwin. The ambulance met us at the airport and she was rushed to the hospital and straight into the examination room. Wal had organised for the surgeon to be waiting. He took only a few moments to arrange for immediate surgery.

For New Year Danielle was in recovery and I was sitting in the hall outside the operating theatre thinking she was still in there. When the nurse took Danielle back to her room from recovery and I wasn't there, she immediately organised a search of the hospital. A nurse found me wringing my hands outside the operating theatre. I was in a worse state than Danielle. Back with her in her room, she managed to calm me down. I must say, she came through the whole thing marvellously. I was a total wreck.

I finally went back to the hotel at around three a.m. and people were still partying. I collapsed on the bed and the next thing I remember was being woken by the phone. It was morning, and it was the girls worried about Danielle. I told them Danielle was now fine, but I was a mess. Knowing their mother, they said they could well understand that.

I told them where we spent New Year and asked them about theirs. They said they had had an early dinner, Uncle Dick and Stumpy had fallen asleep watching the movie and gone home to bed at about nine-thirty. They opened the champagne alone, at about ten-thirty, drank the lot and fell asleep.

The 2nd of January was Danielle's birthday. I tried to buy her a birthday cake, but all the cake shops were still closed, so I finally bought a frozen strawberry and cream sponge. Armed with this, candles, plastic 'Happy Birthday' writing and various presents, I arrived at the hospital. Danielle blew out her candles and opened the gifts and though she was in pain if she moved or laughed, she had a nice birthday.

Not long after his return from America, Charles had another bout of pneumonia. After that he never seemed to regain his zest. His character changed and he no longer had that incredible enthusiasm that everyone relied on.

For many reasons, the Montejinni abattoir never got off the drawing board, and Charles and Gus argued incessantly. Montejinni was put on the market and sold at the beginning of 1982. Most of Charles's profit from Montejinni went to paying debts that were about to destroy Bullo.

Looking back now, I think Charles knew he would not live to a ripe old age, because instead of investing the balance in improved breeding stock or upgrading some of our miserable equipment, he bought a very beautiful forty-four-foot sailing boat. It was a clear and attractive red with white trim, just recently finished.

It was called the *Mary Blair*. He actually paid someone to research the name and history of *Mary Blair*, convinced that there must have been some famous sailing ship by that name. This was no small undertaking—we are talking about Lloyd's register in London. However, the only shipping vessel on the register with that name was an old barge on the Thames, and it was named after a prostitute. So Charles immediately had the boat painted white.

By the time he had purchased the boat, changed the colour, equipped the boat with all the extras, given me some very beautiful but extravagant jewellery, bought an aerobatic plane for Bonnie, bought a few goldmines, and paid the running costs and repairs on the boat and plane for the next year or so, the station was in debt again.

Charles announced to the world, or I should say the Melbourne papers, that he was going to sail to America with an all-girl crew. A few reporters called wanting to know my feelings on this.

'They're welcome to him,' I said.

He had hurt and humiliated me but there was no way he

was going to know it. He came back to the station and we eventually made our peace. It was then he asked me if I would look after the station for the next five years. He would sail and this would cure his lungs. Maybe then we could try our marriage again.

I told him there was no way I could run the station, and he agreed, saying he didn't expect me to. I wasn't capable. I was just to caretake, for eight months of the year, and he would return for the mustering.

I argued that the station needed a lot more than four months' attention each year. There wasn't a decent fence standing, we needed more paddocks, more watering points, and that was just the beginning. The girls would regularly feed this information to me hoping I could get something for these so badly needed improvements.

He wouldn't listen. He said that we would put the station in shape at the end of the five years, when he was cured.

'There won't be any station left to put in shape in five years.'

'Don't be cheeky.'

I walked away knowing I was wasting my breath.

The year 1984 looked daunting before it even began. We had the BTEC programme on our hands. This was a nationwide cattle programme to rid Australia of TB and *Brucella* bacteria. We had to test the required number of cattle, and keep them separated once tested. We didn't have enough fences for this, and we didn't have enough money to buy hay to hold the cattle while testing.

Charles was sailing until nearly the end of April. He met Bonnie and me in Melbourne in late April. April 20th was Bonnie's 21st birthday. She had been working at the R. M. Williams factory in Adelaide learning saddlery and had met Peter Williams.

She called from Adelaide to ask if she could bring Peter to the small dinner we were having in Melbourne for her 21st. As usual, it was a rushed affair and I felt the young people found it a duty. Peter was quite nervous in Charles's presence, as was Bonnie.

Soon after we headed for Bullo, and Peter back to Adelaide. He was going to drive up to Bullo the following month to help us with the coming season's musters.

The first week in May had the season off to a start, with Bonnie in charge of the cattle under her father's direction, and Marlee, bush, chopping fence posts. Charles would endlessly demote Bonnie and promote Marlee only to change it around when Marlee displeased or disobeyed him. The major difference between the girls was that, when he gave his instructions, Bonnie would listen until he was finished, say nothing, then do exactly what she thought best. Marlee, on the other hand, would point out that various orders were impractical or not possible, given the time factor, or distance, or lack of machinery, feed or people. The girls' ideas were similar, but Bonnie didn't voice hers. Marlee on the other hand could not remain silent. So she found herself mostly demoted and cutting fence posts.

The usual chaos prevailed and visitors and friends filtered through the pandemonium as the season progressed. Peter arrived and not long after an ABC 'Big Country' crew turned up to film a followup to 'The Developers'—the documentary they had made in 1964, twenty years earlier.

We made a wonderful friend in Matthew Flanagan, the producer of what was later called 'Henderson's Daughters'. Matthew is one of those rare species who manages to instil his enthusiasm for life into every day.

He spoke in a delightful lilting Irish brogue and whenever we had finished acting out a scene he would say:

'Ooooh, that was wonderful, but do ya think you could do it again?'

In one scene, Marlee was heaving a quarter of meat onto the back of the Toyota. When she had finished Matthew came out with his usual line.

Marlee jokingly replied, 'Like bloody hell!'

Matthew, a vegetarian, quietly picked up the quarter and moved it back into position for the second take. Now that's dedication to your profession.

During their stay and as part of the documentary, Bonnie and Peter had their engagement party. It was a lovely night with many friends coming to Bullo to help us celebrate the occasion, and it was nice to have it on film.

It was time for the crew to leave, and Matthew was saying his goodbyes and kissing the girls. He had kissed Bonnie and was moving on to Danielle, when Bonnie said, in a perfect imitation of his Irish accent, 'Oooh, that was wonderful, but do ya think you could do it again?'

As the glamour of the cameras faded the station settled back into mustering mode. By September the mustering was over, and so was the new engagement. It was never exactly explained why, but Peter just left.

Charles went sailing, Bonnie went flying, and Marlee, Danielle and I were to take care of the property.

Before Charles left, Marlee came to me and asked if she and Charlie could become engaged. Marlee had known Charles Ahlers for three and a half years. He was the chief pilot for Slingsby Helicopters out of Kununurra. He was raised on Outback cattle properties—his family property is on the Peninsula in Queensland. Charlie literally flew into Marlee's life one day when her father hired helicopters for one of our musters. Charlie was one of the pilots.

It wasn't love at first sight however. Charlie came to Bullo for about three or four musters that season before I noticed the sparkle in Marlee's eyes and that extra special preparation of dress, make-up and meals. I was delighted. Charlie was the kind of man every mother hopes her daughter will bring home one day.

Marlee was worried that because Bonnie's engagement had just ended, her father might not be in a receptive frame of mind. However, his only reply was, 'About time!' The engagement party was arranged for December and Charles left to go sailing.

In December we all arrived in Katherine from various points of the compass to celebrate the engagement. As usual Charles held court. He discussed cattle with Bonnie, fencing with Marlee, gold mining operations with the current geologist and avoided money with me. The attendance of many friends made it a memorable evening.

After the party, Charles went back to sailing, Marlee and Charlie to Charlie's family station in North Queensland for the rest of the wet, Bonnie to Darwin flying and Danielle and I to the station to take care of pets and animals in general.

Bonnie and Charles arrived back on the station a few days before Christmas and Danielle and Bonnie cut down the traditional tree. However Christmas was a sober affair—everyone went through the motions, but disagreeable undercurrents were slowly surfacing. Bonnie was flying in Darwin and dating a man whom her father did not approve of.

Around this time there arrived on our doorstep a delightful person by the name of Fairlie Brooke. Charles had met her in Melbourne through her husband Geoff, and finding out that she was an artist, invited her to come to the station to give the girls some lessons. I am sure he probably had more ideas which he didn't voice, but for once his silken charm just kept sliding.

Fairlie still talks about the art lessons in the kitchen by candlelight. She remembers thinking, How stupid can a situation get? Giving lessons on shading, pointing out the light and shade of a drawing, when it is all in darkness, shaded by candlelight.

Charlie, being the strict task master he was, insisted the girls have the art lesson every day, but what with mustering cattle and other work until dark, art lessons did not start until eight at night. Many a time, Fairlie would finish with them all asleep on the breakfast counter. She was the perfect guest, always a help, never a problem. However there was one part of my 'housekeeping' that Fairlie could not accept—leaving the washing on the line when it was raining. To me it seemed perfectly sensible—why drag it all inside wet, only to hang it all out again. Also, our bore water was very hard, and the rain gave the clothes a lovely fresh water rinse.

Fairlie, however, could not bear to see washing sitting on the line for days, and at the first drop of rain would be galvanised into action.

'Rain!' she would shout, disappearing out the door, only

235

to reappear fifteen minutes later under a pile of now thoroughly soaked washing.

At this time we were building part of the back section of the house and that morning, part of the existing roof had been removed to enable the new roof to be joined to the old roof. The missing part was over where Fairlie had carefully stored the washing.

After about the third 'Rain' dash of the morning, I heard this woeful noise coming from the washing area. I found Fairlie standing in front of a pile of very wet, in fact saturated, washing. But she wasn't looking at the washing, she was gazing up at the sky which had, of course, been a roof an hour before.

'What happened to the roof?' she asked in a mystified voice.

The most famous event of Fairlie's visit was the 'snake in the swimming pool' episode. Because of the heat, Fairlie spent a fair time in the pool.

After a dip one day, she said to Bonnie, 'What's your pet snake's name?'

Bonnie, always flippant, replied, 'George.'

About three days later, Fairlie walked into the kitchen and said to me, 'George and I had a lovely swim today.'

'Who's George?'

'Your pet snake,' said Fairlie hesitantly.

'We don't have a pet snake.'

'But . . . but . . . I've been swimming with him for three days!'

'Well I suggest you don't swim with him any more because he's not a pet.'

Fairlie went quite white. It turned out that she had been swimming up and down the pool with a deadly five-foot king brown. We told her she should take up snake charming.

It was discovered that the snake had a hole right beside the pool and would slither in for a dip whenever the fancy took him. Of course after that, no one would put a toe in the swimming pool for fear of meeting George in a deep dive.

About five days later Danielle saw George slithering into the pool. Bonnie raced to get the shotgun. Out in the bush we never touch them, that is their home, but a snake living

236

that close to the house was too risky. However, by the time Bonnie returned, George was halfway down his hole. She grabbed his tail and gave a mighty heave—he went flying through the air and landed about twenty feet away. She picked up the gun and shot his head off. And that was the end of George.

In February 1985, Charles said that he and Gus were going to settle their affairs once and for all and make a legal deed of settlement. Charles insisted I come to Darwin with him, while it was done.

We spent eleven days at the Darwin Hotel, according to the hotel bill on file. They really were most interesting days. It had been a long time since I had seen Charles and Gus together, but it was clear that the old magic of 'our friendship can survive anything' was gone. Friendly bantering had been replaced by serious innuendoes and accusations. They went back over every detail of their long association, right back to their first business partnership at the age of eight mowing lawns.

Many bottles of rum later they finished up with two sheets of yellow pad paper, representing the end of their long association. The lawyers then transformed these two pages into thirteen pages of legal jargon.

Charles flew to Sydney and left on a trip around the Pacific. He called me from places I had never heard of and transferred so much money out of the bank account in such a short time that the bank manager called me voicing his concern.

Somehow we made it to the next season and managed to pay all the summonses that had accumulated over the wet season. We continued the BTEC programme. Halfway through the mustering season it became clear that we were simply sliding further into debt. However Charles was determined to sail, so he borrowed more. He also continually destocked the station for further cash but he soon went through it.

Near the end of the mustering season he needed money again—to sail till December, then visit his mother for Christmas in Maryland. We also needed money for the running of the station during the six months of wet season.

Under Charles's supervision Bonnie had been in charge of

the mustering for the last three years, while Marlee had been relegated to the outer fringes, cutting fence posts. Charles said she was too rebellious.

It was now September and there was one more muster to go. Bonnie had left the station at the end of August. She was to be away for the weekend but she called to say she would be delayed. Finally she called to say she would not be back for the muster.

Marlee and I discussed the situation and I told her to go ahead and arrange the muster. We couldn't contact Charles and time was running out—it would soon be too hot to muster.

'Right now we must carry out that Paperbark muster and get some money in the bank.'

So we ordered the helicopters, assembled the portable yards, and cleared a road to the site. It was a good muster and we managed to move the cattle out with surprisingly little fuss, unlike the usual panic of a 'Charlie' directed muster. These had left everyone in a state of collapse.

Eventually Charles called and I told him that Bonnie had decided not to come back. He said he would fly home to supervise the last muster, but I said there was no need.

'You don't think you can do it, do you?' he said in an impatient voice. 'No, I'll have to come home.'

'Don't bother, the muster's already done, and the cattle have been sold.'

'Good, you can send me some money.'

I said, 'No,' very quietly. He just hung up.

I knew he would call the bank and instruct them to telex funds to him, so I opened a second account and put the money in that account. The main account was totally overdrawn. When he realised he couldn't get any money, I didn't hear from him for a while. The next time he called, he was in Sydney, working full steam on a tourist deal which he said would make us millions.

I had been hearing of the millions we were going to make for years now. He had been working on this scheme most of the year. He was still going to America to see his mother for Christmas and when he returned, the tourist venture would solve all our money problems.

His plan was to buy the *Oriana* which was up for sale for scrap metal price. The ship could no longer maintain Lloyd's certificate, so could no longer sail with adequate insurance. Charles was going to moor the ship at the entrance to the Bullo River on the Victoria River and offer 'the ultimate luxury in the wilderness' type of holiday. To get the idea up and running would cost about twenty million dollars. Charles never believed in doing things by halves. To solve our half million plus debt, he was going to borrow twenty million more. Not to mention the headache of a thousand tourists and eight hundred staff on the *Oriana* out in the middle of nowhere.

'Nothing to it,' said Charles.

The aerobatic plane was put on the market in December before he left for America. The plane was sold for many reasons, but the main reason was lack of money in the bank. Of course this caused a serious rift between Bonnie and Charles. The plane aside, Charles had basically asked her to choose between flying and the boyfriend in Darwin. Charles and I had many arguments over this. To Charles's amazement she chose the boyfriend—Charles had been so sure of emerging the victor.

Charles left for America in late December, Bonnie was living in Darwin, Marlee was in Queensland with Charlie visiting his parents' property, so for Christmas it was Danielle, Uncle Dick, Stumpy our stock camp cook and me. It was the smallest Christmas yet on Bullo.

Charles called on Christmas Day and we talked to the family in America, Marlee called, and I called Mum and my sister, so we were all united by phone, except for Bonnie.

In January I received a phone call from Wal Tracey, in Darwin.

'Charles has arrived home. He's very sick, so sick he can't travel to the station.'

❖

1986

I flew to Darwin. Charles was staying at the Darwin Hotel and I got a shock when I saw him. He looked absolutely terrible.

One lung had collapsed and Wal had him on antibiotics. But a few days of attention and pills and the recovery was amazing. Charles thrived on attention, and that he received. I massaged him for hours on end. He looked a lot better after a week, but he was still a very sick man.

Wal sent him to Sydney. He said Charles needed a specialist now. There was nothing more he could do. I put him on a plane to Sydney and went back to the station. I now regret this action. If I had gone to Sydney with him, maybe the events that followed would have been different.

He called to say he was going to have an operation.

'What type of operation?'

He said his lungs would be opened up and all the cysts stapled and this would improve his breathing capacity. I didn't want him to have the operation, but he wouldn't listen.

'If I'm going to be a vegetable, I'm not interested. This operation can fix the problem once and for all.' This was Charles's opinion, but no one else's, not even his doctor's.

The year before he had had two operations six months apart to remove cataracts from his eyes. These operations had been so successful that his sight was restored to almost 20/20 vision. Before that his eyes had been so bad that I had to send one of the girls flying with him to point him in the direction of the strip.

I think he was so excited with the eye operations that he

thought all his problems could be cured with an operation. He had renewed both his eyes, so why not both his lungs?

He also told me on that call that in four days' time we would have a business meeting to discuss the plans for the coming seasons. He obviously considered Marlee and me as new recruits, although he made it quite clear that he thought he would have a difficult time directing us. However, in about six weeks he would be back on the job, so as long as we did as we were told, we couldn't make too much of a mess in that short time. Needless to say I ignored most of these remarks.

Charles's operation was on the 18th of March 1986. When the doctors opened up one lung, it was far worse than the x-rays had indicated. In fact, there was very little they could do to improve the situation. Janie called to say the operation had gone okay and Charles was recovering. Janie had sailed on the *Mary Blair* with Charles from the first trip around the Pacific. She deserves a medal for her patience and understanding. During the next four horror-filled months she was as strong as steel, yet gentle and always thoughtful. I could never have made it through without her.

My other great close-at-hand support during this terrible time was my brother Blue and his wife Margaret. Except for a few short stays in a hotel near the hospital, I lived with them at Palm Beach from April to June. Blue and Margaret own and run a kindy in Mona Vale, and busy as they were, they always helped when I had problems, and I had non-stop problems.

Charles and I had separated in 1983 when he bought the boat and hired his all-female crew, but now he was sick and needed me, and I didn't hesitate to be with him. I knew he would have done the same for me. We argued like hell, but we were friends.

Charles had a cut from under his arm, around the fourth rib, across his back and up to the top of the shoulderblade and nearly over to his spine. It was a shocking wound. Three weeks after the operation he was not improving. The lungs were not responding, the wound had become infected and

Charles was not in good spirits. As the drugs increased, his character changed. On Marlee's birthday on the 8th of April, he spoke to her on the phone. He could hardly get out 'Happy birthday, I love you.' Marlee burst into tears, I burst into tears and Charles did too. Great birthday, all alone on the station, waiting to know what to do.

A few weeks later Charles's lung collapsed. He was already on pills for everything you could imagine, but he was given more.

I moved into the hotel just down the road, 'just in case' were the doctor's words. Janie and I sat at his bedside all day and until ten or eleven each night. We massaged him and read to him and followed his endless instructions. He started to improve. His lung started to inflate and the ghastly draining machine attached to his side was taken away.

It was as if the sun had emerged from behind a dark cloud. Charles was smiling again. His lungs were far from good, but I read to him about a chap who with only one third of one lung had passed the army fitness test. Each day Janie and I watched as the fight slowly came back into his eyes.

It had been a close call—I thought we had lost him. Yet all through that terrible period, I remember clearly thinking, Of course Charles will make it, he can beat anything.

During all that time, Marlee was alone, back at the property, waiting. She was not alone in the sense of no people. Uncle Dick was always there and by April there were a few staff starting on the endless fencing. But she had no family. Thankfully she did have her Charlie. He dropped in in the chopper whenever he was in the area. It was now the beginning of the mustering season and, being chief pilot, he was very busy, yet he still managed to check on her regularly.

I was dozing by the bed when one of the nurses came into the room. 'You're wanted on the phone, Mrs Henderson.'

It was my sister Sue, calling from Queensland. When she said my name my heart dropped. There was something wrong.

'Sara,' I held my breath, 'Mum has had a stroke.'

My legs turned to jelly. Slowly I sat down in the chair at the desk, trying to breathe. My brain wouldn't follow any normal procedure, it just kept screaming 'First Charles, now Mum, first Charles, now Mum,' over and over.

'Sara, are you alright?' She went on to say that Mum was in hospital. It had been major. At the moment she was out of danger, but they were not sure how things would progress. It would be weeks before they could tell us anything definite.

'I'll come straight away.'

'No, she doesn't know anyone yet, so wait. I'll call you as soon as there's any change.'

She asked about Charles and Marlee. Danielle was going to school in Bundaberg and living with her and her husband Ralph. She told me Danielle had been a great help, going to the hospital and doing all she could.

Charles improved steadily and the doctors said he could move to a convalescing home. He wouldn't hear of it—he was going to the boat. The argument went on for days. The doctors told me I had to get the message across, they didn't have time to argue. Of course Charles only wanted to argue with the doctors. They were worthy opponents, not me.

He now started his underground network. Because I wouldn't do as he ordered, he went around me. He arranged to move the boat to a serviced marina—until now she had been at anchor in Palm Beach. He arranged to have an oxygen machine set up on the boat, emergency power—the list was endless, not to mention the money being spent.

I think the morphine was having an effect on his thinking. At this stage he was even talking about sailing to America. When I asked him how he would get oxygen in the middle of the ocean, he said he would take enough for four months. The power equipment alone would have filled up the boat.

Charles was very excited the day he was to leave hospital. Janie and I were terrified. He was convinced there would be no problems, I saw thousands of problems. But he was determined to get out of the hospital, and I couldn't blame him for that.

My brother Blue was waiting with the car, Janie had packed all of Charles's belongings, and we were ready.

The doctor came into the room and said they were ready to go to x-ray.

243

'What? We're about to leave!'

He looked puzzled. 'Leave where?'

'The hospital. Charles has been discharged, hasn't he?'

He asked me to wait. Charles tried to bulldoze his way through. 'Forget him, let's go.'

'No, we'd better wait.' I could smell a 'Charlie manoeuvre'.

Another doctor arrived and said, 'We'll take an x-ray, and if it's clear, we'll talk about leaving.'

We silently went down to x-ray. It was the door next to the front door. We waited for the results.

Then we were back in the lift, on our way back to that terrible room. The x-ray had revealed a large bubble in the lung. He needed complete rest and no movement until it could be brought under control. He was back on that awful draining machine, with tubes inserted into his side. I watched the excitement in his eyes slowly fade, until he stared at me with blank openings.

The drugs increased and his behaviour became unpredictable. He demanded that the bank manager appear at the foot of his bed at a moment's notice, only to issue 'office boy's orders' to him. He had the entire hospital in an uproar. He told me to hire security guards as the nurses were trying to kill him. He wouldn't eat any of the food—Janie and I had to bring all his meals in from outside.

Some nurses requested not to be assigned to his room. He refused to follow the hospital routine. He wrote out his daily routine and told them to follow that. One morning they called me to come to the hospital as he would not allow them to come into the room until ten a.m. These were the instructions he had given to the night nurse to hand over to the morning nurse.

His health started to improve again, if not his manners. The dreaded draining machine was removed and he was actually walking from the bed out to the balcony. He was on the up road again, the second time he had won the battle. But he would not do any physio work for his lungs. One walk down the hall and he flatly refused to do it again.

I pleaded for days, to no avail. I think he couldn't bear

being so helpless, having to be supported by women in order to walk. So he wouldn't do it. I finally convinced him to walk around his bed behind closed doors, and he did do this, but the physiotherapist said he needed to stretch and strengthen the lungs, and that required walking the length of the hall and up and down stairs.

The 'pass-out' from that place was the length of the hall and two flights of stairs and back again. I would run up and down four or five flights daily because the lifts were so slow, and I would meet the poor patients on the way, labouring a step at a time with two minutes' rest on each step, trying to qualify for the 'pass-out'.

My sister called.

'Mum is out of the coma, Sara. She's paralysed down the right side.'

My heart cried. Our Mum was a wonderful person, always on the move, she never sat still. Even watching television she would knit or crochet. She devoted her life to helping others. Now she was paralysed.

'Sara . . .' There was more. 'Mum cannot speak.'

I put the phone down and cried. At that moment in my life I really didn't want to go on. I felt as if the problems were closing in around me, crushing the life out of me.

Charles was acting strangely. That was normal of late, but he still sensed my sorrow and when I told him about Mum, he insisted I go and visit her. He said he was feeling better every day and by the time I returned, he would be able to leave the hospial.

I flew to Bundaberg. Mum looked like a little girl in that big bed, very small and frail. Her face beamed when I walked in—she recognised me immediately. She took my hand and although she could not speak, she could certainly verbalise. It was the quaintest language and although I could not understand what she was saying, the meaning was clear: 'I love you, and I'm so glad to see you.'

I heard the doctor's report. 'Ninety years of age, not much hope of recovery, possibility of another stroke any time. Best put her in a nursing home.' Home! That dreaded word. All

Mum's life she had cared for and visited people in homes. She would say to my sister and me, 'Please, if I'm ever old and cannot care for myself, please, never put me in a home. That's all I ask.' And all her life, that was all she ever did ask of us. It was now our turn.

The doctors warned us of the cost of looking after her at home. They also said if we didn't send her from hospital to a nursing home, she could lose the bed she was entitled to. We did discuss the plan and the decision split the family. But we eventually decided to get her back to her own home. Later, the look on her face when she got there made it all worth it.

The first step was to get her out of that bed, get her moving. She was despondent, listless. I would ask her what the matter was and she would pat my hand and chatter. Ralph, Susan, my brother Tod, his wife Frances, and I took turns at the hospital sitting with her through the day, so she had constant company. Yet at night, when I went to leave, she would cling to my hand.

I spoke to the doctor. What about physio? He said she would not cooperate. Now I had two of them! But it was not like Mum not to want to fight this. I stumbled onto the problem accidentally.

In desperation I said, 'Well if you don't get out of that bed, you can't go home. Wouldn't you like to go home?'

On the magic word 'home', all the light came back into her eyes and she made a noise that was her version of 'home'. Seeing what a wonderful reaction this comment had elicited, I quickly continued.

'Yes, you walk, and we can go home. The hospital will let you go home.'

When I said 'hospital', she hit high 'C'. After many hours of charades, I gathered that she had thought she was already in a 'home'. When I said it was only a hospital, she cried out for joy.

After that it was plain sailing. You couldn't keep her down. She amazed the doctors and hospital staff.

Mum had a beautiful singing voice and was a wonderful

dancer, so I bought her a Walkman. She had never seen a Walkman before and looked worried when I started to put the earphones on her head. I told her to be patient, one thing my mother never was. I put the tape of one of Mum's favourite operas in the machine and turned it on.

The expression on her face when the music started was wonderful. She listened, mesmerised for the first few moments, then took off the earphones and turned them around. She listened into one earphone and hearing the music again, smiled at me. Then with her good arm she handed the earphones to me— I was to put them back on her head. She closed her eyes and sang along with the score. The only drawback to this otherwise wonderful scene was that, along with her speech, Mum had also lost her lovely singing voice.

I started her dancing to strengthen her leg. I would put her paralysed foot on top of my foot and lift it. We were dancing around the bed, Mum singing off key at the top of her voice, when I turned and saw the doctor standing in the door.

'If only I had a hundred of you!' he remarked.

That night Janie called to say that Charles had again taken a turn for the worse and was acting very strangely. He had told her to get out and never come back. Janie was very upset. I said I would be there the next day.

How to tell Mum? We decided that it was better not to say anything. Ralph, Sue, Tod and Frances would keep going to the hospital and continue the singing and dancing.

I arrived back in Sydney late, checked in at the hotel down the road, and walked to the hospital. The Charles I saw that night was a stranger. He was raving, aggressive and vicious. He accused me of doing terrible things behind his back, of selling Bullo to his enemy. Janie was part of this plot, so he had sent her on her way and now, he was sending me on my way. I was to sign the station back to him and he was changing his will and cutting me out of everything.

Very few people knew that all the shares in the station were in my name and had been since the early seventies. In fact, everything he owned at that stage was in the company's

247

name, so legally it belonged to me.

Charles had received various visitors and phone calls while I was in Queensland and obviously some of the outrageous acts he was accusing me of were the result of these—along with the morphine he was taking.

I snapped! I was feeling desperate and so tired. I'd had enough.

'Okay, it's all yours. I'm tired of the whole thing. After all we've been through and you behave like this! You seem to kick the people who help you and you're nice to people who only use you. So take the stupid station, it owes more than it's worth, and by the time you get Bonnie and your sons out from America to run it, the bank will have sold it anyway.'

Part of his unbelievable plan was that his sons in America would drop everything and come out to run Bullo. I don't know if they were privy to this plan at the time, but later events seem to indicate that he could have had conversations with them along these lines.

By this stage, Danielle had gone back to the station to help Marlee, so there were his two daughters working their guts out for him and he was going to call in other family members—who had left to do their thing—to run the station because he thought we weren't capable.

I took the chequebooks out of my handbag and threw them at him. 'Here, take them. There's nothing in the bank anyway, but no doubt you'll manage to run up some more debt.'

I ran to the elevator and pushed the button furiously. The night nurse came running down the hall and said Charles wanted me to come back.

'Tell him from me, "Get stuffed!" ' She looked at me in surprise, but I was past caring what anyone thought.

I hailed a cab. I couldn't go back to the hotel—he would have called me all night. I had to get away. I told the driver to head for the city. I had him stop at some hotel and I booked in. I had a hot bath and sat and cried. When I had calmed down a little I realised I had not eaten since breakfast, so I ordered a meal.

'Would you like wine with your dinner, madam?'

I was about to say 'No' but said 'Yes'. Food and a whole bottle of wine later, I was feeling a lot better but was completely drunk. After a few more drinks on top of the wine, I was completely smashed.

I awoke the next morning feeling like death. I crawled to the bathroom and drowned under hot and cold showers for hours. After some hot coffee and dry toast, I convinced myself I would live.

However the problem still had to be faced. I regretted my outburst. Charles was the sick one, chained to an oxygen hose in the wall. I headed once more for the hospital. In any case I needed one of the chequebooks to pay my hotel bill.

When I walked in he smiled at me sheepishly. He was in one of his normal moods. I didn't give him a chance to speak. I launched into my little speech.

'I only came back because I need money to check out of the hotel I stayed in last night.' He started to interrupt and I said, 'No, let me finish, then you can say something if you want. I thought long and hard last night. I really didn't think you could hurt me any more than you already have in our life together, but I was wrong. What you said to me last night finishes everything. I no longer want anything to do with you or the name Henderson. I want out. I'll sign all the shares back to you. All I want from you is a release from the mortgage guarantees I have signed. I'll have to start again and when I do make some money, I don't want to find I'm suddenly paying back your debts again. I need a bit of money now to get to my sister, and that's it.'

'What about me?'

'You seem to have a nice network going for you here, all these people running around at your beck and call. If you wave Bullo under their noses they'll all dance to your tune. Just don't tell them how much money you owe.'

'I don't want them here, I want you.'

'Well you've a funny way of showing it. What about last night? What about that lady friend who always scurries away when Janie or I arrive?'

'I want you here.'

'Well you'd better inform her of your views because she thinks it's her you want.'

Again he told me he wanted me to stay. He said he had not meant any of the things he had said the night before. He was jealous, Janie had let on that I was seeing a man.

I had met someone the year before and he was in Sydney on business so we had been to dinner a few times, the only bright spots in my months of darkness. Charles wanted to know his name, but I told him no way. I knew all his little tricks and even though he was sick, he could still have reached far from that bed. He said he was worried this man was after my money. I laughed.

'What money? Anyway, he has his own money and I'm sure his business is in better shape than Bullo.' He realised it was a closed subject. He gave back the chequebooks and promised to behave.

He had more x-rays. He was not improving; in fact he was starting to lose weight rapidly. Up until now, he had read and written all day. Suddenly, he stopped. He became obsessed with time and he looked at his watch incessantly. If the nurse was ten seconds late with his pills, he would fret. He had a schedule written out and he would tick it as each pill was taken.

Janie and I were showing signs of wear, so we started running for an hour in the morning and we split the shifts so we could get a break and do other things in our lives.

It was now the end of May and it seemed as if this life was going to stretch on forever. The hospital asked me to make arrangements to move Charles.

'Move him where?'

'Home.'

'Home is a cattle station two thousand miles away, fifty miles off the road and two hundred and fifty miles from the nearest town.'

'Oh well, he can't go there. But he can't stay here any longer. There's nothing else we can do for him.'

Sue and Ralph said we could come and stay with them

on the beach until he was stronger and then we would work something out.

More problems. His lungs were in such a terrible condition, he could not fly in a pressurised plane. But if we drove, Janie and I would have to carry him in and out of the car, and anyway the trip in winter would be too much for him. As we discussed different possibilities time passed, and he lost more and more weight.

It was Queen's Birthday weekend and I was about to become a patient myself. My periods would not stop, I suppose due to the stress. They were up to ten days long and that morning the flow had increased noticeably. I was supposed to take Charles out of the hospital in a few days and I was on the verge of collapse. I spoke to the doctor and he sent me to the women's hospital across the road. I was examined. The doctor said everything seemed okay. He gave me an injection to control the blood-flow, and said if it did not stop in forty-eight hours, I would have to go into hospital and have a curette. It was a miserable weekend, but the flow corrected itself and I was saved from the operation.

The next big event was Charles leaving the hospital. We hired a limousine to drive him to the house I had rented in Palm Beach. The plan was that we would stay there for six weeks and when he was stronger, we would move to my sister's at Bargara. After that was months down the track, so we would worry about that then.

In the meantime there was the problem of the station. Over the last month, Charles had showed no interest in it at all. When I asked him for instructions he simply wouldn't answer. I finally told Marlee to start mustering, work out a plan for the year and do the best she could. I had called her the week before and given her the phone number at the house. Charles was to leave hospital on the 14th of June—the date of the first muster.

The car drove up the drive at Palm Beach. The house was right on the water, very quiet and peaceful. From the bedroom you could see the *Mary Blair* at anchor. This cheered Charles greatly.

We settled him into bed and he seemed the best he had been for a long time, although the trip had exhausted him. Janie and I sat with him as the sun set and we talked and joked about the exercise routine we were going to put him through. He asked me to sleep in the room with him that night, so I put a mattress on the floor next to his bed and he was happy. He dozed for a while then became restless. He said he was not getting enough oxygen. I called the hospital and they said to increase the flow. An hour later he said he needed more. The first doctor had gone off duty, but the new doctor said to increase it again.

By one o'clock Charles was panicky and so were Janie and I. I called the hospital again. None of the doctors who had been treating him all those months was on duty, but the doctor in charge said he was probably having an anxiety attack and would soon settle down.

'Sit and talk to him,' he said.

So we did, and it did help. But it now seemed we were running out of oxygen and this really panicked him. So we called and ordered more. The people were very sympathetic and sent it in the middle of the night. The driver was a wonderful man. He had a cup of tea and sat and talked to Charles about war, Charles's favourite subject. He finally left around three a.m. Janie went to bed and Charles and I talked some more.

At around four a.m. he said, 'Thank you for being with me tonight.'

'That's okay, I can sleep here every night if it helps.'

'No, tonight is special, thank you.'

I drifted off to sleep holding his hand.

Janie was whispering in my ear. I sat up. 'It's seven o'clock. Will I wake him?'

'Well, we only went to sleep after four, maybe let him sleep.'

'If I do that all his pill times will be messed up.'

'I guess you're right, we'd better wake him.'

I went to get the water. I was half way to the kitchen when Janie called out. I raced back to the room.

'What?'

'He's stopped breathing. I helped him up to take his pills, he mumbled something and then he stopped breathing!'

The rest of the day was a nightmare. I raced to call the ambulance and Janie started mouth-to-mouth. She was wonderful, she didn't stop until the ambulance arrived. Blue and Margaret arrived and we sat silently as the ambulance men took over from Janie. But it was no good, the lungs had just stopped.

Blue and Marg took me home. Their house was just up the road. I don't remember much. Blue gave me a stiff scotch and I slept most of the afternoon.

The next week was a haze. Friends in the Australian Army arranged a wonderful service in Charles's honour. I then flew some of Charles's ashes back to Maryland to be buried in the family plot in Easton. With all the problems awaiting me on the station, flying to America was the last thing I should have been doing, but there was no way I could just send his ashes to Maryland. I had to take him home. I knew he would want this. Marlee and Danielle understood and went back to the station to start the season again.

I thought a lot on the long flight to the east coast. This was my third trip to Maryland. Christmas 1966 had been my first trip, when Charles and I had been married six years. When we were married in 1960, Charles had sent his mother and father a telegram which read, 'Marrying Australian native 4th July. Love Charles.' It was one of Charles's many sick jokes.

When I married Charles, he had not spoken to his father for many years so I assume the telegram was aimed at him.

The second visit was with Bonnie when she was about sixteen. Charles decided she could not go alone, so I had to go along. He told me that she was not to date boys. Bonnie was asked on many dates and Charles's sister and mother were very surprised when I wouldn't let her go. Bonnie wasn't interested, so it didn't worry her. I finally gave them our phone number in Australia and told them to call her father.

'He said "no dating". If he says "yes", she can date.' The subject of Bonnie's dating was not mentioned again.

Now here I was again, taking Charles's ashes home to Maryland.

We had a small gathering of close relatives at the family plot and part of Charles was laid to rest. The next day there was a memorial service and, afterwards, friends and family gathered on the lawns of Lloyds Landing. That afternoon many facets of this unusual man were revealed. As I watched the large group of people I marvelled at the enormous impact Charles had had on so many. For all his faults, there is no doubt that on the 15th of June 1986 the world lost a remarkable human being.

I never thought Charles would die, and I am sure Charles was of the same opinion because he never talked about what kind of burial he wanted. However, he loved Maryland, he loved Bullo, and he loved the sea. So now part of him is in Maryland, part of him is on the highest point of the mountain range overlooking the Bullo Valley, and part of him is with the sea. I think he would have approved.

CHAPTER 19

❖

1986

The problems I returned home to in Australia were quite unbelievable. First there was the bank. I managed to convince them that my daughters could run a cattle station, and I was aware of the recent loans because we had just started with this bank. But those debts were only the tip of the iceberg. When it all came together, I was staggered.

I was feeling my way through the meeting with the bank, when the manager said, 'Now, will the company settle Mr Henderson's personal overdraft, or shall we file it with the estate?'

'Personal overdraft?'

'Yes, he took it out a few months ago.'

He told me the amount and I stopped breathing for a few minutes. 'The company.' I couldn't manage any other words.

I was home just over a week when Gus called to say we were out of time on the delivery of the cattle according to the deed and he was suing me for half a million dollars. I asked him what he was talking about, and said we fully intended to deliver the cattle. We would have them ready within the week, surely he wouldn't do this to us when Charles had only just died?

He did!

We were still reeling from this blow when our lawyers called to say my daughter Bonnie was suing me for forty thousand dollars. No, she said, she wasn't suing me, she was suing Bullo River Pty Ltd. That was different?

While Charles was in hospital, he had asked Bonnie to

come to Sydney to see him. I was in Bundaberg visiting Mum in Hospital at the time. He gave her a cheque. Of course there was no money in the bank, so when the bank talked to Charles about not meeting the cheque, he cancelled it. Charles was a director of the company so after his death, Bonnie sued the company.

The next news was that Charles's sons in America had a lawyer in Sydney looking for a will that left everything to them. The lawyer wrote to Charles's lawyer asking about such a will. He was informed of the only will on record and nothing more was heard through legal channels, although some of the boys called me to ask if I knew of such a will.

If I had never known the feeling of complete and utter annihilation, I knew it now.

With a heavy heart I picked myself up, and Marlee, Danielle and I began the long battle to survive, to save Bullo, to pay all Charles's debts and to defend ourselves in the courts.

We finished the mustering season as best we could and withdrew for the wet season to recuperate and prepare ourselves emotionally for the battles that 1987 promised.

Most of the wet was spent answering letters and cards from friends and people who had known Charles. It was a very sad time. I found myself crying for hours on end.

Some letters poured out praise, some apologised for not liking him, some told of their fascination, some criticised. Charles evoked every possible emotion in people.

Very few people had known the true Charles, but one person who had was Major General Ron Grey. Not a longstanding friendship, Ron had met Charles only eight years before his death, but after a few initial rounds of sparring, they had settled down to a rare friendship. They would debate and argue for days, with Ron patiently listening, while Charles told him how to run the police force, the government, the army, the world.

In his letter to me Ron quoted parts of Tennyson's 'Ulysses'.

I cannot rest from travel: I will drink
Life to the lees: all times I have enjoy'd
Greatly . . .

256

Tho' much is taken, much abides; and tho'
We are not now that strength which in the old days
Moved earth and heaven; that which we are, we are;
One equal temper of heroic hearts,
Made weak by time and fate, but strong in will
To strive, to seek, to find, and not to yield.

Charles left me with insurmountable problems and unbelievable debts, but all these pale into insignificance beside the gift of friends.

'If there is anything I can do to help the Henderson family, please just ask.' This was said to me over and over again, and it gave me the strength to stand up and fight.

In the new year Marlee and Charlie went to Queensland. After a month there, Marlee called to say she and Charlie had found a great 6×6 ex-army truck. We needed this type of truck to complete the equipment for our bull-catching operation and though we were spending money we couldn't afford, the 6×6 would make money next year. I told her to go ahead and purchase the truck. I should have known it wouldn't stop there—then we had to fill it up.

'Well Mummy, it's silly to drive the truck all the way back to the station empty.'

By the time the truck left Queensland, it had one of the famous Bullo loads. Whenever one of our trucks went to town, it would finally leave loaded down with anything from a shower curtain and drums of avgas, to a beach umbrella and a windscreen for a grader.

There were endless phone calls.

'Mummy, can we buy a washing machine for the staff quarters? It's so cheap.'

'Mummy, if we buy some milking cows, we won't have to buy powdered milk.' Three milking cows later.'

'Mummy, a friend of Charlie's has a magnificent breeding bull. He's the only one left and we can have him at discount. He's De Manso blood and really lovely.'

'Oh Mummy, I've found the perfect stallion.'

Charlie finally said, 'No more!' and Marlee reluctantly had to stop her gathering.

When they were ready to leave I called Bob, our insurance agent, and started to list the contents of the truck. Halfway through the list, he interrupted me.

'Is all this on one truck?' he asked.

'I suppose a more apt description would be "Noah's Ark".' Bob named the policy 'Operation Noah's Ark'.

When the 'Ark' finally arrived at Bullo, the animals all marched off like little angels.

'Aren't they well-behaved!' I said.

'Should have seen them last week,' grunted Charlie.

The first day of this long journey they had just loaded all the animals in together, with no division, and waited. Of course Marlee had given them all names. Our first super-duper, papered stud bull, she called Henry VIII, because he would have so many wives, about thirty-five in all. The milking cows were Pickle, Pumpkin and Daisy, and the stallion, whose registered racing name was 'Grey Cab', she called Rastas.

Henry and Rastas chose opposite corners with their backsides jammed up against the truck, as far away from each other as possible, and Pickle, Pumpkin and Daisy all put their heads in another corner trying to hide.

Marlee hung hay nets all around the sides of the crate and strapped an awning to the overhead framework. There was thick hay on the floor for them to rest on. They didn't give the animals too much time to decide if they liked their travelling companions—the idea being that if the truck was moving, they would have to concentrate on standing and would leave each other alone.

When they stopped for lunch, the animals had not moved. Rastas and Henry were still having a staring contest and the girls still had their heads in the corner.

Marlee had arranged resting yards each night along the way. The first night the animals could not wait to escape and retreated to the furthest corners of the yard, trying to ignore each other. They had not touched the hay in the nets, so they spent most of the night eating.

The next morning at loading time they were not keen to reboard. Charlie had to almost throw them on. The second day was the same as the first. Henry and Rastas continued their 'Mexican stand-off', and the girls hid in the corner. No one would eat. At the end of that day, they again exploded out of the truck in their rush to get away from each other.

By the third morning, things were tense. Charlie, who liked things to be orderly and systematic, was feeling the strain of this slow trek across Australia with an unwilling menagerie. He threw the animals on the truck again and the morning passed in silence. Lunch also passed in silence, and so did the afternoon. By unloading time things were grim. The animals did their usual bolt into the furthest corners of the yard and Charlie walked away throwing his hands in the air.

However, maybe the animals realised all the trouble they were causing because the next morning, much to Charlie's surprise, they walked quietly onto the truck.

More surprises were in store. When they stopped for lunch, all the animals were sitting down on the hay. Granted, they were still in their respective corners, but they were sitting. After that it was easy. Some nights when Charlie opened the crate, they would look at him from their reclining positions and not even move. The end of the trip found them all true friends. Henry and Rastas would sit in the middle of the crate back to back, using each other for support, and the cows would sit on Henry's side.

For the next few months, the animals stayed in the garden, until they became acclimatised. Their friendship never wavered. When Henry fell into the swimming pool one day they all rushed anxiously to the side and watched every move of the rescue operation. And when he was safely on land, the cows sniffed him all over to make sure he was alright—even Rastas gave him a casual inspection.

259

CHAPTER 20

❖

1986-1987

From July 1986 to September 1987 I played the stock market. In July 1986 I had listed all the debts I knew, and Marlee, Danielle and I had had a directors' meeting.

'We have three choices,' I said. 'We can sell and probably walk away with nothing, we can struggle on for the next twenty years in the same half-baked way we have for the last twenty years, or I can try to make some money on the stock market to get us through to next year at least.' In fact, we really didn't have three choices because there was not enough money to get through to next year and there was no way I could ask the bank for more.

I told them I would sell everything we had except the station and cattle, but that we needed money in the meantime to operate and pay the large outstanding loans. The only way to get some money quickly was to gamble, either on horseraces or the stock market. Horseraces were out, but the stock market seemed very good at present, and Charles had said gold was going to move soon. So, if we bought gold shares, we might just pick up some extra cash. Enough to help us survive for the moment.

The girls looked at me. Not knowing anything about the stock market, it didn't mean much to them.

'However,' I continued, 'I know nothing about the stock market and I could blow the only money that stands between us and food for the next six months. If I lose it, the game could be over.'

With complete blind faith they said, 'Go for it, Mum.'

In the next twelve months, Bullo River made one hundred

and fourteen thousand dollars in trading shares, and a little less the following year. It was the most remarkable run of luck. No matter what I touched, it turned to money. If I had not been so unsure of myself, I could have made ten times that.

The first share I bought was Chillagoe. I purchased these shares because a mining geologist who had been drilling for oil on Bullo the year before had come from the town of Chillagoe. I saw the name 'Chillagoe', the shares were very low-priced and Chillagoe was a goldmining company.

Within a week of me buying my shares, the managing director went to Europe and bought the patents on a new system for producing washing powder in condensed form—a kilo packet of washing powder would now be the size of an aspirin packet. Apparently the publicity was endless, but of course we missed the lot.

We had no television, no radio and no newspapers. Our only contact with the outside world was limited to the radio telephone and sometimes it took days for people calling in to get through. Calling out usually took about a half-day. So I knew nothing of the patent purchase, or the price rise, or the change in the company name.

The broker finally reached me by phone. He said he thought I should sell my Viking shares. They were having trouble with the patent in Europe and if it could not be resolved soon, the shares would start to drop.

'But I don't have any Viking shares,' I said. There were a few 'Yes you do', 'No I don't' exchanges and then he told me what had happened.

'So your fifteen cent Chillagoe shares are now Viking and at present, they are trading at . . .' pause as he clicked keys on the computer, 'seventy-eight cents.'

Did I want to sell? Until now, I had been very hesitant in this stock market venture, but that win had a marvellous effect on my confidence and I immediately ploughed back in. I bought all low-price shares and sold as soon as they moved a reasonable margin. This was my little plan. I suppose this is done by professionals on a larger scale but I don't really know.

I would buy ten thousand shares, hold them for ten days and sell with a three thousand dollar profit. I achieved this about two or three times a month, not all the time of course, but fairly regularly, for about eight months.

I bought Esmeralda shares because I once had a mythical maid called Esmeralda. Charles used to say, 'Why isn't this clean? Why hasn't that been put away? Where is my lunch?' and so on, and I would say, 'Good heavens, you just can't rely on staff today. I distinctly told Esmeralda to do that. I really must take that girl in hand.'

When I saw Esmeralda listed in the mining shares, it was a must.

'What did you buy today, Mummy?' the girls asked when they came in that night from the yard.

When they heard 'Esmeralda', they both laughed. They had grown up with Esmeralda, the mythical maid.

Another big killing was a complete mistake. A friend gave me a tip that something big was about to happen and Elders shares would really rise. I think it was when they were going for a brewery in England. But their shares were five dollars plus. This was getting way out of my depth. I anguished over it for days. I usually bought ten thousand shares, my plan being if the share rose ten cents, I made one thousand dollars. With five and ten cent shares, this was fine, even up to eighty cent shares, but five dollars? That would be fifty thousand dollars I was gambling. But then there was the other side of the argument—you also made big money. I wrestled with it for another day. We needed the money, no two ways about that. I decided I would go in, take a reasonable profit, and get out quickly. I didn't say anything to the girls.

I felt quite ill when I put the phone down. My hands were shaking. I had just gambled fifty thousand dollars.

A few days later my friend called.

'Bad luck about our Elders shares.'

My heart hit the floor. 'What happened?' I croaked.

Apparently the shares had dropped by dollars and were still dropping—they had lost the brewery deal and further trouble was rumoured.

I stopped listening. All I could think of was that I had just wiped out around twenty-five thousand dollars. I was sick for days. What was I to do now, sell and take the loss, hold on and hope that maybe they would pull off the deal? I decided to wait.

I went back to my ten cent shares and my little regular profits. I had a lot to make up.

I was buying another 'hunch share' about three weeks later when the broker said, 'You certainly made a smart move with your Elders shares. Are you going to hold them much longer, or take the profit now?'

'Are you being sarcastic?' I asked. He hesitated, so I said, 'What do you mean "profit"?'

'Well they've gone up substantially since you bought them last month.'

I was completely mystified. I had the listings in front of me from a three-day-old paper and unless some miracle had just occurred on the floor this Monday morning, I was twenty-eight thousand out of pocket.

'How much have they gone up?'

'About one dollar twenty.'

I nearly dropped the phone. 'What shares did you buy me?'

'Elders Resources, of course.'

Because I only bought gold shares, when I told him to buy Elders, he didn't even think of Elders in the industrial shares, which of course were the shares I was told to buy. I had been worried sick over the last month watching the shares drop and thinking of all the money we were losing when we were making money all the time. Bullo ended up making about twenty thousand dollars out of that mistake. But I had learned my lesson—no more tips from the experts. My stockbroker gave me a few good suggestions, but my regular profits stayed with the hunches.

The market was moving so fast that I could buy one hundred thousand five cent shares, the price would move five cents in a few weeks and I would sell and make five thousand dollars. It was heady business for me, so I can just imagine what those big guys were doing.

263

Another big profit was a share I bought because it had the same name as our dog. I found out later it was an aluminium share. I bought these shares a week before trade sanctions were imposed on South Africa. South Africa had been the world's biggest producer of aluminium, now it was Australia. The price went up.

The luck was not only in buying the shares. Sometimes a company announced an issue, and I made money. One day I bought a share and the price went up the very next day. I asked the stockbroker if he knew any reason—were they about to announce a good result in the mine, or was it a merger? His reply was, 'I really don't know why these shares are improving Mrs Henderson, maybe they found out you bought some.'

One day he said to me, 'Mrs Henderson, in the last ten weeks, out of the shares you have bought, there have been four mergers and three share issues.' He then asked me if I knew that insider trading was illegal and that receivers of information were also guilty.

I asked him what insider trading was. He gave up. I guess he finally believed that my amazing luck was just that, luck.

But our really big win has to be laid at Charlie's feet. About twenty months before his death, he had told me he wanted to buy some shares. He thought the share market was about to move, especially gold. This was my first introduction to the stock market. We were in Sydney and we had lunch with the stockbroker, then we visited the stock exchange. Charles, with introductions from the right quarters in Sydney, opened a share trading account.

He wanted to buy into a certain company. A friend's father was the managing director, and Charles had met him at lunch and was very impressed. In Charles's usual form, he had most of the facts wrong or had forgotten them, but he told me to call our new stockbroker and buy the shares.

'The name is North . . . North . . . North something, the mine is in the Northern Territory, they're mining gold, and it's a fairly new company.'

I told Charles I couldn't buy shares when I didn't know

the name of the company, but he said there couldn't be many gold companies in the Territory with a name starting with 'North'. I gave him one of my, 'Oh come on Charles' looks.

'Don't be cheeky.'

'What if there are four?' I asked patiently.

'Buy the lot.'

'Charles, why don't you just ask Peter the name?'

'What, and let him think I wasn't paying attention?'

'Well obviously you weren't.'

I called our new stockbroker with our first order and told him what I knew.

'Buy shares like this often?' he asked.

The stockbroker came back and said there was one company that fitted the description and the name was North Flinders. I told him to buy. This done, we forgot all about it.

Now, two and a half years later, this sudden and short urge of Charlie's was about to surface and help lift us out of our deep hole of debt. Well, not right out, but it was a rope for us to climb.

It happened a few days after my arrival back in Sydney from America. The broker tracked me to my brother's house and called, wondering if I wanted to sell my North Flinders shares. I said I didn't think I had shares in that company and he said I had bought them in 1984. I then remembered the great first share purchase. He said the shares had improved and made a good profit and I should sell. Indeed, the shares had doubled in price. I suppose I should have been delighted to find this nice little nest egg in a sea of debt, but my instincts said 'no'. The broker seemed to have gone to just a little too much trouble to track me down. I said I would call back if I changed my mind. I called my friend of the 'Elders tip'. He lived and breathed shares.

'North Flinders? No, you're a bit too late for that gravy train. Absolutely no seller at any price, those stocks are about to m–o–v–e.'

It seems the company was about to sign an agreement with the traditional owners and a new mining shaft was about to open. If this happened, and it seemed sure it would, the rumours were 'Lasseter's Reef proportions' in returns. It happened and the price went up and up.

This was the agony and the ecstasy to its fullest degree. During the next day I would calculate, by the hour, our profits, then all night I would have nightmares. They ranged from the stock market crashing due to world problems and gold losing its value overnight, to the mine collapsing and everyone being killed. I would wake the next morning exhausted. Each day as the amount increased, so did the strain. Weekends were really bad.

I chickened out at thirteen dollars, partly because thirteen was Charlie's lucky number, and partly because I hadn't slept in three weeks. Also, the bank was wanting the great meeting. The shares continued to increase and so then I worried about all the money I could have made but didn't! They finally levelled out at seventeen dollars. I calculated the amount I could have made if I had stayed in, and berated myself for weeks.

The really amazing part of this story was revealed to me a year or so later. Charles had bought shares in the wrong company. He had, at a later luncheon, told Peter's dad he had purchased shares in his Northern Territory gold company, North Flinders, and said what a great company it was. He told Peter's father to keep up the good work.

Peter's dad later told Peter of this strange conversation he had had with Charles. It seems Peter's father had been retired for years. The company he had been a director of was in Victoria, it was not in gold, and it was not a new company. So our biggest stock win was a complete fluke.

It was luck again when I sold most of the shares. It was the end of September 1987, and I was visiting my mother and sister in Queensland. The station needed money to bring in the fuel for the wet season and I was gambling with the money for these expenses. Also, I was on my way back to the station where the radio–telephone made share-trading a nightmare. So, having access to a normal phone, I sold the bulk of my shares and left just a few five cent hunches here and there, hoping they would take off. They did—right off the board when the crash came.

CHAPTER 21

❖

1987

In March of 1987, Marlee's Charlie decided he had been flying helicopters too long and wanted a break. So he came to Bullo to help us run the station. What a marvellous man. It is said, to really get to know someone, you have to live in the same house with them. It was a privilege to get to know Charlie. He was one of those good, strong, silent men who could always solve the problems. He was big, six foot three, capable and goodlooking. When Charlie walked into the house, you had that feeling, 'Everything is alright now'.

Charlie was our knight in shining armour. Marlee loved him, Danielle adored him, and if I had ever had a son, I would have wanted him to be just like Charlie.

The mustering season started to move along, we began improvements on the property, repairing machinery and so on, and also looked at our long-term plans for the future. The biggest problem was lack of cows—thousands had been destocked between 1983 and 1985, and no cows meant no babies, no babies no steers, and no steers no money. We had to get breeders.

I wrestled with this problem for weeks—it meant going further into debt. But the choice was clear, either expand, or sell. For years Charles had been running a half-baked programme, always in debt, always behind at the beginning of each year, not a decent bit of equipment on the whole place, miserable cattle. I wanted no more of this way of life. We had all worked our hearts out for years, only to go further into debt. However, there was so much to think about, I put the problem of breeders temporarily back on the shelf.

The 1987 season was good. Marlee, Danielle and Charlie were a wonderful team. Charlie and Uncle Dick had all the machinery humming, and the musters, despite some problems, were going smoothly and successfully. In the background I was busily working the stock market to produce what we considered great returns. Things were looking bright.

I was in Sydney with Danielle. She was going to America to visit her grandmother for a few months. Danielle had not been back to Maryland since she was two, so she did not know 'Bomma', her grandmother. One of Charles's many requests during those long months in hospital was that Danielle meet her grandmother, and I promised him I would do my best to get Danielle home to Maryland. Charles's mother was ninety-six years old so it could not be a long range plan. However, as I write this today, she is approaching one hundred and one years and is hale and hearty.

The visit would be very beneficial for Danielle. Apart from boarding school in Adelaide and school in Bundaberg, she had lived all her life on Bullo, which was a hard, harsh way of life. What she needed was a look at a 'world', worlds apart. The beauty of eastern shore Maryland was just the place to send her. She would also meet a whole family she had only heard about and seen in photos.

We rushed around town buying warm clothes. After giving her pages of instructions on what to do and what not to do, and a credit card, I waved goodbye. Within the next few days, the stock market did its amazing plunge, but I had no time to think about my few shares that were also crashing by the minute because my sister called to say Mum had had another massive stroke.

They didn't think she would come through this one. I dropped everything and flew straight to Bundaberg. There was a terrible storm approaching from the northeast. The sky was a black inky blue. It rushed to meet us as we drove from the airport to the hospital. I was quiet. I knew Mum was leaving us. Ralph was also quiet, so we stayed with our own thoughts as we drove to the hospital.

I had visited Mum as much as I could over the last eighteen months. On my way home from America for a short time, then in January 1987, and a few times during the year on business trips. She had moved out of the hospital and I had just spent a few weeks with her. We had some wonderful times, a lot of laughter, but there were also tears.

She had great difficulty in trying to communicate. She could not write, and all her speech came out as gibberish. But one of the biggest problems was that she did not know her speech was gibberish and became more and more frustrated with our lack of comprehension.

One day she was really throwing a tantrum. She wanted me to do something, that was clear, but I had no idea what. She could say a few words like yes, no, look, oh dear, and there, but that was about it. This particular day she was on the verge of despair.

'Look,' she said, and then launched into her own language, rounding it all off with, 'there.'

I sat for a while and then said, 'Now I'm supposed to do something?'

'Yes.' The tone was impatient.

'It's very clear in your mind what you want me to do.'

'Yes.'

'But you see, I haven't a clue what's in your mind because when it comes out of your mouth, it's gibberish.'

'No,' she said, shaking her head from side to side.

'Yes,' I said, nodding my head up and down.

'Look,' she said, and after that one clear word she lapsed back into her unintelligible jabber, although she enunciated each garbled word slowly as if I was a bit simple.

'I should understand what you've just said?'

'Yes.'

'I'll try to repeat it back to you and then you think about it, okay?'

'Okay.' She watched me closely.

So, as best I could, I repeated the jabber. Her eyes widened as I mimicked her.

'No,' she said, shaking her head again. My sister walked into the room.

'Sue, Mum doesn't believe she sounds all garbled when she speaks. Doesn't she sound like this . . . ?' I mimicked her gobbledegook again.

'Yes, Mum, that's exactly how you sound.'

At last it dawned on her. You could almost see her thought process—'and all that time I thought the whole world had gone mad and no one could understand me!'

Every night Sue, Ralph and I would all put her to bed. She really loved this little routine and would direct the whole procedure. The sliding door into the garden had to be open just so. Ralph would deliberately open it to the wrong position and he would be told in very definite gobbledegook that it was wrong.

Then Ralph would say, 'How about there?'

After several of these exchanges, she would realise he was teasing her and with a smile and wave of her hand, look the other way and ignore him. He would then put the door in the right position.

After the door, we would go through the same procedure with the blanket. The last was the positioning of her slippers and walker, so she could go to the bathroom. We would then kiss her goodnight and she would try to hold three hands and pat them all at once and tell us how lucky she was to have us. Her eyes said it all.

Of course usually it was only Sue and Ralph there to say goodnight. Tod would also do night shifts, and Fran day shifts. Ralph slept in the guest room after the day help had left. He is a great reader and listens to the radio most of the night. He said he would be reading late at night and Mum would go past his room with her walker and wave to him as she passed.

Ralph was wonderful to my mum during those eighteen months, as were Sue and Tod and Fran. It's the constant day in and day out care that is the hardest. They made Mum's last years on earth very happy and I will always be grateful to them for carrying my part of the load.

The district nurse came every week to record Mum's progress and to answer any questions the family had. I was there one day when she arrived. We chatted over a cup of tea.

'Visiting your mum is the highlight of my week. She's so happy and always so beautifully dressed.' Sue made Mum lovely colourful caftans and put make-up on her every day. 'It's such a pleasure to see an old person in her own home, surrounded by her family and people she loves. If only all old people could have this, what a wonderful world it would be.' She indicated the lovely view of the ocean across green lawns to a sandy beach. She patted Mum's hand and said, 'You're very lucky, Ida.' Mum smiled, and her eyes said, 'Indeed I am, indeed I am.'

'We're here, kiddo.' Ralph stopped the car. I took a deep breath and prepared myself. I met my sister in the hall. She said Mum did not know anyone and was in a semi-coma. I went into the room and saw her frail shape in the bed. I took her cold limp hand in mine, kissed her on the cheek and whispered in her ear, 'I'm here, darling.' Her eyes rolled back as if she was fighting to open them, but she couldn't. The fingers came alive and I felt the pressure of her fingers on my hand, very slight, but it was there.

Sue and I sat each side of the bed and talked to her about things we knew she would enjoy hearing. She quietly left us, holding our hands. She was with Dad again.

Every night in the last twelve years, up to the first stroke, Mum said her prayers. When I visited her, I could clearly hear her from the guest room. It is very nice to hear your mother bless you in her prayers. She would say the Lord's Prayer and a few other old favourites, and then she would bless the whole family. It would take about five minutes. She would work through us all in order of age, with husbands and wives and offspring, and would finally get to, 'And Sara, Charles, Marlee, Bon and Danya.' She would close with, 'Good night Aubrey, be with you soon.'

The closing lines of her prayers passed through my mind as I kissed her goodbye for the last time. I put my head on her shoulder and cried and cried. I felt as if part of my being had gone, she was such an important part of my life. I still cannot think of her without tears. I am crying as I write this. She was a mum who was always there for you, and the gap that she left is something I will have to live with for the rest of my life.

CHAPTER 22

❖

1987-1988

I was back on the station for Christmas. Marlee and Charlie stayed for Christmas Day, and left for Queensland in the new year. We had a quiet Christmas at Bullo, the loss of Mum was still heavy in my heart. But I was certainly learning fast that no matter how sad you are, life just keeps moving along and if you don't keep pace, you get steamrolled.

We spent the wet season working on more fencing. All the fencing on the place was useless, only three wires. The cattle just stepped through it as if it didn't exist. And the maintenance was endless. We pulled the fences down an area at a time and replaced them with good strong fences that the cattle stopped at, then walked along, not through. With half a million acres to do, it was going to take a few years.

Fencing and machinery repairs took us into the new year of 1988. We were so tired on New Year's Eve, we went to bed early, saying we would get up around eleven-thirty to celebrate the new year. We slept through it.

We had one very exciting plan for January—a wedding. Marlee and Charlie, being very practical people, had decided they better get married while there was a lull.

As Marlee put it, 'We've been engaged since December 1984, and if we don't marry this coming wet, I can't see another chance for years.'

So amidst cattle planning, yard planning, and money juggling, a section of January was shaded in and marked as 'wedding time'.

One of the hardest decisions was where. January ruled Bullo

273

out—the station is completely cut off during the wet. Most of our friends who lived in Kununurra and around the station area came from Queensland and New South Wales and were usually on holidays in January. Charlie's family came from near Cooktown, and most of our family and friends came from New South Wales and Victoria. So we decided to hold it in Brisbane, as this was the most central spot.

Marlee and I went to Brisbane in early December to order and print the invitations. We had already called most of our friends by phone from the station and told them about it, saying the invitations would be along later. I was sure it would take weeks to organise the invitations, but not so. The wedding industry really has its act together.

Before we could print the invitations, we had to decide on where to have the reception. So the night of our arrival, we sat and pored through the part of the yellow pages marked 'wedding receptions' and I wrote down about fifteen likely places. The next morning, armed with our list, we went to see them. Some places I wouldn't even get out of the cab, and Marlee said I was a snob.

'Maybe so, but I would rather have no reception at all than have it there.'

We were up to about number ten and I was starting to think maybe I was a bit too hard to please. We stopped in front of the next place and before we stepped out of the cab, I said, 'This is it!'

Marlee looked at me and rolled her eyes. 'Oh Mummy, how do you know? We haven't even been inside.'

'This is it!' And it was.

It sat on a high hill overlooking Brisbane and was a beautifully restored old home. That's what I liked about it— it looked like a home. It had charm and warmth, which is difficult to achieve when you have hundreds of people passing through every day. Of course they were booked out on Saturdays for fifteen months ahead, so that was how we ended up with Sunday, the 17th of January.

We mentioned invitations and within the hour a man was showing us samples. We picked a style and told them to hold

274

the printing until we gave them the church information and the next day the invitations were delivered to our hotel. We mentioned flowers, same thing. The florist met us the next day and the flowers were decided. Photographer, ditto. Talk about one-stop shopping!

With all this attended to, we had to find the church. Charlie was Catholic but not a churchgoer, Marlee was Church of England or Episcopalian as it's called in America and also not a churchgoer. So they were not really interested in a church wedding, but Marlee had carefully explained to Charlie that I was religious and they had to have a church wedding.

So it was back to the yellow pages, this time under 'churches'. I saw Church of England, Petrie. The wedding reception was at Petrie Mansions, so we assumed the church was close by. I called the church and spoke to a charming minister. I explained that we were from the Northern Territory and didn't know Brisbane very well and were wondering if it was far from the church to the reception house, as we thought it would be nice for the guests to walk from the church.

'It depends on how much you like walking,' he replied. The suburb of Petrie was twenty kilometres from Petrie Mansions. 'But a friend of mine has a lovely church in the street just behind the mansions. Give him a call.'

We did and made an appointment for the next day. We stopped in front of the church and, like the reception house, I knew it was the one. It was a little old wooden church nestled in amongst tall trees. When we walked inside Marlee too fell under its spell. The whole church was polished wood—floor, walls, ceiling and altar. It was beautiful. Just sitting there made you feel happy and at peace.

We went into the office to make the arrangements. When we said the seventeenth, the minister said the date was available, but he would be on holidays. This was a disappointment as we had both liked him immediately.

'But don't worry,' he said, 'my brother-in-law is a minister and he's looking after my Sunday services while I'm away, so there should be no problem.'

He said he would arrange the marriage certificate and all

we had to do was call his brother-in-law the week we arrived. One meeting and a rehearsal on Saturday night before the wedding should be enough. I mentioned that I would like someone to sing and he said his wife had a friend who sang at weddings, so he could contact her as well.

We had no time to have a wedding dress made but luck stayed with us and we found a beautiful dress, ready-made. It was lace, with a long plain bodice and a dull satin skirt forming a small train at the back. A headpiece of wispy flowers and a fluffy white veil, and Marlee looked gorgeous, even in the fitting room. I knew without a doubt that on her wedding day she would be breathtaking.

After finding some lovely aqua dresses for the bridesmaids, Danielle and a cousin on Charlie's side, we returned to the station. We worked until a week before the exciting day, then we once more departed for Brisbane, this time with Danielle and Charlie.

I called the minister the day after we arrived and there was no answer in the office, but this didn't worry me unduly as it was only Monday and we had until Sunday.

What a week! On top of the thousand and one things that needed to be done, Marlee decided Charlie should have dancing lessons so he would look right dancing the bridal waltz. Friends and family arrived from all over and there were dinners, luncheons, afternoon teas and cocktails, an endless array of events.

One very happy arrival was Peggy and Jack Cater. Jack was 'giving' Marlee away which was wonderful, as he had also given me away on my wedding day in Hong Kong twenty-eight years before. I know Charles would have thoroughly approved of Jack as his stand-in. Brigadier General John Keldie was to be master of ceremonies, and was handling all his duties as smoothly as a military operation. We had settled into the wedding mode.

Around Wednesday when there was still no answer at the church office I started to feel a bit worried. Thursday morning we went to the church. The house and office were locked up as tight as the church. We wandered around and found a door open in the church hall, just behind the church.

An art class was in progress. Most of the people were church members but the only information we could obtain was that the minister standing in—at least we knew he was a brother-in-law, they didn't even know this—arrived on Sunday morning, unlocked the church, gave the sermon, then locked the church and departed until the following Sunday. We asked if there was somewhere we could contact him. There was a five-minute debate over his name.

We went back to the apartments and I called the head office of the Church of England in Brisbane. The next day they called back to say sorry, they couldn't help. At this point I spoke my mind, and it wasn't pleasant. I explained, very firmly, that we had made a special trip to Brisbane from the Territory in December to arrange all the details, and now, when we arrive for the wedding, the church is locked until Sunday morning, we do not have the stand-in minister's name and it appears that no one else, including the church, does either.

'This is not acceptable, and I want answers within the hour.' I gave the poor girl my number and told her to get busy. It was Friday night. Marlee, Charlie, Danielle and the rest of the bridal group all disappeared to dancing lessons and on to dinner, and I worried.

I was called by some man in the Church of England offices who gave me the number of the head of the church committee for our little church. I thanked him curtly and called the number. This man was no help at all, he didn't even know the minister's name.

'Are you telling me you have a minister preaching in your church and you don't know his name?'

'Oh, it's not as it sounds. He only came to us last week and he was late. Seems a very busy man. He gave the service and we were all waiting to meet him over tea after the service, but he rushed away saying he was late for an appointment and would have time to talk this week. So you see, we're still waiting.'

'If by any chance you do see him before Sunday, could you please ask him to call me?'

He said he would. One consolation was that the wedding was after the service, so we had a chance he might turn up.

Saturday arrived and we still didn't know if we had a minister. I thought we had better start a back-up plan. John Keldie said that if he didn't arrive at the church for the rehearsal that night, he would make arrangements for an army minister to come from the headquarters in Brisbane. I relaxed slightly.

Marlee, Charlie and the mob disappeared to dancing lessons again and I took an aspirin.

Peg and Jack, bless them, wandered over to the church and found a lady there arranging flowers for the wedding. They called me and told me there was also a lady there who said she was singing at the wedding. I quickly called the dancing studio and told the wedding group to meet me at the church.

Our holiday minister had arranged for the lady to meet us to discuss the flowers. Apparently she always decorated the church for the weddings. She had it all in hand. The next day the church looked beautiful.

Next, the lady who always sang at weddings sang for us and she had a delightful voice. The organist had also turned up and she accompanied our singer. So it was almost perfect, except we still didn't have a minister.

We were still hopeful; everyone else had arrived, so surely he would. He did, and what a character! It was eight-thirty, he raced in, gave Marlee and Charlie a non-stop lecture on married life, duties to their children, and so on, all interspersed with directions on how to walk down the aisle, what he would say to them tomorrow, and directions to the organist and singer. He shook all our hands, said he would see us tomorrow and was gone.

We wandered to our cars in a daze. I suppose we were so glad to have a minister, we really didn't care if he was a bit eccentric. Saturday night we celebrated—we finally had a preacher.

Sunday dawned dark and rainy. The photographer had wanted to take photos in the park so all morning there were phone calls back and forth.

'It's stopped raining. We can.'

278

'It's raining. We can't.'

I finally said 'no'. I could just see Marlee tiptoeing through the mud in the park and being drowned by one of the sudden squalls that were racing over Brisbane at regular intervals. The sun came out and we had a peaceful photo session in the foyer and garden close by.

We finally arrived at the church and it was Peg who mentioned we still did not know the minister's name. She was right. In all the panic and fuss of the previous night, he had left and we still didn't know his name. Peg said she would find out. I didn't mind, just as long as the wedding ceremony was pleasant. I didn't care what his name was.

As we were doing the final adjustments for Marlee to walk down the aisle with Jack, Peg came over to me.

'His name is Hall, Reverend Hall.' The bridal march started up and I slipped into the church to be in place to watch my daughter walk down the aisle.

What a picture she was: absolutely radiant. At that moment I felt great joy and a little sad. If only Charles and Mum could have lived to see this day.

The minister was a sheer delight. He rambled on, sang a few bars of different hymns during his sermon, lost his train of thought a few times and wandered onto completely different subjects on the punchlines of funny stories he was relating. But, as eccentric as he was, the most amazing thing was still to surface. We were all standing in the courtyard talking after the ceremony when Peg mentioned she lived in Hong Kong.

'Oh, my uncle was in the church in Hong Kong,' said Reverend Hall. His accent was cockney Australian with a Queensland overtone, if you can imagine it. We were all stunned.

Peg broke the silence. 'You can't mean Bishop Hall?' Bishop Hall was a quiet, soft-spoken, English gentleman with a very British accent. He seemed worlds apart from this jolly Australian.

'That's him.'

'But we've known Bishop Hall for over forty years. He married Sara in Hong Kong in 1960,' said Peg.

279

'Well, what do you know about that?' And he was off to another appointment.

We went to the reception still shaking our heads. What an amazing coincidence. Marlee did not know any of this and Jack included it in his speech.

'We sometimes wonder if events are coincidence or planned by fate. A remarkable event has happened today. Sara was married in Hong Kong in 1960 to Charles, and they were married by Bishop R. O. Hall, Bishop of Far East Asia. When Marlee was born, Bishop Hall did Charles the honour of accepting to be her godfather. He visited her in Manila when she was four years old. I had the pleasure of giving Sara away. Now, twenty-eight years later, I gave Marlee away to another Charlie and the minister that performed the wedding was Bishop Hall's nephew. Now if that's not predestined, I don't know what is.'

Marlee looked at me amazed, her eyes asking, Is this true? I nodded and she smiled.

The wedding was a great success and the dancing went on and on. Eventually I told Marlee and Charlie it was time to change and say goodbye. 'No way!' they said. They were having too much fun to leave. The only way around this was for them to go through the goodbyes, leave, and come back in the other door. This they agreed to. The circle was formed, Marlee threw her bouquet and they left through one door and, one minute later, came in another. They danced until three.

As Charlie said, 'I'm not wasting all that money spent on dancing lessons.'

As a surprise, Danielle and I had booked the bridal suite in the apartment building where we were staying. We had looked at it during the week. It was all white, even the carpet, and had a spa bath and enormous bedroom and bed. We bought some lacy bits and pieces for Marlee, some unmentionables for Charlie, and put champagne and strawberries in the fridge. We told the girls in reception to tell them that due to a breakdown in the airconditioning, they had to be moved to another apartment for the night. The surprise was complete and Marlee called at three-thirty in the morning to tell me.

We stayed in Brisbane for a few more days and then Danielle and I headed back to the station, while Marlee and Charlie went on a driving holiday up the coast, ending up at Charlie's family's property near Cooktown. They were going to stay there for a few months until mustering started at Bullo.

CHAPTER 23

❖

1988

Mustering began around April and it was wonderful to have Marlee and Charlie home. For the first time in years, the station began to show signs of care, with functional yards, and water and feed for the cattle. No more complaints, as in the old days, of cattle arriving at the meatworks too weak to stand. But we had a lot of work ahead of us.

At one yarding alone we had eight hundred unbranded, fully grown cattle, in a yarding of seventeen hundred head. This showed bad mustering techniques and cattle control. Apart from these problems, there was the other major problem which we had discussed in 1987 of not enough breeders. This year it was even more evident. We were simply not producing enough steers.

Around May/June, after our two major musters, we sat down and discussed the problem again. It was clear we couldn't put off the decision any longer. We had to buy more breeding cows and bulls if our herd was ever going to improve. Queensland was still in drought and the stations were selling more and more breeders each year as the drought continued. A lot of properties were down to their best foundation stock. If we were going to buy breeders, now was the right time to get top quality for a reasonable price.

I was still struggling, paying Charles's debts. I had sold the house in Queensland, a gift from Charles which I had never even slept in; I had sold his boat which was in such disrepair that her value was dropping by the month; and I had sold some gold leases that had cost a fortune to buy and maintain and yet we had never had the money to do anything with them. All the money from these sales, and my lucky run on the stock market, had brought us back to a point where we could service the loan still outstanding. Now to go back into the realms of uncertainty and debt again . . .

But the facts could not be ignored: we had to bring in more breeders, now. We also had to remove all the old scrubber bulls and buy more good Brahman bulls.

Charles had bought good Brahman bulls way back in 1975, but the herd did not improve. This was because we had too many wild scrubber bulls serving inferior inbred shorthorn cows, while the good Brahman bulls sat under a tree and sulked.

Our first move was to buy a short wheel-base Toyota and turn it into a bull-catcher.

Marlee had been taught the technique of bull-catching by two of the top bull-catchers in the North—Tommy Teece and John Kirby. Of course she didn't actually have lessons. In 1983 and 1984 when Charles destocked cows under the BTEC programme, he also hired contract bull-catchers to bring down the wild bull problem. Our bulls were such that the difference between what was termed a scrubber and what we had to work with as a breeding bull was scarcely discernible. So Marlee would drive around with the bull-catcher telling him which bulls we considered to be breeding bulls and which scrubbers.

During this time, she perfected the art of bull-catching. With the little 'green machine'—that is the bull-catcher's name—Marlee catches, on an average, one hundred and eighty bulls each year, and has done for the last four years.

It is not hard to see why the Brahman breeding bulls Charles had bought over the years did not have much chance to do their thing. Along with the contract bull-catching done in the early eighties and the regular yearly turn-off in the last four years, we have removed close to two thousand scrubber bulls and mickies (baby bulls) from the property. This has not only earned us good money, but it has also had a marked effect on the quality of the herd. The Brahman bulls are no longer sitting under trees sulking.

With the bull-catching programme now at least started,

the next immediate step was to buy quality breeders and bulls. So it was back to the bank. I enthusiastically outlined the great plan Marlee, Danielle, Charlie and I had drawn up. They listened and said it sounded good, but could I present a feasibility study? I told them timing was of the essence—if the drought in Queensland broke, cattle prices would go up and the herd we proposed to purchase of one thousand breeder cows and sixty breeder bulls would double in cost. The price we were working on per head was our limit. But still, they needed a feasibility study. I had seen a few of these so-called 'feasibility studies'. Charles had had some done for his wondrous schemes. They were enough to cure me of 'feasibility studies' for life. But the facts remained: no feasibility study, no loan.

When the accountants told me how much the feasibility study would cost, I was stunned. I had had no idea I had hundreds of thousands of dollars worth of this humbug sitting in Charles's 'wondrous schemes' filing cabinet. The extraordinary amount the accountant quoted, plus a time frame of six months to complete a professional feasibility study, was out of the question. So I did my own feasibility study.

I locked myself in the office for five days and nights and came up with what I considered a fair presentation. I made a graph of the new herd with the yearly calving expectancy, the turn-off (steers sold), the value of the turn-off, the value of the heifers that moved into the herd as breeding cows, and what it would all mean to the overall operation of the station over a period of ten years.

I used the format of one of Charles's super-expensive feasibility studies, substituting our idea and plan for his idea and plan. It worked. The bank came back after ten days and said to go ahead. However, even with all this speed, we missed the herd of cattle we had had all lined up to buy. We received the bank's approval around midday and went straight to the owner with a firm offer, only to be told the cattle had been sold the night before.

So Marlee and Charlie started looking for another large herd on the market. This was not that simple. There were plenty of cattle for sale, but we had to find a good bloodline of Brahmans raised on hard country as cattle from 'soft' country would not survive up here. So we really had to do our homework.

The court case of Bonnie versus Bullo River was now looming on the horizon. The feelings this provoked would fill many books, but I will not even attempt to record mine. I was so down, I knew that if I tackled the problem, it could finish me. I had to walk away from it, bury it very deep. I told my lawyer to settle out of court on the condition that I did not have to see Bonnie or her husband in person during the settlement. I was not acquainted with the legal procedure, but apparently this was in fact the norm rather than unusual.

On the 2nd of August, 1988, in my lawyer's office in Darwin, I signed papers pertaining to and finalising this dreadful affair. Somewhere, in another office, I assume Bonnie did the same, and on the 2nd of August, 1988, I lost a daughter.

A film crew from Germany arrived at Bullo. Hardy Krüger wanted to film us and Bullo as part of a series to be shown in Germany called 'Hardy Krüger's Weltenbummler'. The series was about Krüger travelling to interesting places around the world. Matthew, the director from 'The Henderson Daughters' Big Country story, came with the crew.

We were busy mustering cattle; we were really too busy to spare the time, and perhaps I should have said no. During the first few days of filming, a bushfire came over the mountain and into the southwestern corner of the valley about twenty-five miles from the homestead. It had to be stopped or it would burn all the feed in that section. Filming was suspended and we all became fire fighters.

With Marlee, Charlie and Danielle directing, we managed to clear a fire break wide enough to stop the fire advancing, and after a few more days of fighting, the fire was contained and slowly burned itself out.

It was the second to last day of filming. The girls and Charlie had been loading cattle on trucks all day, and did not get back to the homestead until nine-thirty that night. They were exhausted, but we still had to do a dinner sequence for

285

the film crew. So at eleven p.m., there we were having a candlelight dinner, with about eight super bright lights all around, pretending to enjoy ourselves. Normally, when we came in at nine-thirty at night after loading cattle, we would grab a bite to eat, head for a hot bath and collapse into bed. Having to shower, dress and sit down to a candlelight dinner and small talk, after seventeen and a half hours in cattle yards, seemed just ridiculous.

However, we eventually did what was required for the camera and could go to bed. At least there was only one more day of filming. Not that we didn't enjoy having the crew, but it meant eight more people to cater for, and the girls and Charlie already had more work than they could manage, without having to do silly things for the camera.

At about eleven the next morning, there was to be the usual galloping of horses past the camera that all crews seem to want. Charlie was rounding up the horses on his motor bike. Then the final scene would be the girls and I standing on the mountain where Charles's ashes are, overlooking the valley.

It was now midday. People had been rushing in and out of the house for the past hour. There seemed to be a problem but I dismissed it as technical. Marlee came into the house and as she rushed through I yelled, 'What's wrong?'

As she ran towards the helicopter, she shouted back, 'I don't know yet.' The helicopter disappeared in a cloud of dust.

Only minutes later, the helicopter landed again and the pilot asked to talk to me. I walked with him into the living room where we could be alone. I knew from his face that something had happened, but even my worst fears did not prepare me for his next words.

'Charlie has been accidentally killed. His motorbike hit an anthill in the grass, he was thrown off. His neck was broken.'

I just stared at him as these words ricocheted around my brain.

'Marlee?'

'She is with him now, bringing him back in the Toyota.'

'No, oh Marlee, no!' The words echoed down a long tunnel.

I was led to my bedroom and I cried and cried. I wanted to go to Marlee but I couldn't bear to see the pain that I knew would be there. She was with Charlie in their bedroom. I knew I should be strong for her but at that moment I was a mess. I had to gather myself.

It took me hours, but I finally said, 'I must go to Marlee.'

She would not leave Charlie, so I had to go into their room. I walked halfway across the room and saw that wonderful man lying there, and Marlee's eyes asking me to make him wake up. I broke. I really don't know what I did. I think I simply collapsed in a howling heap.

I remember Danielle saying, 'Take Mummy out of the room, quickly.'

Once away from that heartbreaking scene, I slowly calmed down.

During the terrible time that followed, Danielle was wonderful. She was a pillar of strength. She quietly organised everything, as well as taking care of Marlee and me.

People were everywhere. At some some time, the film crew departed, the Timber Creek police arrived, Ralph flew over from Queensland, Charlie's father and brothers arrived, as well as many friends. I think I did speak to them all, but I do not remember clearly.

Danielle came to me. The police had to take Charlie away and Marlee wouldn't let them. Even Danielle could not convince her. She was now in deep shock and firmly believed he would wake up and everything would be back to normal.

I had to go back into that room. I had to find the strength. I walked in and we looked at each other in silence, tears streaming down our faces.

'He is going to be alright, isn't he?' Her eyes pleaded with me to say yes. I quietly shook my head. We cried together for a long time. Eventually there was a knock on the door.

'You have to say goodbye to Charlie, darling, he has to leave us now.' She did, and her pain and agony broke my heart.

After he had gone she curled up on the part of the bed where he had lain and softly cried. Danielle brought in two 'knock-out' pills and we both found respite in oblivion.

Marlee stayed in deep shock until well after the funeral. She had wanted Charlie to be buried here on Bullo, but his parents asked if he could be buried in the town of Mareeba, the town nearest their property. Marlee granted them this wish, so we flew to Cairns.

It was a terrible journey. Such sadness is hard to describe. Our wonderful friend Peter Roberts flew from Sydney especially to take us to Cairns. He picked us up in Darwin, flew with us to Cairns via Alice Springs, and then flew all the way back to Sydney. He did this simply to ensure our grief could be private. I feel very privileged to have a friend such as Peter.

Watching Charlie's coffin being lowered into the ground sent a cold, numb feeling through me. We were now alone again.

On our sad journey home another thoughtful friend, Jim Craven, made the journey bearable with his help and thoughtfulness. Jim had helped us over the years with many machine and truck purchases, and he and Marlee's Charlie had spent hours discussing machines whenever Jim visited the station. So in our darkest hour, many friends put out their hands to help us.

We returned to the station. Marlee was so sad that nothing except silence was appropriate. I slept in the room with her and helped her through some terrible nights and nightmares. Some nights were so bad, I was ready to give in. There seemed no way we could climb the mountains of grief.

I was now fifty-two years old. I had lost my husband, my mother, a daughter in litigation, my son-in-law, and now it seemed Marlee was lost in grief forever. She would take a knock-out pill and sit in a daze all day. She hardly ate, and was losing weight at a frightening rate. I couldn't see the point of going on.

But then what would happen to Marlee? Filters of light started to flicker through my gloom. Danielle's lovely face would smile wistfully at me whenever she found me sad. Slowly I realised I had to keep fighting. I still had Marlee, Danielle, my family and many wonderful friends. I had my health and

I had a home to fight for. And I just couldn't give more grief to my daughters.

I decided the first thing I had to do was get those knock-out pills away from Marlee. She had to face the grief without the dope and then I would know if I would ever see the Marlee I once knew again. We would start the very next day.

The next morning I found her in the kitchen. 'Marlee, you must get off those pills. The few days I was on them was terrible. You've been on them too long.' She turned to me and I could see immediately her eyes looked better.

'I just flushed them all down the toilet, and I didn't take one last night.' We put our arms around each other and cried.

'We'll make it, darling, we'll make it.' Danielle came into the room and put her arms around both of us. We all cried.

In normal times, Danielle and Marlee fought like cat and dog. They fought over anything. But during this time Danielle was the sweetest of sisters.

Each day saw a step along the recovery path. Of course it would take years to conquer the grief, if ever. But you learn to live around it. You laugh and appear happy and seem to be enjoying yourself while all the time the grief is alive and well inside you. The secret is to control it, so that you can live with it, so that it doesn't destroy you. Marlee has achieved this, but only after a long, hard, sad road. She presents a smiling face to the world, but, being her mother, I can see behind this. Her eyes say, 'Sorry, I can't help still being sad' and my eyes say back. 'It's okay, be sad, just keep it with us'.

We still have a good cry, but over the years the hopelessness of the grief has faded slightly—it's become a soft, acceptable sort of grief that can even tolerate a sad smile now and then.

CHAPTER 24

❖

1988-1990

After what is considered, in the business world, a reasonable time, the bank reminded us of the loan money sitting waiting. I thought it would be good to get Marlee away from the station for a while, so she and Danielle drove to Queensland to buy breeders. Most of the legwork had been done by an old friend, Alan Woods, who, through an agent, had narrowed our purchase down to a selection from four properties. True to form, he led us to top quality cattle and the purchase was made.

They drove back with the cattle trucks, resting the cattle along the way. They arrived on Bullo with decks and decks of beautiful Brahman breeders and a few decks of gorgeous bulls. To see those animals walking regally down the ramp was marvellous. They were Bullo's future. They had cost a lot of money, but they were worth it.

Now when I drive through the paddocks and see the beautiful little Brahman calves frisking about, I remember Charles saying, 'Some day on Bullo there'll be top quality cattle grazing on improved green pasture for as far as the eye can see.' When he said that he was looking at inbred shorthorns chewing on stubble on the salt flats.

We are getting there, Charlie, we are getting there.

April 1989 was the courtcase with Gus. I tried to settle out of court again, not that this case would affect me emotionally. It was upsetting—I had known Gus since our airport meeting in 1960—but it could not hurt me in the way that an entanglement with your daughter could. Financially, it was a different matter. And that was why we ended up in court, because of money—half a million dollars.

In the deed signed in 1985, Charles and Gus had agreed that Charles would deliver eight hundred head of breeder cows and thirty bulls. In the hand-written contract they both signed, it was stated that delivery would take place over three years with one last year for any shortfall. Charles had written the delivery as four years, two hundred head per year. Gus said he wanted as many cattle as possible in the first year. Charles said he didn't think the Bullo herd could stand losing more than two hundred the first year. They finally agreed to change the first year's delivery to four hundred breeders on the understanding that if Charles could not deliver all four hundred, then the shortfall, indeed any shortfall over the three years, would be made up in the fourth year. In Gus's own handwriting, on the first handwritten draft contract, and in his own diary, he said, 'Henderson to have the option to make up any shortfall in 1988.'

As I said to my lawyers, 'This is the truth and it is in Charles's and Gus's handwriting. This is what they agreed, yet you tell me this cannot be used in court.'

'The court will only look at the final deed.'

'You mean the ambiguous jargon the lawyers wrote?'

'Yes.'

'No one is interested in the truth, a loophole has been found and now there will be endless exchange and manoeuvring of fact and laws, and the truth is out the window, forgotten.' He had the grace to look uncomfortable.

So we were in court arguing over an ambiguous clause, even though Marlee and I had agreed to deliver all the cattle to Gus in the three years without the fourth year's grace. The year Charles died, which was the second year, we could have delivered all that year's cattle to him, except that it would have been three weeks late. We had one hundred and thirty-three of the two hundred head in the yards and he refused to come and inspect them. The next year we wanted to deliver all the cattle and finish the contract, but he refused to accept them, saying that they were 'out of time'. Because of these

291

so-called 'out of time cattle' he was suing us for half a million dollars.

So the ponderous wheels of litigation started to move. I knew nothing about courts of law. Except for a few minutes in the courtroom during one of Charles's endless legal encounters, I had no idea of court procedure.

Apparently, the first step was to obtain a barrister. Gus Trippe had a top Q.C. from Sydney, so we picked a top Q.C. from Brisbane. He was obviously a good choice because after our lawyers had spent some weeks briefing him, he was appointed a judge. This was February, and the case was in April. Richard, our lawyer, then approached a Q.C. in Adelaide and he agreed to take over the case. After another period of briefing, arrangements were being made for him to come to Darwin when a murder case he was handling was rescheduled to our dates in court, so he had to hand back the file. Richard then approached a local Q.C. Time was running out but Richard said that as the Q.C. lived in Darwin, we would be able to make up for lost time. More briefing. By this time I was feeling more than anxious. It was bordering on lunacy.

Richard called a week before the trial.

'I don't know how to tell you this.'

'Let me guess, our Q.C. has been made a judge?'

'No.'

'He's been hit by a bus?' I would have believed anything.

'No, he has a trial that will now run over into the first three days of our trial. So he's called to ask if his junior counsel can handle it for that time.'

'A Darwin junior counsel against a top New South Wales Q.C.? Why bother going into court?' I was desperate.

'Leave it with me, I'll see what I can do.'

I put down the receiver. Did I have any choice?

It was Wednesday, five days before the trial, when Richard called. 'Good news, we have a Q.C. I've already started briefing him. Can you be in Darwin on Saturday to talk to him?'

'Yes. And do you think he could lock himself in the courtroom incommunicado until Monday?'

Richard laughed. 'His name is Graham Hiley.'

I put the phone down. I thought, well, I suppose a Q.C. five days before a trial is better than no Q.C. at all.

Where had I heard that name? I opened the file on the case and flipped through the endless notes that had accumulated during the build-up, I found his name way back at the beginning. I had called a friend in Sydney for advice, and he had come back with the name Graham Hiley. He was considered to be the best Q.C. in Darwin. My heart jumped— we had landed on our feet, we were back in the ballgame.

We met Graham on Saturday and Marlee and I spent many hours telling the story and answering questions. We both left Graham's office feeling much happier than we had for many months. We had liked him instantly.

Monday arrived. Nerves were top billing. Richard told us Marlee was allowed to hear the opening address by both counsel, but then she would have to leave as she was a witness. The Q.C. for Trippe opened. Ten minutes into his address, I felt sick. If he proved any of the things about us he said he would, we were good candidates for the devil's job. Marlee looked at me and our eyes said the same thing, 'We are in trouble.'

This man was certainly living up to his reputation. We were in the right, but I quickly realised that in the courtroom this was irrelevant. It was how you played the game and we were up against a top pro. I was feeling very sorry for myself when one of the court's officers came into the room and went up to the judge. Trippe's Q.C. stopped as the judge held up his hand. The officer whispered something to the judge. He called Graham and the other Q.C. over to the bench. They spoke for a while in hushed tones. We gleaned that this was not part of normal procedure because Gus was asking his lawyers what was happening.

Gus's barrister had to leave immediately, his father was critically ill and he was needed back in Sydney. He excused himself and left the courtroom. There was stunned silence.

The junior counsel stepped in and the address continued. Then Graham spoke and on it rolled. The case really revolved around one side saying each load of cattle had to be delivered in the year stated with twelve months' grace for each year, and the other side—our side—saying three years to deliver eight hundred head with one year, the fourth, for any shortfall, as per the handwritten contract. But here we were day after day laboriously wading through a mountain of seemingly unrelated facts and reports. What a nightmare. My only advice on going to court is, don't! If there is any way of settling your differences out of court, take it.

The biggest blow was yet to come. Trippe informed me that Bonnie was to testify in court. So, in fact, he was able to hurt me emotionally. To watch your own daughter standing up in court and willingly testifying against you is more than any parent should have to endure. I felt completely cold and empty inside. I didn't think she could hurt me any more, but I was wrong.

When it was all over we had to wait for the decision. Richard said it could take months, but for the first few weeks we jumped at every phone call. Then, as the weeks passed, the urgency did too. We still speculated endlessly but we were now very busy with the mustering. In June, Richard phoned.

'We won!' he shouted down the line. I closed my eyes and said a silent thank you to God. 'All in all a fantastic result,' Richard went on.

All I could get out was, 'Oh Richard, that's wonderful!'

'Of course it's not over yet, he could appeal.'

'What do you mean, not over, we won didn't we?'

'Yes, but he could appeal.'

Here we go again. I just knew Trippe would appeal. 'Okay, what happens now?'

So Richard outlined the complicated procedure of an appeal.

'But if in twenty-eight days he doesn't file an appeal, it's over?'

'Yes.'

Another twenty-eight days. We put our heads down and worked to stay sane. Twenty-eight days passed—no appeal. Again a silent prayer of thanks. For the first time in months we went about our work with some lightness in our hearts.

After many years of forward planning, the army's 'K89' was

finally moved into gear. What a massive undertaking. Most people have no idea of the work entailed in moving men and equipment on this scale. K89 was the largest peacetime exercise in the world and stretched across three States, Western Australia, Northern Territory and Queensland. Most of the Engineer Regiment was stationed on Bullo—about two hundred plus.

By the end of the exercise, I am sure most of the 'goodies' and 'baddies' had had tea and banana cake at the Bullo River homestead. At one stage of the 'war', I was baking ten supersize cakes a day, and I gave up icing them as they were still hot when the last piece disappeared from the plate.

The association between Bullo and the Australian Army goes back to 1972. Charles regarded the Australian Army as one of the best fighting units in the world and always welcomed it on Bullo. I suppose in return for this continued support, the army offered to build a causeway across the Bullo River. The Department of Roads supplied the materials, the army, the expertise, and Bullo nine hundred banana cakes and thousands of gallons of tea.

The war over, and the causeway completed, on their last night we had the opening ceremony. The men were not allowed to drink alcohol, but nothing was said about eating, so Marlee and I made a massive fruitcake and used one gallon of rum in the making. By the night of the ceremony, every soldier within one hundred miles knew there was a gallon of rum in the fruitcake.

Marlee and I iced the cake and decorated it with 'Thank you', and put it safely on the back seat of the Pajero, or so we thought.

About ten miles from the causeway, a wallaby suddenly exploded out of the grass on the side of the road, with two dingoes in hot pursuit. He tried to jump the Pajero, failed, and crashed into the window behind me on the passenger's side. The window shattered into a thousand pieces, and they all showered down onto the beautiful rum-laced 'thank you' cake.

When we arrived at the causeway we told the tale of the wallaby. But the anticipation of one gallon of rum was too much and the glass-covered cake was whisked away to the operating table where, with surgeon's skill, the glass-impregnated icing was delicately removed. The fruitcake was then enthusiastically consumed in record time.

The dust having settled after the mass exodus of machines and men, we looked forward to a period of relative calm. No such luck. Ten months before, we had bought three hundred breeders from a 'clean' (no TB), completely destocked, restocked property. It now seemed that this property had just had what was termed a 'breakdown', which meant that TB had been found in the herd. And because we had bought cattle from there, our cattle were now suspect.

This event happening hundreds of miles away had the following effect on Bullo: we could not sell these cattle, or any of their offspring, except for immediate slaughter—their offspring had been meant for the live-steer export trade. We could not move them to any other part of the property, and the area they were in, which had been classed as clean, was now infected. So our eight-year programme of testing to achieve 'clear' status was now possibly down the drain and we had a quarter of the property isolated. Also, the herd was not there alone. With it was a herd of four hundred that had tested clean through the programme, plus sixty breeder bulls, which had been about to move around the property as they were now old enough to work, and eight hundred other breeders bought in Queensland. We were talking about fifteen hundred head of cattle.

Marlee and I listened in silence as we were told we had to shoot all the beautiful breeders we had worked so hard to buy. At that stage we were working extra bulldozing contracts and entertaining tourists on top of all our other work in order to keep up our interest payments until the breeders' offspring started to bring in money. Some days it was from four a.m., working cattle in the yards and bulldozing, and then sitting down to dinner with twelve or sixteen guests until midnight. Marlee would slip away around ten and I would stay until the guests went to bed. She would then be up at four a.m.

and I could sleep till six. Now we were being told it was all in vain. We came out with the same words in unison.

'Over my dead body you will!'

Something in our voices must have conveyed our determination because they then brought up the option of testing the herd. The discussions which followed stretched over eighteen months. In the halls of the offices of BTEC, Marlee and I became known as 'the Henderson ladies', and an awful lot could be read into that phrase.

The animals in question had been established in an area termed as 'bush'. This means a large tract of undeveloped land with very little fencing. In this particular case there was no internal fencing at all. There was a fence at twelve-mile. This was across the valley from mountain range to mountain range and the 'twelve-mile' meant it was twelve miles from the homestead. The next fence, again across the valley, was at twenty-two-mile. So the area was roughly ten miles by eighteen miles. Our plan before the breakdown had been to establish the young breeders in that area and let them settle down the first year, then muster them the following year. With the cattle now suspect, we couldn't do this. We had to muster and test them all, hold them for a period, and then test them again.

This entailed all kinds of problems. It would take us the rest of the season to build fences to enable us to muster them and by the time we had finished there would be no more time to finish our yearly mustering to earn our income. We said we couldn't achieve this immediately—it would have to be at the beginning of the next season after the wet. After much debating and arguing, they agreed. Over the wet we would build the fencing needed to successfully muster that big area. We finally achieved the testing by about September of the following year and came up clean!

However, this was another twelve months down the track. At present, it was near the end of the mustering season 1989, and apart from the suspect cattle problem we had had a good season, and both court cases were over.

Danielle had met 'Mr Right'. He had his own business in

Queensland and he could not come to Bullo, so she wanted
to go and live in Queensland for a while. But she felt she
was letting us down by leaving. However, as I explained to
her, 'Martin is unhappy because he can't see you, and you're
unhappy for the same reason.' And this wasn't helping the
happiness situation on Bullo, because Marlee and Danielle were
back to their regular arguing. We would miss her dreadfully,
but I thought it would be good for her to go out into the
outside world on her own. So in November we sadly waved
goodbye and I watched 'my baby' take that big step into the
outside world and womanhood.

Marlee caught scrubber bulls with the 'green machine' until
the rain made it impossible to continue and around the 20th
of December we rushed into Darwin for Christmas shopping.
While we were there, we visited Richard, our solicitor, and
he told us that Trippe had filed an appeal.

'How can he? What about the twenty-eight days? They
were up five months ago!'

'They're claiming the judgment is not complete until costs
are settled and that was only done a few weeks ago.'

Richard did not feel that this was likely to get approval,
so our lawyers lodged an objection to the right to appeal.

New year wasn't much to celebrate—we had the BTEC
problem to solve, the court case was back on the agenda and
the interest rates were climbing daily.

One bright twinkle was 2nd of January, Danielle's twenty-
first birthday. She had always complained that her birthday
was so close to Christmas and New Year that it did not get
the proper attention. So I knew I would have to give extra
special attention to this one or I would be in strife.

Danielle had been away since November and because of
their workload, she and Martin had not been able to come
to Bullo for Christmas. I thought I would plan a lovely dinner
and dance twenty-first in Darwin with close friends. But when
I presented this plan to Danielle, she said there was too much
work on their agenda and there wasn't enough time for them
to go to Darwin. So that was the end of the dinner dance.

Marlee and I called her on the morning of the 2nd and

wished her a lovely day and we sent her three big bunches of flowers hourly for three hours. She liked that. Then, after much talking, Marlee and I decided the best gift we could think of was a Toyota utility. We delivered it a month or so late. Marlee loaded it on our seven-ton truck and took it to Cloncurry in February.

Between 2nd of January and delivery, there were endless phone conversations about the mystery gift. Questions like:

'Is it wood?'

'How big?'

'Is it useful?'

'Steel?'

'Have I ever had one before?'

'Oh, Mummy, please tell me what it is!'

I stayed home to look after the animals and pets on the station, so there were many phone calls between Marlee and myself regarding the strategy of delivery. Marlee arrived in Cloncurry and unloaded the Toyota at a trucking yard. I had arranged for a large basket of flowers with long ribbon streamers and Marlee sat this on top of the bonnet. The Toyota was white and the flower arrangement was pink and white, so it looked very feminine, or as feminine as a Toyota can look.

She then sneaked into the street, parked it in front of the house next door, and went back and got the truck.

She told Danielle she had to call me to say she had arrived safely. She whispered to me the Toyota was parked outside the house next door and gave the phone to Danielle. Now our Danielle is a very composed type. If you think something is exciting and you tell Danielle, the response is usually, 'Oh yeah.' But we got her this time.

She said hello and I said, 'Happy birthday, darling, your present is out the front of the house.'

There was silence and then she said in her usual dry tone, 'What? The white truck?'

'No, a bit further along the street.'

Marlee said when she saw the Toyota she just walked out the door with her mouth open. On my end of the phone it was, 'Where down the street? I . . . Oh . . .' And she dropped the phone.

'Are you there, Mummy?' asked Marlee.

'Yes. Does she like it?'

'Does she ever, she's out there patting it. We did it Mum, we finally got a reaction out of Danielle!'

The Outback can sometimes make the simplest of chores life-threatening. During the wet of 1989 we had friends staying with us. The rains had been continuous all through December and January and now Homestead Creek had flooded. Uncle Dick and the cook were on the other side, so the problem was how to get their nightly beer rations to them.

Marlee sweetly asked one of our guests if he would do this small thing for her. John readily agreed.

'But how do I get there?' he asked, after looking at the one hundred and fifty yards of flowing water.

'Oh it's quite shallow. The creek is only deep in the middle. Take the Lilo out of the pool and put the beer on it like a raft. Just walk it to the deep part and then swim the last few yards to the other side.'

He waded into the water. The first fifty yards was easy as it was the quiet backwater of the flooding. Dick and the cook were waiting on the other side, eyes glued to the beer carton.

'Don't drop the beer!' they kept shouting. When the Lilo hit the current, it started to buck and weave, and the shouts from Dick and the cook grew louder and louder.

Terrified of losing the beer, John wrapped his arms around the carton and the Lilo and locked his fingers. He did many complete somersaults and each time he came up, Dick and the cook renewed their shouting, 'Don't drop the beer!' He was kicking with his feet, but with no hands he was at the mercy of the current. He finally bumped into the bank on the other side and willing hands dragged the waterlogged lump from the water and separated him from the beer. They left him sitting on the bank gasping for breath.

'See ya' tomorrow night,' they called back as they walked off.

'That's what you think!' he said.

The next night John made a small raft out of two flour drums with a loop of baling wire over the top. Uncle Dick and the cook were shouting various instructions to the 'young city slicker' as they had dubbed him, when he walked to the edge of the fast current, hurled a weighted rope to them and called 'Catch!' They scrambled for the rope and tied it to a nearby tree.

'Okay, pull the guide rope.' He took his end and tied it to a tree and Uncle Dick and the cook hauled in their beer raft. It was then returned to the supply side, where it was secured until the next supply was due.

'Look at that, only wet to the knees!' called John. Uncle Dick stopped calling him a 'city slicker'.

CHAPTER 25

❖

1990

In March 1990 a sudden urge came over me to go to Hong Kong. I am not a sudden urge person, but one morning I woke up and decided. Marlee agreed. I hadn't had a real holiday for a while and apart from needing the break, I wanted to wander alone for a while.

I called Peg and Jack and told them I was coming to Hong Kong and in their usual delightful way they welcomed me with open arms.

It was almost thirty years since I had been in Hong Kong. What a change! As the plane banked to approach the airport, this strange skyline greeted me. Rows and rows of tall apartment buildings covered the shoreline. A new shoreline that didn't even exist when I was there in 1960.

Peg and Jack had been in Sydney while Charles was in hospital, and in Brisbane for Marlee's wedding, so it was not thirty years since I had seen them. They drove me through parts of Kowloon that had not changed at all and then into areas so new and completely different to the old surroundings it was like a time warp.

We talked non-stop, trying to bridge the long time gap that letters and phone calls never seem to cover adequately.

During their decades of contribution to the efficient running of Hong Kong, Peg and Jack had lived all over the area. From the White House in Tai Po to the Peak to Kowloon and back again.

'As you know, we moved to this house last year,' Peg said as we drove in the gates. I just sat there looking across the road. There on the corner stood Grand Court, and there on the top floor was the room where I had spent my first night in Hong Kong thirty years ago, in Dick Kirby's apartment.

We drove in and the gates closed. What a beautiful walled garden. The house was only a stone's throw from one of Hong Kong's busiest roads, but you would never know. It was surrounded by a high stone wall, with a garden full of big trees and plants bordering a small lawn. The house was also stone, with ivy climbing all over it.

Inside were the marvellous high ceilings of the tropics, spacious open rooms, parquet floors, and all the beauty of the Orient in paintings, rugs and furnishings. It was a perfect setting of elegance and harmony created by two people whose love for this fascinating place showed in every treasure they had gathered around them.

The pace and schedule of Jack and Peg's lives had not changed much in thirty years. They still both had three times the normal workload to achieve daily.

Peg apologised the next morning at breakfast, saying the next few days were going to be hectic. I said I was quite content to tag along or, if this was not convenient, she could drop me off downtown or I could just sit in the garden.

She said unfortunately that morning she had to go to a funeral, but I could sit in the park or go shopping. I decided to go along. Living in the outback 250 kilometres from the nearest town makes attending church slightly difficult, and though nightly I sit and look up at the heavens and stars and have a heart to heart with God about daily events, there is something about a beautiful church. We stopped in front of the Hong Kong Cathedral, where thirty years ago Charles and I had been married. In less than twenty-four hours I had returned to where I had spent my first night in Hong Kong, and to where I was married.

I sat in that beautiful old church and in my mind's eye watched the years slip away until I was back at the beginning. I remember thinking, 'What would I change?'

It is a strange thing about life—we constantly say, 'I wish this' or 'If only that', but when faced with a choice, it is

303

difficult to make a decision.

I had spent thirty years saying 'I wish this' or 'If only', but when I asked myself 'What would I change?', I could not make up my mind. How can you change anything? The knowledge you gain from your experiences, good or bad, would not have been gained if you had not had the experiences! You must experience to grow, with growth comes knowledge, and with knowledge you change. I interrupted this philosophical debate with myself. What was the point in going back to ask what I would change? What has happened has happened; it is now in the past. Think about the present and the future.

So I did. I looked at it as a new beginning. Thirty years before, I had started out in this church to build a life with a very unusual man. Now, thirty years later, I was back again, alone. Did I have another thirty years to live? Would I be alone? This time around I was captain of the boat, so all the decisions were mine. Would my decisions be good ones? What would I do with the years remaining to me? What lessons had I learned from the past?

When I walked out into the sunlight, I walked out in both person and spirit—I felt I had found the sun again. Since Charles's, Mum's and Charlie's deaths, I had been digging myself deeper and deeper into a hole, burying myself in work, shutting out the world, hiding in my grief. Now I was ready to start again.

The next morning, Peg said, 'We may as well make it three out of three—would you like to go to Repulse Bay today?'

The road to Repulse Bay had changed drastically, a few old landmarks showed their faces as we whizzed by, but there were many more new faces. I closed my eyes briefly to conjure up a picture of Repulse Bay as it had been on the day of my wedding. I saw the curved hills and the Repulse Bay Hotel nestled at the bottom of the hills on the water's edge. A little piece of England in a tropical setting. The hotel had dominated the bay, not by size, but by being almost the only thing there. Peg brought me back to the present.

'Brace yourself! It's changed.'

By comparison to my mental picture, it was like stepping

out into the French Riviera! The entire shoreline was wall to wall highrise. It saddened me to see the change.

The hotel itself had been a magical place, but it was gone, replaced by yet another huge concrete block, this one in shades of pastel. A small attempt had been made to recapture the romance of the past: the old hotel's famous verandah, the scene of many gin and tonics, brilliant debates and wild and fanciful dreams, had been recreated on similar lines. But it was new, out of place with the rest of the buildings, something tacked on as an afterthought.

We finished the day with a four out of four. We went to Tai Po to see the White House. Again the picture in my mind was of a lovely white house on the side of a hill with a long flight of steps to the top, a train track at the foot of the hill, and a sleepy bay with a fishing village along the shore.

The bay was completely gone! Filled in and covered with tall white apartment buildings. Where the train track had wound around the bottom of the hill, there was now a six-lane expressway to Canton. The White House is still there, but trees have covered the view and I could only get a glimpse as we streaked past. Peg asked if I wanted to get off the freeway and drive back, but I said no. We went on through the New Territory, which thirty years ago had been all farms and dirt roads. Now we whizzed along highways all the way back to Hong Kong.

The following days were filled with long chats, meeting friends, some old but mostly new, then all too soon it was time to go back to my wilderness.

It was a very bracing visit, weatherwise and mindwise, but I felt for Hong Kong. It is changing. I could see it on the faces, I could feel it in the air. My flight home was occupied with sobering thoughts of Hong Kong, past, present and future.

On my return home, one familiar face was missing from the welcoming committee, my German shepherd, Donna. She was very old and I knew in my heart when I left for Hong Kong that she might not be there to greet me on my return.

Marlee had put her body in our special pet area and even though we had said goodbye when I left, I wandered over and had a few words to her again. She was a special dog. She started out as a Christmas present to Danielle from Uncle Gus. She was one of a litter from his German shepherd.

Like all children, Danielle played endlessly with Donna as a pup, but as the puppy grew into a dog, the interest was not there and I found I was feeding and brushing and caring for her so much, she became my dog. She was the family dog, but I suppose really she ended up my dog. When those beautiful eyes said goodbye to me when I left for Hong Kong and thanked me for her life, I felt I should have been thanking her. Always faithful, tolerant of my moods, silent companion in my sadness, wonderful walking mate, faithful guard, she was part of my life for well over a decade and I knew I would miss her very much.

Marlee decided a Donna replacement was needed. She asked if I would like a Rottweiler. Marlee's dog, Hunter, is a Rottweiler and he is a beautiful animal and was almost as big a favourite with me as Donna. At this stage I didn't think any dog could replace Donna, but I agreed a female Rottweiler would be nice. She called the lady who bred Hunter and the earliest date for a female was November. She ordered one.

By April the heavens told us the wet was over for another year and we moved into top gear to start the new season. The rains had been good; short, but good.

At the end of the 1989 season, we had bought a small TB-tested buffalo herd from Tipperary Station. We did this for many reasons: to establish a commercial herd for the future, to save them from being shot under the BTEC programme, and to quieten some of them for the tourists.

Sceptics said our country was too dry and buffalo would never survive on Bullo. When they first arrived, we handfed them in the yards for a few weeks and gave them showers three times a day. After a month they would stand and lick the water dripping off your foot. We then left the gates open and they grazed in the laneway, coming back into the yards for water. The laneway was an electric fence area. During the next month, they became acquainted with electric fences. They learned to respect them so much that when we wanted to put them into their final home paddock, they would not go through the gate in the electric fence. We left the gate open and it took about six days for them all to convince themselves they wouldn't get a shock passing through the gate.

When the ground dried the next season, and we could finally drive into our lower paddocks, we were greeted by fat, healthy buffalo with lots of baby buffalo racing around in the long grass. So much for the sceptics.

There are four babies that now graze right outside the garden fence. The other day a visitor said whenever she saw photos of the North, there was always a buffalo there somewhere, but since she had been in the North, she had not seen one. I pointed out the window and there were the babies, a mother and a big bull. She grabbed her camera and disappeared out the door.

When we first mustered the cattle out of their paddock, I wondered if we would have trouble with the buffalo, but they just grouped themselves together and moved politely to one side as the cattle trotted by. Of course I didn't expect any less from the buffalo. I had seen many in the Philippines, magnificent beasts with massive horns plodding along the road with eight or ten children on their back. It's all in the training.

The evidence of our purchase of one thousand Brahman breeders and sixty bulls was everywhere. The calves and growing stock were a pleasure to watch walk through the yards. Of course we still had our poor old run-out shorthorns here and there, which had not had the advantage of a cross with Brahman blood. But some of our shorthorn cows had produced some stunning Brahman cross babies. Considering they are the product of a wild herd that had never seen new blood from the time they landed in the valley they are not bad 'old gals'.

Each year 'our girls' become less and less in number as our herd moves to a more uniform Brahman cross quality. But I will never forget them. They, and their mothers before them, were our foundation herd when we collected them out of the bush over twenty years ago.

Marlee had stared our weaning programme. The idea of this is to give the cow time to recover—from October to December, when our feed is at its worst, a big weaner calf can mean the difference between life and death for an older cow, indeed any cow. But to wean calves, we had to have more paddocks and more feed, all of which meant time and money.

In the year before we had weaned two hundred and fifty babies. This year we weaned eight hundred, and as we build more paddocks, we will double that number. Twelve hundred or more calves were left with their mothers as they were too small to wean. With more paddocks and feed, we can do a second weaning and let all of our cows have that vital yearly rest.

In August, in the middle of mustering, 'Current Affair' turned up to do a human interest story on these females battling it out alone in the Outback. I am always very quick to point out that we are not macho female types proving we can do without men. I think man was one of God's great creations. I didn't start this adventure, Charles did, it has just been dumped in my lap. So we are not out here without men because we want to be; we are busy saving our home and it doesn't leave much time for socialising. And of course we employ loads of men every year. So, when the media want to present it other than it is, they don't make it to the property. 'Current Affair' showed it as it is—two females giving their all to save their home and carry on a dream.

After the excitement of being filmed at every turn, our stock camp settled down to work again. We had a great crew—our cook was a delightful Irish girl from Margaret River near Perth. Her name was Siobhan McNeal. As well as cooking for the mob, she raised two little baby joeys whose mothers had been hit by the big cattle roadtrains that carried our steers away.

The babies were found a few weeks apart and so grew up together as Siobhan's twins. They were called 'Skippy' (very original), and 'Barney'. We phoned a lovely lady in Darwin who was an expert on raising wallabies for advice. She said it was not an easy task. They might seem to be coming along and then suddenly they would just die, so she said to be prepared to lose them.

I think the thing that brought our twins through was the attention. Siobhan made a pouch out of an old sloppy joe and the joeys would spend most of the day in it, underneath a cooking apron. It was also not unusual to walk into the camp and see a big burly stockman feeding a joey the size of his hand with an eye-dropper.

They grew very fast and with Siobhan as their mother, they were very spoilt. When the stock camp came back to the homeyard and Siobhan was cooking in the homestead, Skippy and Barney had their first taste of discipline. They didn't like not being able to run riot through the house. I was patient, as they were cute little devils, but the day they jumped right into the middle of the lunch table I put my foot down. We had American tourists arriving in the next few weeks and I could just imagine their reaction if Barney landed in their lunch.

So Barney and Skippy were introduced to the garden and soon realised that this was to be their playground, not the living room, dining room and kitchen. Our tourists were completely charmed by the little rascals and took hundreds of photos.

CHAPTER 26

❖

1990

One morning I walked into the office and found Marlee sitting at the telephone desk waiting for the trucking company to call back with the arrival time of the trucks coming to load our steers.

'Look what I did.' She handed me a page out of the *Bulletin*. 'I nominated you for Businesswoman of the Year. I just faxed it to Sydney.'

'Oh Marlee, you are a silly goose. Good heavens, you can't think in a million years they would consider someone in the Outback.'

'Why not? You go through the same business procedures as any woman in the city, under far more difficult conditions, plus you do all the work and the administration. So you do more, in much harder surroundings. Why wouldn't they pick you?'

'Well I'm telling you, they won't.'

'Well I'm telling you they will. It's got everything that will appeal. Just you wait and see!'

The form said the judges would announce the results on the 13th of November. 'We have a few months to wait then, because it's in November. And, darling, thank you for thinking I'm so great, but don't pin your hopes on it.'

'No hoping, I know you'll win.'

The phone call she was waiting for came through and I walked away shaking my head.

About three weeks later, I answered the phone. A woman asked to speak to Marlee.

'She's out mustering, can I take a message?'

'Is this Sara Henderson?'

'Yes it is.'

'My name is Glennys Bell of the *Bulletin*, and I wanted to talk to Marlee in regard to her nomination of you for Businesswoman of the Year.'

'Oh dear, she shouldn't have done that . . .'

Glennys interrupted me. She said that they were very interested in our struggle in the Outback. So much so, that she wanted to run a story on me, along with stories on a few of the other nominations the *Bulletin* had received. We had a long chat and she asked many questions. The article was in the next *Bulletin*.

'See, I told you,' said Marlee. But I said it was general interest, nothing more.

A few weeks later, my banker and accountants had to be given permission to answer questions. It seemed I was approaching the quarter-finals.

By now Marlee was jumping up and down saying, 'I told you, I told you!' And I kept on telling her not to be silly. I didn't believe for a moment that it would happen.

But Marlee kept saying, 'Just wait till November, Mum. Better get your speech ready,' and 'Can't wait for November, then everyone will know what a great Mum I have!' Marlee is a great tonic for a middle-aged mum.

From October 18th, life became a little more hectic than usual. Bob Doyle and Pauline Rainer of Northern Territory Tourism came to Bullo with David McNicoll of the *Bulletin*. David was visiting all the old Second World War airstrips in the Territory. Marlee quickly pointed out the *Bulletin* connection, but I just as quickly pointed out that Pauline had called me before the fax had even been sent. This did not dull her enthusiasm.

However, we didn't have time to dwell on any implications because on the 20th, a planeload of tourists from Melbourne arrived. There were seven doctors, plus a pilot and a stock investment broker. What a mob! They had a wonderful time. I know this because on the last night they made endless speeches

311

saying so. They had more camera equipment between them than a movie crew, and took hundreds of photos, many of which they sent on to us as gifts. When they finally took off in their private jet, we all collapsed for the day. The next day Marlee moved the camp out to twenty-two-mile, our last muster site.

It was the 26th. I was alone in the homestead. About an hour before lunch the phone rang.

'Hello, this is James Hall, editor of the *Bulletin*. I would like to inform you, you have been selected as *Bulletin*/Qantas Businesswoman of the Year.'

I have been lost for words many times in my life, but this time it was complete. Not even a squawk.

'Hello, are you there?'

I managed a feeble, 'Yes.'

'Good, well congratulations! How does it feel?'

After a few 'Ahs' and 'Ohs' had come out, he realised he wouldn't get much more.

'Our people will call and tell you of all the arrangements. See you on the 13th of November.'

He reeled off various names and telephone numbers, but I was still looking for a pen long after he had hung up.

After the shock had worn off slightly, I suddenly realised it was true! I jumped all around the house, but there was no one to tell. Daisy, our milking cow, was watching my crazy antics. I rushed up to her and took her head in my hands.

'Daisy, I'm *Bulletin*/Qantas Businesswoman of the Year! How about that!'

She let out this tremendous bellow and backed away, quite sure I had gone crazy. After dancing three rounds of the house, I settled down and called my sister and Danielle. I was sitting at the phone desk, wondering what to do next—it seemed an anti-climax to go back to office work—when Wayne Tregaskis, manager of corporate advertising and promotion for Qantas, called with the outline for the next two weeks. They wanted to send up a cameraman to film me in my office and surroundings. It was a rushed affair as they had to get to Bullo from Sydney, film, and be back in time to get everything ready for the 13th.

He then said, 'Now don't tell anyone until the announcement—this must be kept hush-hush until then. We had to have so much leadtime with you because we have to get to Bullo and back to process everything.' I quickly hung up and called my sister.

'We have to keep it a secret until it's announced on the 13th of November.'

I noticed she quickly finished the conversation, no doubt to call everyone she had told. When I called Danielle, the same. It probably went on all day, but it wasn't too bad. We managed to keep it fairly quiet.

Marlee returned late at night. She had been away setting up the twenty-two-mile mustering camp. When she came into the house, I acted very seriously and said there was a fax she must look at immediately. Because of all the problems we had at the time, she expected the worst and followed me quietly into the office with a worried look.

I solemnly handed her the congratulatory fax that Wayne had sent. She read the first line, squealed, threw the fax in the air, hugged me and twirled me around and around shouting, 'You won! Told you so! You won! Told you so!' She put me down, gave me another wonderful hug and said, 'My mum!' with a look of obvious delight glowing on her face.

Glennys was the *Bulletin* part of the crew that arrived and, on their return to Sydney, she had to work non-stop to have the written story ready ahead of time for printing. But like the video, the story was terrific, only she did have us loading a D8 bulldozer onto a front end loader instead of a low loader. Very few people would have picked this up, but of course it was the first thing Jim, our heavy equipment expert, noticed.

A few reporters started sniffing around after the *Bulletin/* Qantas team came to Bullo, but I told them they had been there for advertising. When one clever one asked if I would be on the station on the 12th of November for a radio talkback show and I told them they would have to call early in the morning or late at night as we were mustering, the interest died down.

The biggest problem was when friends called. 'Been doing

anything interesting?' they'd ask.

It was very hard to keep the excitement out of my voice and say, 'Oh nothing much, just working.'

The excitement kept building daily and by the time Marlee and I stepped on the plane, I had difficulty sitting still. Danielle was going to meet us in Sydney. On top of the excitement was the nervousness of making my first speech. I had nightmares about my first school play. I knew the lines, but the words would not come out of my mouth. During the weeks up to 13th of November, I had this terrible dream over and over.

I was asked if I wanted to rehearse, but I declined.

'I will jump in at the deep end if you don't mind. Don't want to make a fool of myself twice.'

I think Wayne was a bit worried by now because Marlee told me later he had arranged for Helen Daley, the Master of Ceremonies who introduced me, to join me again on stage and interview me if I suffered stage fright. And of course Marlee and Danielle were going to rush to the stage and help me if I floundered.

The big day arrived! I had the morning for hair and so on. Marlee and Danielle had been 'last minute' shopping and we all met at the hairdressers. My hair was washed and I was sitting waiting for the dye to cover all the grey hair, when this man walked into the salon.

'I'm from the Water Board and I'm here to disconnect the water.' I closed my eyes and visualised myself on stage with brown guck all over my head. Marlee took over.

'You can't turn it off for another half hour. My mother is "Businesswoman of the Year" and she is having her hair set for the award luncheon and she has to have her hair washed in twenty minutes.'

'Well, I have to do my job.'

'You do your job somewhere else and come back!'

He wisely agreed.

Marlee had let the cat out of the bag, but it was only one hour before the luncheon so it didn't really matter. We were now running out of time. The owner was busy calling people about the water, but we finally persuaded them to finish our hair. To compensate for the inconvenience, they wanted to put my make-up on. I was so upset I agreed. Anyway, I was shaking too much to do a good job myself.

That morning I had had two pre-scheduled television interviews that would go to air the day after the announcement. At each studio, they had piled stacks of make-up on my face so this touch-up was the third. My face was starting to feel as if it would crack.

It could have been the mixture of products, all the excitement, or just plain allergy, but as I rode up in the lift at the hotel my face started to prickle. By the time I reached the room and looked in the mirror, the make-up was bright orange and my face was stinging as if a thousand needles were being stuck into my skin.

I quickly washed my face clean. Now I was a shiny red. I had fifteen minutes before I had to be downstairs. I put a bucket of ice in the handbasin and froze my face back to normal by submerging it in the ice for long breath-holding periods. It was great for my face, hell for my hairdo.

I showered, blowdried the wet part of my hair, dressed and applied a light moisturiser and powder, my usual make-up. My hair had that flyaway look and my face just glowed, but I passed for normal. I headed downstairs.

I had drinks with the other finalists, they still didn't know which one of us had won. Mrs Hawke was there, as well as officials from Qantas and the *Bulletin*. We moved into the dining room and were seated. Lunch looked wonderful but by now my stomach was such a mess I didn't dare introduce it to anything but water. My mind kept going over my speech, hoping I wouldn't forget it. I had had a trial run on the station, reading it to myself, but found I was so nervous I fogged up my glasses and couldn't see the words. So I had memorised it. Of course in Sydney, in November, with airconditioning, my glasses would not fog up, but I didn't think of that back on the station.

I was thinking silly things like, how can I walk from here to the stage? I know I will fall going up the stairs. All this was racing through my head while I was trying to conduct intelligent conversation with the people at the table.

Marlee and Danielle just kept grinning and patting my hand. Mayor Sallyanne Atkinson spoke about women in general, Helen Daley's speech was excellent, as was Mrs Hawke's. Then the room dimmed as Helen said that they would first like to show where the new Businesswoman of the Year lived.

The screen was massive and the magic of Bullo filled the room. When the lights came on, there was stunned silence. If anyone had had doubts about someone so remote and removed from the everyday world receiving the award, I think that five-minute video would have silenced them. The size and magnitude of the girls' and my challenge was vividly brought home. I knew Bullo, and I was awed!

'Mummy.' Marlee was tugging at my sleeve. I came back to my senses and heard my name being called.

I don't remember walking across to the steps. I didn't fall, but Mrs Hawke did drop my sculpture. I picked it up and thanked her, then turned to face my first audience. The moment I had been dreading had arrived. Having had non-stop nerves for weeks, I was now fairly calm. Still nervous but not nearly as nervous as I had imagined.

Mrs Hawke went to put the award on the stand behind me and it nearly fell again so I took it and put it on the podium. This brought forth laughter and from then on it was easy.

I looked out at that sea of friendly faces and launched into my speech. I didn't forget it; I did leave a bit out, but it still flowed freely. So much so that someone congratulated Wayne and said it was a good idea to have a speechwriter write the speech.

Wayne said, 'No way, it was all her own work!'

I had come through with flying colours, their choice had been signed, sealed and approved! Everyone could relax. Well, they did, I didn't. Newspapers, radio, television, it was one continuous round.

My marvellous publicity co-ordinator, Tracey Dean from Australian Consolidated Press, kept me sane. We finally made dinner at about 9.30 p.m. I had not eaten all day so I really enjoyed it. Tracey disappeared at about midnight saying she would see me bright and early for the 'Today Show'. We made it back to the hotel at about 2.30 a.m. and had to be back in the foyer at 6.30 a.m. The whole day had been amazing.

Marlee came to my room the next morning at six.

'I just walked down a hallway wall-to-wall with my mum.'

'What?' I said. She threw *The Australian* on the bed and there I was spread across the front page.

'What would Nanny think?' We all laughed. Danielle had joined us by now, and we all knew what 'What would Nanny think?' meant. When the girls started dating I had told them what my mother had always told me. 'Don't do anything you wouldn't want to read about on the front page of the morning papers.' But I knew if Mum could have seen that headline, she would have been very proud . . . Maybe she could see it.

That next day was bedlam. Danielle, Marlee, my publicity co-ordinator and I answered phones and raced to radio and television stations most of the day. By three p.m. I had not eaten any food and could not even go to the bathroom in peace. There was a telephone in the bathroom and it started ringing while I was sitting on the toilet! Now whoever heard of answering the phone while sitting on the toilet! Reclining in a bubble bath, perhaps, but sitting on the toilet! I ignored it.

The next day was more of the same. I just don't know how people in the public eye cope. One more day and I had had enough. We moved to another hotel. Danielle returned to Queensland and Jim arrived in Sydney and the three of us acted like tourists for a few days. Then it was back to work.

It was hard to settle down after all that glamour, attention, flowers and champagne. I found myself gazing across the valley to the distant mountains wondering why this had happened to me. Would it change my life? The last week had certainly been different, but I knew life couldn't go on like that for long, so what would change?

There were signs. Already I had been approached by several

publishers, interested in a story on my life. Several agencies had also called me about doing speaking engagements.

The phone calls and letters and congratulations streamed in non-stop for months, and not only from friends. I received hundreds of wonderful letters from people who had read our story and just wanted to write and say, 'Good on you!'

I met someone last week who is on the land, and he congratulated me on the award, but the words that concluded his little speech were the most significant. He said:

'I can't tell you what a boost your winning this award has given the people on the land. For an Australian that everyone can relate to to win something like this is tremendous. It gives people the courage to keep going.'

I have lost count of the number of times this last sentence has been said to me.

In November the phone rang on average every five minutes. It was an amazing experience: people I went to school with, people I had played tennis with, people I had met at a dinner party twenty years ago. People sent photos they had taken of the family and station over the last twenty-six years. Phone message, faxes, and letters—they just kept piling up. Eventually a friend who was a legal secretary came to visit, and what a friend! She helped me attack the mountains of correspondence and finally, well into 1991, all the letters and cards have received a thank you.

Most of the speaking requests were for eight to twelve months in the future, and they came in so thick and fast I had to put a hold on them. As I explained to the people who rang, my daughter and I were still working about eighty hours per week keeping the station operating and if I had accepted even one third of the requests, I would have been travelling full-time.

I then received another request. Again I began to explain that I could not afford the time when the voice on the other end interrupted.

'Oh, you are paid.'

This was news to me. Still I said, 'I really don't think so. I get so nervous, I don't think I could.'

'They want you to speak in Hawaii, first class travel, five-star accommodation. You can go for the whole week of the convention at their expense.'

All that made me stop and think. Then they mentioned the fee and that floored me.

'You can't be serious. They'll pay me all that money on top of airfares and accommodation?' Nerves or not, I couldn't refuse so much money for a half-hour speech. We worked thirty hours to achieve the same results. So, with my eyes on the money, I accepted. It was four months away, I could get nervous later.

CHAPTER 27

❖

1990-1991

Later in November, my Rottweiler puppy arrived. She was gorgeous. We called her Jedda. I can't help but wonder at all the bad press these fine animals have been receiving lately. I don't care what any expert says, it is all in the training.

I suppose many people would say we are eccentric when it comes to our animals—we speak to them as we do people. But there are very few who have not commented on how wonderful our animals are—our dogs, our cat, our stallion who stands in the middle of the living room under the fan, our milking cows who go to the bedroom window of the person who is milking them to moo if the person is behind schedule.

Recently an English boy was here who was so scared of Hunter, our male Rottweiler, he would not even come into the homestead garden. When we found this out Marlee decided to introduce them properly. The boy was very ill at ease but he agreed.

'Hunter, this is Dave and he's very afraid of Rottweilers, so you be very nice to him and show him how lovely you are. Say hello.'

Hunter quietly walked up to Dave and put his massive head on Dave's lap and looked into his eyes. It was love at first sight and from then on, whenever Dave was near the house, he would be found playing with Hunter.

The training of people does not differ greatly. Anyone who throws an empty can on the ground at Bullo is fined fifty dollars for littering. It does not take long to train each new group. Their names are written on the bottom of their cans for the first few weeks, and usually this is enough. And like an old sheep dog training a young pup, the current group of stockmen will always train the next group.

'Don't drop your cans on the ground—fifty dollar fine.'

Marlee said one morning they were all driving out to a new section of fence they were building when Dave shouted, 'Stop! I left a Coke can standing on one of the posts in the yard!' Marlee assured him it was safe until lunchtime and if I found it, she would give evidence on his behalf. Despite this reassurance from Marlee, she said he was fidgety all morning and only returned to normal when he got his hands on the empty Coke can again.

We had friends and employees for Christmas, so it was a busy, cheerful time. The phone stopped ringing every five minutes and we had lovely rain. Magically, as it does every year, the vast golden brown valley turned lush green and the cattle waded through feed knee high and ate until they were rolling fat.

The wet of 1990–91 was our first normal rainfall since Cyclone Tracy. Our rainfall until 1974 had been thirty to thirty-five inches, but after 1974 it dropped back to between twenty and twenty-five inches. However, at least we had rain.

People say to us how brave we are, fighting the wilderness, braving the isolation of the Outback. But these are easy opponents, compared with drought. To watch your land shrivel and die, year in and year out, to see beautiful fields turn to dust bowls, to watch your animals starve and die. To suffer all this, only to be then washed away in a flood, your home and your family treasures lost and destroyed. And to then pick up the pieces and start again. The farmers of the South are the brave!

Compared with these people, we live in luxury, a harsh and demanding luxury, but with rain every year, no devastating floods, control of fire by our natural boundaries, and plenty of ground water, it is a sort of luxury. Living in isolation and carving something out of the wilderness is only development.

Part of our development this last wet was to grow our own hay. As each year passes and the control of our herd improves, we need more and more hay. So given the increased tonnage required, the cost of transport and the increasing cost of quality hay, we decided to grow our own. Of course, it was not that easy.

We knew nothing about farming, so we had to learn from the ground up, so to speak. We had tractors, but we needed a plough. Jim to the rescue again. He lent us a plough and seeder, and also told us what to do.

I think everyone gets a thrill out of growing something. To see tilled rich brown earth all neatly ploughed and, after a shower of rain, row upon row of little green shoots is very satisfying.

Until 1960 Bullo was an isolated valley, a part of Auvergne Station. It was a little pocket to one side of a five-million-acre property. When Charles bought it in 1962, the land was in its natural state. It had a gravel airstrip and a donkey track over the mountain rather optimistically referred to as an 'access road'. And that was the full extent of its development. So the first tilling for our small one-hundred-acre farming project was quite a momentous occasion, as it was the first time the soil had been turned by a plough.

As well as growing sorghum to feed our animals, we were attacking our weed problem. Weeds come with development. In the early days, we did not have weeds, but when our road improved and cattle trucks came into the valley, the weed problem came too. The seeds drop off the trucks along the sides of the road and with a fifty-mile access road, it was not long before we had weeds. This problem was further aggravated by heavy stocking in paddocks for the testing of cattle during our BTEC programme.

Since starting the programme back in 1983, we have increased our fencing to such an extent that we can now rest paddocks and attack the weed problem. We started with one hundred acres of thick cida weed. We ploughed the cida, turning the roots over to the sun, and left it for about ten days. We then ploughed it all again. The skies were getting blacker by the day and we managed to plant and fertilise just in time for a lovely shower of rain. Of course it entailed much more than these few lines indicate. We had Jim constantly on the line, and on weekends we had lessons 'in the field'.

We had to plant where the crop was protected from the cattle until it was hay. Because of early rain, paddocks in low areas that we had set aside to plough became too wet. There was not enough time for further fence-building, so we utilised the airstrip. The airstrip is nicely fenced and stock-proof. We left a narrow strip down the middle for the planes to land, and the rest was ploughed.

Of course one thing we had not thought of was that eventually the sorghum reaches a height of twelve feet. It closed the homestead in and, looking across to the mountains, we couldn't see the cattle grazing in the paddocks. Watching the planes land was very amusing. They would approach the airstrip and then disappear into a field of sorghum.

I went out to meet a plane one day and the pilot was quite relieved to see me appear.

'I was getting worried. It's a bit like a maze. I thought I could be searching for hours, looking for the homestead.'

Then there was the mowing and baling. I thought that growing the stuff was the hard part, but little did I realise . . . On the airstrip we had the additional problem of having to move the machines into a corner every time a plane wanted to land. The 'machines' consisted of a mower conditioner and a baler. Both machines were second-hand as new was not within our budget.

The mower conditioner was almost new and it was a gem. It never missed a beat, did everything the operator's manual said it would, and under instructions from Jim, we cut the crop at the right time and were ready for baling.

The baler was another matter. I knew absolutely nothing about baling machines, but when it was started I knew we were in trouble. I have never seen so many moving parts on one machine in all my life. There were spikes and belts and flaps all moving at once in different directions. We had no end of problems and, unfortunately, Jim was not up on balers. But over the next few months, like us, he became an expert.

David, who drove this ghastly machine, had the patience

323

of Job, although I suspect that out in the field it was a different David to the one who pored over the instruction book with me when Jim wasn't there. David is a marine biologist who wanted to be a farmer, but after growing and baling one hundred acres of sorghum on Bullo, I think he went back to the sea.

The baler tried our patience to breaking point. Uncle Dick nearly rebuilt the whole machine. Mention the word baler and his eyes cross. The machine is supposed to gather up the windrows of cut sorghum and roll it into large bales about five feet in diameter, wrap string around the bale and spit this finished product out the back. 'Supposed to' is the key phrase. The baler would jam repeatedly after making the core of a bale and to unclog this monster, poor David had to nearly stand on his head, down in amongst spikes, and pull all the sorghum out by hand. To add to this problem, David suffered from hay fever. Many a time I would find David head down, tail up, muttering to himself, and sneezing and sniffling with sorghum flying in all directions.

Finally, after Uncle Dick had replaced almost everything he could, we found the problem. At the bottom of the machine is a drum with ridges running along it every four inches. The drum turns, pulling the sorghum into the part of the machine that rolls the bales. The ridges had worn smooth and the sorghum was slipping and not feeding into the machine evenly. Uncle Dick welded new ridges onto the drum and we were suddenly baling sixty to eighty bales per day.

It is a great sight, 660 five-foot bales of sorghum hay— at roughly four to a ton, that's 165 tons of hay. It filled one whole holding paddock near the house and every animal within ten miles had one ambition, to get into that paddock.

At the Katherine Show in June 1991, Bullo River won first prize in Pasture Regeneration, section 'H' agriculture, class H44. Our little venture was really a three-in-one project. We had ploughed in the weeds for weed control and when we planted the sorghum, we had also added grass seed, so with any luck, when it rains this wet, we should see one hundred acres of improved pasture of buffel and verano. This wet we hope to plant two hundred acres of sorghum and improved pasture.

324

But I will be really happy when we are up to two thousand, and just imagine twenty thousand. Now that's a dream to aim for—all our beautiful cattle knee-deep in feed every October and November.

In February one of the big farming concerns on the Ord River irrigation closed down: machinery, workshop, ploughs, tools, everything was up for sale. Auctions are more addictive than drugs. Everything you see, you need, want or must have. I could quite easily have bought everything there—and waved a magic wand to move the magnificent storage shed over to Bullo. And of course everything I needed, which was almost everything, Jim needed. We would walk up to a lot and say, almost in unison, 'I could use that.' But everyone else there could no doubt have said the same thing; that was why we were all there.

Between us, Jim and I bought a good percentage of the sale. Marlee would rush up to us and say, 'Gee, that was cheap, we should have bought that.'

'We did.'

'Oh, good!' And she would disappear into the crowd only to reappear and go through the same conversation.

The third time this happened, she just looked at me and I nodded.

Later she said to me, 'I never saw Jim bidding.'

I explained that you never see experienced auction goers bidding. I had been to an auction once with my sister Sue, and we had sat there for hours with Sue not moving a muscle.

Later, at lunch, I had said, 'Well, that was a slow morning. Do you think you'll buy anything this afternoon?'

'I bought most of the sale this morning.'

I was amazed. My sister, before she retired, had dress shops in Sydney. At one time, she had three shops. She bought bankrupt stock and sold it at bargain prices. She ran a very successful business and had a talent for buying at auctions that was superior. Apparently it was all done with the eyes.

Jim had a similar technique. I didn't see him bidding, but somehow I would end up the owner. Of course I let him buy for me. When you have the talents of a professional at your

325

disposal, I am a firm believer in standing back and letting them do their thing. Jim bought us a semi-trailer full of useful machinery and tools. Marlee was delighted.

After the auction we flew to Cable Beach and enjoyed a week out, then it was back to the ever-expanding work load— Jim to his machines, and us to our cattle.

On the 23rd of February I signed a contract to write this book. It was my dad's birthday. I had agreed back in November to write a book and had, over the wet, put more than a third of it on paper, but the final contract was not signed until February. When I wrote the date after my signature and realised it was Poppa's birthday, I thought, well, that has to make it a good book!

Because of Saddam Hussein's antics in the Gulf, the week in Hawaii was now a week in Cairns, which was a disappointment. I had to speak for forty minutes. As I was writing my speech, I realised I might be receiving a lot of money for the forty minutes it took me to say it, but it took days to write it. I ended up with twenty-two pages. After some weeks of changing and shaping it a few hundred times, I typed it up neatly and decided it would have to do. As the day approached, I became more and more nervous. Everyone around me noticed.

'Come on, Mum, you can do it!' Marlee kept saying. Dick also voiced his confidence.

The speaking agency had given me pages of information on matters like what to wear, for example! But on the important details, such as, what the people were like, what walk of life, what age group and so on, nothing. I asked most of these questions myself but when I finally arrived for the great event, I realised I had been given the wrong information. I arrived Sunday night and was not speaking till Tuesday, so I spent Sunday night and most of Monday labouring over the rewrite. I am glad I did because the result was well received.

In the Cairns newspaper the next morning, the reporter said I had started down the road of a new career!

I then spoke on the Gold Coast for the Life Education Centre, Smile for Life. I spoke with Kay Cottee and Diane

Cilento on courage, strength and success. Kay was courage, I was strength, Diane was success. I was very nervous that night but Kay and Diane were delightful and soon put me at ease.

These two speeches were only two days apart, and afterwards I flew to Caloundra to spend a few days with Susan and Ralph. They had moved there recently and I had only seen photos of the house. It is called 'Pandanus House' and what a delightful home. It is very old and sits on the river bend, looking up the river and down the river and out to sea. All around is bushland and across the river is parkland, so sitting on the verandah, you cannot see any other houses. Then it was back to the station and mustering.

At the beginning of April, the travel editor of the London *Sunday Times*, Mark Ottaway, arrived on Bullo to write a story about us. This was real prestige—the London *Sunday Times* no less. Mark is a terrific person and we had no end of fun during his stay. He sent us a copy of the article and said it was the biggest spread the travel section had done on any one place in twenty-five years.

Soon after Mark left I was off to Rockhampton for my next speaking engagement. This was to open 'Beef Expo 1991'. I wished so much that Marlee could have been there—all those magnificent cattle gathered together in one place. The Expo lasted for over a week, but I could only stay for the opening and the cattle judging the next day. Marlee was in the middle of a muster and had to be away from the homestead all day and most nights and it was difficult for her to run the outside and the inside operations. Marlee is always glad to see me home as she really doesn't like the business part.

It was then into Katherine as Marlee was in a play. This was to raise money for the 'Outback Hall of Fame' women's wing. It was a play about pioneer women and Marlee played the stockwoman working side-by-side with the men; it was the perfect casting for her. It was now her turn to be nervous and my turn to say, 'Oh you'll be alright, Marlee, nothing to it.' Of course she carried it off beautifully. Then it was home again to mustering and to appear in a video for the

327

Department of Primary Production and Fisheries for promotion of the Northern Territory overseas. I appeared in the land and cattle section of the video.

I was now racing in and out of the station almost every ten days. Before the award, if I had left the station four times in a year it was considered a lot. Marlee said I was so busy she would soon have to make an appointment to see me. Between her being out mustering for days and my leaving every ten days, we did spend most of our time talking on the two-way radio, saying hello and goodbye.

Our next muster was in the home paddocks. The yards are only one mile from the homestead, so Marlee was home at night. This was nice because I was off again soon, to Townsville.

The 15th of June was the anniversary of Charles's death. It was now five years since he had died. I had a drink at sunset, in the usual sunset drinking spot he had always favoured. I raised my glass to him and listened to Tchaikovsky's Piano Concerto No. 1, our favourite piece of music. There was no sudden upheaval or bolt of lightning, so I suppose he was pleased with our work to date. I sat there until it was quite dark.

The next day we mustered and drafted out all the steers for export. We then booked the trucks to move the cattle to Wyndham wharf for live export.

The cattle had been loaded and the truck was leaving the yards when I received a fax from the buyer asking us to load two extra steers. I won't go into the comments this request brought forth, first from me, then from Marlee, then from the truck driver, but we all reasoned he wouldn't ask for them if it wasn't absolutely necessary.

The driver turned the big rig around on the flat outside the homestead. As I went back inside he slowly drove onto the causeway that approaches a small bridge near the generator shed. A few moments later, one of the kitchen staff came into the office.

'Would you come and look at the truck, it doesn't look right.'

The road train had gone off the side of the causeway and

was lying on its side with one hundred and fifty head of cattle on board. 'That's not right, is it?' said the girl.

We ran from all directions. Marlee found the driver walking around the rig shaking his head in disbelief. But this only lasted for a few seconds, then everyone was galvanised into action. He opened the emergency hatches on the trailers and released the cattle. As amazing as it sounds, not one was hurt. The last trailer had not rolled, but was teetering on the edge of the causeway and shuddered every time the cattle moved. Marlee quickly chained it to the steel culverts under the causeway to stop it rolling as well.

You normally unload the bottom deck of a double decker first, but of course, normally, half the trailer is not hanging off a causeway. We had to get the top deck of cattle off first. It was a twelve-foot drop from the top deck to the ground, so Marlee piled a huge ten-foot mound of dirt up against the trailer with the front end loader.

Then we watched as fifty steers one by one did a fantastic swallow dive off the twelve-foot deck into the soft mound of dirt. There was definite Olympic material there. Some of the stockmen jumped on their horses and mustered the cattle back to the yards.

The road train was standing almost on its head as it was on the slope of a five-foot embankment. It was decided the causeway would have to be bulldozed away to get the truck upright again or too much damage would be done to the truck pulling it up and over the embankment. So Marlee revved up the D8 bulldozer and removed about one hundred and fifty feet of the causeway. With lots of instructions, many chains and the D8, Marlee finally stood the road train upright again.

Uncle Dick checked the motor, the driver did a few trial runs around the flat, and it was back to the yards. The cattle were loaded again, including the extra two, and they finally arrived at the ship with about five minutes to spare. We had worked all through the night.

We waved goodbye to the truck at 5.30 a.m. and were just drinking a cup of coffee when three helicopters appeared over the horizon for our next muster. We mustered eighteen hundred head into the yards and then, at twelve noon, I stepped into the four-seater charter plane to fly to catch the jet to Darwin. Then, early the next morning, on to Cairns and Townsville. That night I spoke to the Townsville Business-women's Network.

People often ask me, 'What do you find to do, to pass the time out there?'

A few days after my return we had tourists from Melbourne and, at the same time, about twenty-two army men on a survival course, living off the land for two weeks.

We waved goodbye to our tourists, a delightful family, at ten on Saturday morning and I had to speak at Carlton Hill Station at about seven that night. It was a six-hour drive from Bullo, I was already exhausted and I still had to write my speech. This life in the fast lane was taking its toll. Jim was driving me to Carlton Hill, so I prepared the speech en route.

Marlee had left for Carlton Hill the day before because her play was being performed again there, and there were rehearsals on Friday.

It was a wonderful night. Dame Mary Durack came back to her country to tell us of the early days, Dame Edna visited the Kimberley for the first time, Ted Egan was there, and also James Blundell, to mention just a few. I sat with Neville and Gabby Kennard, who were passing through Kununurra on a flying trip and had dropped by for the night. I had met Gabby at my award luncheon in November and Neville had visited the station earlier in the year. I caught up with many friends, some of whom I had not seen for years.

We didn't have time to dally as the ABC crew that covered the night at Carlton Hill was coming on to Bullo to film Marlee and me, and our life away from the stage! The footage of rehearsals, the actual night and our life on Bullo will all end up in a half hour programme of 'Big Country'.

We have had many film shoots on Bullo over the years and all the crews have been terrific. Our new friends this time were Varsha, Laurence, Gunter and Colin. They arrived feeling travel-weary and sore, but after a hot shower, a large steak and some good wine, along with a royal greeting from our Rottweilers and Boots our stallion, standing in the middle of the living room, they brightened up considerably.

We had a great few days filming but soon it was time for the crew to leave. We were truly sorry to see them go— they had settled into the Bullo routine like oldtimers. But we all had to continue on our various paths—Varsha out to Kakadu, Laurence and Gunter to Darwin, and Colin back to Sydney, and the Bullo mob back to work in the bush.

I also was off again, this time to present the Northern Territory Businesswoman of the Year award in Darwin. This was a first time for the Northern Territory—I suppose my winning the Australian award inspired a local one. The AMP sponsored the night and a great deal of effort was put into the event. Again I saw old friends, some going back twenty years.

The next day I flew to Sydney. Sebel Furniture had asked me to be part of their promotion for a new Executive Chair. They wanted an executive with a difference.

I decided that fate or opportunity had been knocking at my door when I received this phone call. A few years before I had invented a 'TV exercise chair' and had been trying to decide which manufacturing firm to approach with my design.

So I said, 'I'll promote your chair, if you'll manufacture my chair.'

As I write this book, my chair is in their Research and Development department going through its paces. God willing, by the time these words are in print, the chair will be on the assembly line.

The photography session gave me a healthy respect for photographic models. My feet ached, my back ached, my face ached, everything ached.

At one stage the photographer said, 'Smile!'

'I am,' I replied.

I had been smiling for so long, I couldn't feel my face muscles. I spent most of the day there. Silly me had thought it would be click, click, click, thank you. Six hundred clicks later, it was, 'Okay, one more smile.'

The next day I delivered the first two hundred pages of this book to my trusting publisher. I told them I had twenty years to go, and returned to the bush.

August found us mustering the furthest points of the station. All the stock camp were camping out as it was twenty-five miles one way. It was fairly quiet around the homestead, so, along with the various other jobs that fill my day, I was busily recording the second half of my life. I soon realised it would be a few years before I could finish if I followed the schedule of the past week. There were too many interruptions. So I started to write at five each morning. This was the solution—I could get at least five uninterrupted hours of writing before phones, faxes, two-way radios, and people started functioning. As I am approaching the end of the book, I am writing most of the day, but I still find the first five hours the most productive.

It is 9.30 a.m. and I have just returned to my desk after rescuing one of the Brahman bulls. Jude, one of the girls helping around the house, came to me and said, 'There's a bull over near the hay paddock and he's lying on his back with his legs in the air—it doesn't look right.'

I dropped my pen and rushed out the door. Indeed he did not look right—he was caught in the fence. Jude's eyesight is not too good over long distances and she could not see that he was caught, only that he was on his back. We drove over. Somehow he had managed to get his back hoof jammed between the straining wire and the top steel rail of the fence. I can only assume he was trying to climb over the fence into the hay paddock, slipped and fell backwards and caught his leg. His hoof was jammed so tight we had to cut the straining wire to release him. He limped away a dazed but happy bull.

Little events like this constantly intrude into my writing day making it impossible some days after eight a.m. to put words to paper. I now know why writers go alone to the mountains or some remote beach house to write—to get away from hay-stealing bulls. I certainly am remote from the outside world, but alone I am not.

My publisher called and said he and the editor were very pleased with the first half of the book and to hurry with the second half. It is a great boost to be told you are doing something well and it had the desired effect—I approached the 'home stretch' with renewed vigour.

The rest of August and beginning of September were continued mustering and more tourists. Maybe we have been lucky, I don't know, but without exception, every tourist who has come to Bullo has been a delight. They do not come in droves and maybe that is the answer. We keep the numbers small and everything has a personal touch to it. They become part of the operation and they seem to enjoy this treatment.

At the end of August it was back to Darwin to be one of the judges for the Engineering Award for the year. While I was there I also visited our lawyer and barrister to discuss the next step in the Trippe case. The appeal was now scheduled for the 2nd, 3rd and 4th of September. We spent the afternoon discussing the plan of attack. After telling them my life and future was in their hands, I departed for the bush again.

The season was moving to a close and our stock camp was reducing in size as each week passed. We had two more small helicopter musters to go, not the two-and-a-half-thousand-head type we had just finished. We were planning to start them the day after we returned from the appeal. A week before we were to leave, my lawyer called to say the hearing had been changed to the 21st, 22nd and 23rd of September. We went ahead with the muster and rearranged our plans, so that while Marlee and I were in Darwin, the yard could be moved to the next and last site.

Being in court again was the same nerve-racking experience. At least we didn't have to go through the cross-examination horror of the trial, but by the time Trippe's barrister had again described our actions, Marlee and I were still top applicants for the devil's job. It is very hard to sit all day and listen to derogatory statements about yourself, your actions, your intentions and your daughter. By the end of the day, I was in tears. But our lawyer said not to worry, it was our turn the next day. I couldn't sleep, and spent most of the night telling the 'supreme commander' up above what I thought of the legal system.

At the end of the second day, I felt a little better, as it was our day. But I can now see how brainwashing can break a person.

At the end of the third day it was over. There was the desire to make just that one more point, but that could go on forever. As I write this in October, we are still waiting for the decision.

The previous January, I had promised to speak for another charity in September, and that date was now upon me, one day after our appeal hearing. I really would have done anything to get out of that speech, but I had said I would do it, so Marlee and I wearily boarded the plane to Perth.

I was asked if I would like to attend the conference, but had to decline as I still had to write the speech. It was received well—one man even asked for a copy, which I consider a big compliment. I spoke at the dinner on Saturday night and our flight home was on Monday morning.

Marlee, who had joined me for a few days break and also, I think, to keep me company, as we were still upset by the appeal hearing, insisted we go to the Perth Royal Show. We had a wonderful day looking at cattle and new machinery. Monday morning it was back to the station.

Our last muster was an area called Paperbark, very wild, very remote. Marlee set the camp up beside Leslie Lake, a particularly beautiful area on Bullo, and a few days later yarded around four hundred cattle; a good result for this area. Catching wild cattle with a helicopter is usually the hardest part of the operation, but, in this muster, it was getting the cattle trucks out of Paperbark. It took close to five days in stops and starts and delays. The first truck came in at night and the wheels of his last trailer slipped over the edge on a tight bend and Marlee had to walk the D8 thirty miles to lift him back on the road. On top of these problems, Marlee sprained her ankle when she turned her foot jumping down from the front end loader. Naturally, the next day the cattle truck got stuck on one of our bad jump-ups. So Marlee had to drive the grader and tow the road train out of trouble while on crutches. Being the great little trouper she is, she pulled it off successfully.

Now, apart from bull-catching, we are watching the heavens. Almost all our home-grown hay is gone, so I have put in an order to 'above' for rain.

The mail has just arrived from Katherine with our 'weed men'— the government helps properties with advice for weed control— and I have received an invitation to the 1992 Businesswoman of the Year awards. So in a few weeks time I will no longer be the current Businesswoman of the Year.

What a year! Although it is drawing to a close, nothing else is—in fact it is all beginning! There are so many opportunities opening up I don't know which way to turn first.

I am negotiating for my TV Exercise Chair to go into production, I have the possibility of a speaking tour in America, I have another invention that could help the wool industry, and if all these eventuate, I will be able to move my ten-year plan to get out of debt forward a few years. And all of this has happened in the last year, since Marlee sent that fateful fax.

So maybe fate has decided to smile on me for a while. I hope it is a fair while. I don't want the world on a platter and I don't mind working all my life—like most people, I just need a fair go.

At fifty-five most women are settling down to knit booties for their grandchildren. When I look at what is on my plate and the possibilities that could be on my plate, it is mind-boggling—the booties will have to go on the back burner.

I was asked at one of my speeches what I would do at the end of my ten-year plan. I replied that I only hoped to be out of debt in ten years.

'Well after you're out of debt and after you carry out your plans, what will you do then?'

'Well, I have a time problem, because our plans for Bullo cover about a hundred years. But there's nothing to stop me working on many things while working towards securing Bullo. And that's what I'm doing.'

So as I look at my invitation and wonder who the 1992

Businesswoman of the Year will be, I wonder if her life will change as drastically as mine has. Will she move into new fields, will she achieve her dreams, will she discover all the wonderful people out there that I have, could she possibly be as lucky as I have been?

For on the 13th of November 1990 in the Regent Ballroom in Sydney, when the words, 'And the winner is . . .' brought me back to the present, and I walked towards the stage with feelings of excitement, pride and humility, the winner really was Sara Henderson.

EPILOGUE

The first words in this book were dedicated to Charlie, so I suppose the last should be too. He always had to have the last word.

I certainly would not be the person I am today if I had not married Charles English Henderson III. I still cannot judge if my life to this point has been worth it. But if I can go on and do something that really counts, something that helps make the world a better place, then the pain, unhappiness and tragedy will not have been in vain.

I know he is sitting up there somewhere, watching me, criticising my every move, but sometimes applauding and saying 'I taught her that!' So in closing, I say this:

'Charlie, you put me through the world's most demanding, humiliating, and challenging obstacle course any human could be expected to endure. It is five years since you left me with this mess and I am still sorting it out! I will survive. Marlee and I will do everything you asked us to, and then I will get on with what I want to do in my life, and you won't say a word. It's time to cut the strings, Charlie. I'm not asking you, I'm telling you. But God, how I loved you, *you son of a bitch, Yankee bastard.*'

·